Dialogue for Interreligious Understanding

Interreligious Studies in Theory and Practice

Series Editors: Aimee Light, Jennifer Peace, Or Rose,
Madhuri Yadlapati, and Homayra Ziad

Palgrave's new series, *Interreligious Studies in Theory and Practice*, seeks to capture the best of the diverse contributions to the rapidly expanding field of interreligious and interfaith studies. While the series includes a diverse set of titles, they are all united by a common vision: Each volume advocates—explicitly or implicitly—for interreligious engagement, even if this involves a critique of the limits of this work as it is currently defined or embodied. Each volume provides models and resources—textual, theological, pedagogic, or practical—for interreligious dialogue, study, or action. The series models a commitment to religious pluralism by including books that begin from diverse religious perspectives. This does not preclude the publication of books dedicated to a specific religion, but the overall series reflects a balance of various faiths and perspectives.

Dialogue for Interreligious Understanding: Strategies for the Transformation of Culture-Shaping Institutions
Leonard Swidler

Dialogue for Interreligious Understanding

Strategies for the Transformation of Culture-Shaping Institutions

Leonard Swidler

First published in 2014 by
PALGRAVE MACMILLAN®
in the United States—a division of St. Martin's Press LLC,
175 Fifth Avenue, New York, NY 10010.

Where this book is distributed in the UK, Europe and the rest of the world,
this is by Palgrave Macmillan, a division of Macmillan Publishers Limited,
registered in England, company number 785998, of Houndmills,
Basingstoke, Hampshire RG21 6XS.

Palgrave Macmillan is the global academic imprint of the above companies
and has companies and representatives throughout the world.

Palgrave® and Macmillan® are registered trademarks in the United States,
the United Kingdom, Europe and other countries.

ISBN: 978–1–137–47118–5 (hc)
ISBN: 978–1–137–47119–2 (pbk)

Library of Congress Cataloging-in-Publication Data is available from the
Library of Congress.

A catalogue record of the book is available from the British Library.

Design by Newgen Knowledge Works (P) Ltd., Chennai, India.

First edition: November 2014

10 9 8 7 6 5 4 3 2 1

Contents

1   Dialogue on Dialogue: Introduction to the *Virtue* and *Way* of
Deep-Dialogue/Critical-Thinking/Emotional-Intelligence/
Competitive-Cooperation—*Dia-Logos*   1

Part I   General Background and Guides

2   What Is Religion?   7

3   The Cosmic Dance of Dialogue: Dialogue of the Head, Hands,
Heart, the Holy   15

4   What Is Dialogue?   19

5   Deep-Dialogue/Critical-Thinking/Emotional-Intelligence/
Competitive-Cooperation: The Most Authentic Way to Be Human   35

6   The Dialogue Decalogue: Ground Rules for Interreligious,
Interideological Dialogue   47

7   Dialogue Decalogue: Pastoral Applications   53

8   The Deep-Dialogue Decalogue: Ground Rules of Personal/
Communal Deep-Dialogue/Critical-Thinking/
Emotional-Intelligence/Competitive-Cooperation   61

Part II   Theoretical Background

9   Introduction to the Basic Documents of Deep-Dialogue/
Critical-Thinking/Emotional-Intelligence/
Competitive-Cooperation   71

10   The Background of the "Way" of Deep-Dialogue/Critical-Thinking/
Emotional-Intelligence/Competitive-Cooperation   73

11   Theory Underlying Deep-Dialogue/Critical-Thinking/
Emotional-Intelligence/Competitive-Cooperation   83

12   Ten Principles Articulating Deep-Dialogue/Critical-Thinking/
Emotional-Intelligence/Competitive-Cooperation   89

13 Three Facets of Deep-Dialogue/Critical-Thinking/
    Emotional-Intelligence/Competitive-Cooperation   93

14 The Global Way of Deep-Dialogue/Critical-Thinking/
    Emotional-Intelligence/Competitive-Cooperation   95

15 Seven Stages of Deep-Dialogue/Critical-Thinking/
    Emotional-Intelligence/Competitive-Cooperation   99

16 Online Course in Deep-Dialogue/Critical-Thinking/
    Emotional-Intelligence/Competitive-Cooperation   103

Part III   Implications

17 Integrated Education through Deep-Dialogue/Critical-Thinking/
    Emotional-Intelligence/Competitive-Cooperation   129

18 Dialogue Institute: "Whole Child Education"
    Exercise in Concept Attainment   139

19 Seven Stages of Deep-Dialogue/Critical-Thinking/
    Emotional-Intelligence/Competitive-Cooperation—Applied to
    Teachers of Whole Child Education   145

20 Toward a Universal Declaration of a Global Ethic   149

21 A Universal Declaration of a Global Ethic   169

22 The Law and Global Ethics   177

Part IV   Potential Applications

23 Eleven-Step Program to Deep-Dialogue/Critical-Thinking/
    Emotional-Intelligence/Competitive-Cooperation   185

24 An Executives' Encounter through Deep-Dialogue/
    Critical-Thinking/Emotional-Intelligence/
    Competitive-Cooperation   189

25 Business in Dialogue: Network for Business Ethical/
    Spiritual Values   193

26 Conclusion   195

Notes   197

Index   207

I

Dialogue on Dialogue: Introduction to the *Virtue* and *Way* of Deep-Dialogue/ Critical-Thinking/Emotional-Intelligence/Competitive-Cooperation—*Dia-Logos*

Dialogue is not just talking together, but is a whole new way of seeing oneself and the world, and then living accordingly. Dialogue must become a Virtue, a Way of Life, penetrating all of life and being expressed in Deep-Dialogue, Critical-Thinking, Emotional-Intelligence, Competitive-Cooperation—in short, *Dia-Logos*.

Why a Dialogue on Dialogue? Answer: Because most people do not understand dialogue as it is often used today. They hear a lot about it, sense that it is growing in importance in today's world, but often are hesitant about it, precisely because they do not really know what it is, or—even more fearsome—what it might lead to. Many reject it out of hand simply because of fear of the unknown. When individuals and groups do begin to test dialogue, they most often begin with a Dialogue on Dialogue, seeking to learn what it is and what it might lead to. I remember that when I was heavily involved in the Christian-Marxist dialogues of the 1960s, until the disappearance of the Soviet Union in 1991, I was struck by the fact that every time a new partner group joined the dialogue, they spent the first two or more years on a Dialogue on Dialogue.[1]

Virtue, Way, and Dia-Logos

This book, then, aims to help those who are convinced, or who at least suspect, that the tried and true but disastrously *unsuccessful* methods of Diatribe, Debate, or any of the other aggressive stances against those who think differently from us, need to yield to the new method—the *Virtue* and *Way*—not of casual, everyday dialogue, but, as I shall lay out in this book, Deep-Dialogue/Critical-Thinking/Emotional-Intelligence/Competitive-Cooperation—that is, *Dia-Logos* in the original Greek. Here are laid out what (1) Religion, (2) Dialogue, and beyond it, Deep-Dialogue, its obverse, Critical-Thinking and Emotional-Intelligence, their action expression, Competitive-Cooperation are, as well as some commonsense guidelines and resources to make them happen. Beyond that, (3) a deeper, a more theoretical explanation of Deep-Dialogue/Critical-Thinking/Emotional-Intelligence/Competitive-Cooperation is also disussed. In brief, the *Virtue*, that is, the *Way* of living every day in Deep-Dialogue/Critical-Thinking/Emotional-Intelligence/Competitive-Cooperation—in *Dia-Logos*—is presented.

Those who are not very used to more theoretical reflection might experience a slight bit of My Eyes Glaze Over (MEGO) in this theory section, but you are urged to persist—perhaps give it a slow, second or even third reading spread over an extended period time. Deep-Dialogue, its counterparts Critical-Thinking/Emotional-Intelligence, and action expression Competitive-Cooperation are virtues, which means that they are not acquired in a flash. Virtues (more on *Virtue* below) are habitual ways of acting. For example, the person who has developed the virtue of courage reacts habitually, that is, automatically, in a courageous manner when a challenge arises. So, too, a Deep-Dialogue/Critical-Thinking/Emotional-Intelligence/Competitive-Cooperation mentality needs to be inculcated to operate habitually; it needs to become a Virtue—a Way of life. Virtues, however, cannot be developed overnight. So, yes, try to put these Deep-Dialogue/Critical-Thinking/Emotional-Intelligence/Competitive-Cooperation ways of thinking, and consequent acting, into practice time and time again, and come back and reread these pages time and time again. It will be rewarding. Then live accordingly the Virtue, the Way of Deep-Dialogue/Critical-Thinking/Emotional-Intelligence/Competitive-Cooperation: *Dia-Logos*.

Then (4) reflections are offered on some of the most important applications of the Virtue, the Way of Deep-Dialogue/Emotional-Intelligence/Critical-Thinking/Competitive-Cooperation, for example, education, global ethics, law, and business. These, of course, are not the only important areas of the out-working of a mentality—Virtue, Way—of Deep-Dia-logue/Critical-Thinking/Emotional-Intelligence/Competitive-Cooperation among the culture-shapers of the world, but they will serve as pump primers for you, the reader, to do something similar in your part of the world—and then share it with the rest of us, including me!

Last (5), a few more practical sample programs are presented on how to apply the Virtue, the Way of Deep-Dialogue/Critical-Thinking/Emotional-Intelligence/Competitive-Cooperation in various settings. These sample programs are projects that organizations like the Dialogue Institute (founded in 1978, www.jesdialogue.org) could undertake or that you the reader can launch on your own, in perhaps adapted form.

Because several of these chapters are also designed as stand-alone documents that readers may want to duplicate, there will be a very minimal amount of repetition of some key material at the beginning of these chapters. Before you complain, I would like to recall a Latin saying I learned in my youth (does anyone study Latin anymore? No? What a loss!): *Repetitio est mater studiorum*, "Repetition is the mother of studies."

So, this book aims at being what I hope will be a helpful combination of theoretical ideas and practical projects that will serve as a sort of *vade mecum* (a "Come with me!"—see, there's that missing Latin study again!) for the twenty-first-century person who wants not just to live out her/his life in reasonable comfort but also to help transform her-/himself and the world for the better—to follow the Virtue, the Way of Deep-Dialogue/Critical-Thinking/Emotional-Intelligence/Competitive-Cooperation—*Dia-Logos*.

Deep-Dialogue and Critical-Thinking/Emotional-Intelligence/Competitive-Cooperation

In recent decades, the term "dialogue" has become increasingly popular. Already over a half-century ago (1957), I started researching the ecumenical dialogue (called the Una Sancta Movement) between Catholics and Protestants that started after World War I in Germany, the Land of the Reformation.[2] Then came Vatican Council II—1962–1965—of the Catholic Church (with its 1.3 billion members!), which totally reversed the Catholic Church's resistance to dialogue and committed it to its full embrace. In the midst of this, my wife, Arlene Anderson Swidler, and I launched the *Journal of Ecumenical Studies* (*JES*, 1964). The subtitle of *JES* was "Protestant, Catholic, Orthodox," but already in 1965, we dropped the subtitle and took on our first non-Christian associate editor, Rabbi Arthur Gilbert. In the next three years, *JES* continued to expand the dialogue (adding Muslim, Hindu, Buddhist... associate editors) so that the initial dialogue among Christians quickly spread to dialogue among all religions and beyond to all ideologies, cultures, and societal institutions.

Already in the late 1960s, *JES* was found in a worldwide survey by the Centro Pro Unione in Rome to be the most important publication in the world devoted to ecumenical/interreligious dialogue. In 1978, I established an outreach arm of *JES*, the Dialogue Institute: Interreligious, Intercultural, International (DI), although the name was modified several times over the decades. In the mid-1990s, I joined with Ashok Gangadean, professor of philosophy at Haverford College, an elite Quaker undergraduate college near Philadelphia, to form the Global Dialogue Institute. We worked jointly with Harry Halloran and Uli Kortsch, local business leaders, as well as Ingrid Shafer, professor of integrated studies at the University of Science and Arts of Oklahoma, a liberal arts college. Together Ashok and I collaborated to produce—in dialogue (!)—several documents, of which a few are the basis of some of the material here.

Thus, I had started out as a graduate student in the 1950s taking up the dialogue between Catholics and Protestants, moved on to Jewish-Christian dialogue, then Jewish-Christian-Muslim dialogue, and further to dialogue with Hinduism, Buddhism, and..., and...by 1968, even atheistic Marxism! I then began to reflect, along with others, about dialogue itself. In 1989, the Berlin

Wall came down, and the Soviet Union (which I and everybody else, including the Central Intelligence Agency [CIA] and the KGB [!], thought would last well into the third millennium) teetered into oblivion. Shortly afterward, in 1993, Samuel Huntington argued that the world had settled back into "The Clash of Civilizations."[3]

He was right. There was/is a Clash of Civilizations. But that did not and does not describe all of the contemporary global scene. The world also dramatically began to move into the Age of Global Dialogue,[4] as I personally can attest. In the same period, that is, between 1990 and 1992, I published 12 books dealing with Dialogue![5] Soon the very term dialogue became extremely popular (but not necessarily the reality!), so much so that it was at times applied indiscriminately or even deceptively. Hence, I began to look for a term that would avoid such light-headed misunderstandings. Thus, my friend and colleague Ashok Gangadean and I, also in cooperation with Howard Perlmutter, a professor at the Wharton School of Business, University of Pennsylvania, in the 1990s came up with the term Deep-Dialogue to indicate that we were talking about something much deeper than mere conversation, something life transforming.

Very briefly, Deep-Dialogue can initially, and still relatively superficially, be described as a "conversation between individual persons—and at times through them, two or more communities or groups—with differing views, the *primary* purpose of which is for each participant to learn from the other so that s/he can grow, which of course means change—and thereby the respective groups or communities as well." Hence, whereas in the early decades the term I used was dialogue, in the materials Ashok and I developed, and those I created in more recent years, I use, or at least mean, Deep-Dialogue, in its profound, life-transforming sense. In addition, I am convinced that the concomitant virtue to Deep-Dialogue must be Critical-Thinking/Emotional-Intelligence and their consequent action expression Competitive-Cooperation—but much more of them below.

Beyond that, however, Deep-Dialogue/Critical-Thinking/Emotional-Intelligence/Competitive-Cooperation needs to pervade all of reality in ways that we humans have not realized—until this new millennium, when we began to reflect even more deeply not just about dialogue. Rather, only recently have we begun to reflect on,[6] and attempt to live out, a whole way of life, the Way of Deep-Dialogue/Critical-Thinking/Emotional-Intelligence/Competitive-Cooperation—*Dia-Logos* (more on the latter below).

General Background and Guides

This section provides an understanding of the basic subjects involved, for example, religion, ideology, dialogue...and the basic tools to deal with them.

Part I

General Background and Guides

2

What Is Religion?[1]

Religion is an "Explanation of the ultimate meaning of life, and how to live accordingly, based on some notion and experience of the transcendent." Each religion has four "C's": Creed (the "explanation of life"); Code (of behavior, ethics); Cult (actions relating the believer to the transcendent); Community structure (monarchical, republican, individualistic, etc.)

General Western Definition of Religion

What is religion? Let's start with the etymological roots of the Western term "religion," even though it turns out not to be particularly helpful. We say in English that we ought to choose good and avoid evil; we speak of being "obliged" to choose the good. Our English word obliged comes from a Latin root, *obligare*, "to be bound to." Hence, we are bound to, obliged to, do the good. The Latin root of the term religion is fundamentally the same as that of oblige, that is, *religare*, "to be bound back." This word root is really more helpful in another way in which we use the term religious, as when we say, "He follows his routine religiously," meaning that he is bound to it. That regular commitment may at times, or even often, be a part of what we normally name religion, but it surely is not its core.

Scholars writing about the meaning of religion often start by stating that it is not possible to give a definition of religion, and then often follow that up with quotations of a number of descriptions by other scholars, and end up nevertheless offering their own description, or perhaps tentatively a working definition. I am more optimistic about the possibility of giving a definition and offer one here at the start:

> Religion is an explanation of the ultimate meaning of life, based on a notion and experience of the transcendent, and how to live accordingly, and it normally contains the four "C's": creed, code, cult, community structure.

Creed refers to the cognitive aspect of a religion; it is everything that goes into the explanation of the ultimate meaning of life.

Code of behavior or ethics includes all the rules and customs of action that somehow follow from one aspect or another of the Creed.

Cult means all the ritual activities that relate the believer to one aspect or other of the Transcendent, either directly or indirectly, prayer being an example of the former and certain formal behavior toward representatives of the Transcendent, like priests, of the latter.

Community structure refers to the relationships among the believers; this can vary widely, from a very egalitarian relationship, as among Quakers, through a "republican" structure like Presbyterians have, to a monarchical one, as with some Hasidic Jews vis-à-vis their Rebbe.

Transcendent, as the roots of the word indicate, means "that which goes beyond" the everyday, the ordinary, the surface experience of reality. It can mean spirits, gods, a personal god, an impersonal god, Emptiness, and so forth.

Especially in modern times there have developed "explanations of the ultimate meaning of life, and how to live accordingly," which are not based on a notion of the transcendent, for example, Marxism or Atheistic Humanism. Although in every respect these explanations function as religions traditionally have in human life, because the idea of the Transcendent, however it is understood, plays such a central role in religion, but not in these explanations, as was discussed above, for the sake of accuracy it is best to give these explanations not based on notion of the transcendent a separate name. The name often used is ideology. Much, although not all, of the following discussion will, *mutatis mutandis* (Latin: "changing what needs to be changed") also apply to ideology even when the term is not used.

It is clear when we say that religion provides an explanation of the meaning of life, that therefore all religion is constitutively related to humans; it is to provide *our* understanding of life. (The great Swiss Protestant theologian Karl Barth agreed with this idea when he argued that all religions are human creations—and therefore will necessarily be misleading, he concluded—but then went on to insist that Christianity was not a religion, for it, alone, was created by God, by the Transcendent, and therefore it alone was not misleading. I am persuaded that he is mistaken in this judgment of his.)

Also apparent in this definition is that religion offers an explanation of the ultimate understanding of life, not just part of it. It is an attempt to get it all together, as the American expression of the 1960s had it. Religion does not just attempt to explain the meaning of physical life, as bio*logy* does, or just psychic life, as psycho*logy*, or life in community, as socio*logy*, or the earth on which we live, as geo*logy*, and so on. Rather, it is an explanation of the meaning of Ultimate Reality and how Ultimate Reality relates to all finite reality, and most especially to us humans. Perhaps the best way in Western languages to speak of Ultimate Reality as Ultimate Reality relates to us is to follow the Greek linguistic tradition reflected in the other "-logys" above: theo*logy*. The ancient Greeks spoke of Ultimate Reality as *Theos*, God. Hence, theo*logy* basically means the study of *Theos* and the relationship of the rest of reality, especially humans, to *Theos*.

I am aware that the term theology is not only culturally a Western term, and therefore has severe limitations, but also that it is a term that has come to mean Ultimate Reality as understood in personal terms, and therefore is still more restricted. Concerning the latter, I do not want to claim that religion must have a personal understanding of Ultimate Reality in order to qualify as religion. That is a matter that is a potentially fruitful subject of dialogue between theists and nontheists.

Concerning the former restriction, the fact is that no term from whatever culture can possibly be without its limitations. Hence, the best we can do is consciously choose terms that we think will be the most helpful—and then always bear in mind their cultural and other limitations. Only thus can we avoid on the one hand being condemned to silence, because we cannot find any words to describe reality that will not be limited and hence distorting, and on the other hand being guilty of idolatry, that is, mistaking our words, the idols (i.e., the images, the symbols, the "finger pointing to the moon") for the reality they are supposed to describe, to image.

There is, of course, much more to reflect on concerning the various explanations of Ultimate Reality and the relation of humans to Ultimate Reality, all of which religion is supposed to provide. Therefore, I mean to return to that subject later.

The Way

I noted above that those explanations of the ultimate meaning of life, and how to live accordingly, which are not based on a notion of the Transcendent will be termed ideologies. The term "philosophy" would seem to be too exclusively cognitive to serve as a generic term embracing both religions and ideologies, and the term "Weltanschauungen" (worldviews) too vague. I suggest that a combination, "worldview and way" might serve as such a generic term. Let me here detail a bit more about the importance of the term "way."

Religion is much more than just an intellectual explanation of the ultimate meaning of life—absolutely vital to religion as that theoretical dimension is. Religion is also "how to live according" to that explanation. It is a way of living, of life. This is reflected in the interesting fact that many major religions of the world have the very term "way," or some variation of it, at the heart of their self-understanding.

For example, in the three Semitic, or Abrahamic, religions—Judadism, Christianity, and Islam—all the following terms mean the way:

Central to Judaism, the Hebrew word *Halacha,* the way, has come to mean the Rabbinic teachings, the legal decisions to be followed, in order to lead a life according to the Torah, that is, as instructed by God (the Hebrew word Torah means "instruction").

At the beginning of Christianity the followers of Jesus (*Yeshua,* in Hebrew) were not called Christians, but followers of the way (*Hodos,* in New Testament Greek[2]), "Rabbi" Yeshua taught and exemplified.

In Islam, the traditional way to live a correct life was to follow the *Shar'ia,* an Arabic term for the way—specifically the path to find water in the desert; it also, analogous to *Halacha* in Judaism, came to mean the myriad legal decisions that should be followed by the devout Muslim.

Much the same is also true for the major religions that come out of India—Hinduism and Buddhism:

In Hinduism, there are three major Ways, *Marga*s in Sanskrit, to attain the goal in life: *Moksha* (Sanskrit for "liberation"), namely, the way or *Marga* of knowledge; (*Jnana*), the *Marga* of works (*Karma*); and the *Marga* of devotion (*Bhakti*).

In Buddhism, the key term meaning way is *Magga*, in Pali, and refers to the Noble Eightfold *Path* (the fourth of Gautama's fundamental Four Noble Truths) to be followed in order to reach nirvana, the goal of life. Moreover, Gautama himself in his first, fundamental, sermon, and Buddhism after him, described his way as the Middle *Way* (*Majjhima Patipada* in Pali) between harsh asceticism and loose sensuality, which will lead to the goal of life.

For the major religions of the Far East too, the term the *way* was central:

> The very name of Chinese *Tao*ism places the Way, *Tao*, at the center, at the foundation of the entire Religion, the goal of which was to discern the *Tao* of the universe and live in harmony with it.

This notion of the way, the *Tao*, was also central to the doctrine of Confucius, who taught that "The Way of Humanity" (*Ren-Tao*) is to follow "The Way of Heaven" (*T'ien-Tao*). for Confucius, Heaven, *T'ien*, was largely personal, *Theos*, although eventually, and especially for the neo-Confucians of the Song Dynasty (960–1279 CE) and afterwards, *T'ien* became largely nonpersonal.

Japan's native religion, Shinto, likewise has embedded in its very name the term the way, namely, *To*, "The Way of the Gods," *Shin-To*. The term was taken from the Chinese with the same meaning, *Shen-Tao*, to distinguish the original Japanese religion (which in pure Japanese was called the "Way of the *Kami* or Gods," *Kami-no Michi*) from that religion of India, Buddhism, which came to Japan by way of China through Korea, also known in Chinese as "the Way of Buddha," *Butsu-Tao*.

Authentic Religion

Ours in the West is largely a secularized society. However, especially after September 11, we have become much more aware of the influence of religion—mostly bad in many people's eyes. This, I believe, is a bum rap for *authentic* religion, which I would describe in a phrase as "within me, and between me and thee."

I cringe, for example, when someone says of a Jewish person that she is "religious," meaning, of course, that she does all the externals. That is not only a wrongheaded understanding of what religion is, but it is *precisely* wrong. To stick with Judaism for the moment, according to the rabbis, the heart of what Judaism is all about is *kavanah*, interior intention. The same is true, of course, of all the major religions. In Confucianism, for example, the rituals, *Li*, are for the sake of forming an authentic human, *Ren*. The externals are supposed to help get our head and heart right, and then to act accordingly—"within me, and between me and thee."

If the externals—which include not only doing all the prescribed things but also saying the correct formularies of doctrines (which is a special problem for Christians)—in fact distract us from the righting of our head and heart and consequent action in the world, we should reevaluate and perhaps even drop them. After all, the greatest sin in the Bible is idolatry. This is so not because God is thereby maligned—surely God cannot be injured by humans. No, there is a constitutive reason why idolatry is the worst sin. Idolatry is so bad because, as long as we hold onto it, we are incapable of becoming authentic humans.

Idolatry literally means "worshiping an image" (Greek: *eidol*, image, *latria*, worship). It is to focus on the finger pointing to the object, rather than on the object. The whole purpose, however, of the pointing finger is for us to look at the object, not the finger. In the case of religion, the finger is the external and the object is the interior thought and desire and consequent action: "within me, and between me and thee."

The two major Semitic religions, Judaism and Islam, both tend to concentrate on *what to do*, on actions, whereas Christianity ("half" Semitic) stresses much more, although of course not exclusively, *what to think*. Hence, the greatest temptations toward idolatry for Jews and Muslims are the external actions: I must not eat certain food; I must stop what I doing and go pray now; I may not join with you at these times. All these prescribed actions are doubtless good, as long as they are for the sake of persons (for we truly "love God with our whole heart" by "loving our neighbor as ourselves"), not for the sake of an action.

For Christians, although they are also tempted to idolatry by way of external actions, the most deceptive temptation comes from their adherence to doctrines. For example, Protestantism classically claimed that truth is to be found solely in the Bible (*sola Scriptura*), and yet in the United States alone there are over 350 different Protestant denominations. Have they made an *eidol* of *their* doctrine of what the *Scriptura* teaches? Catholicism, of course, is not any better off, with its doctrine of papal infallibility. Has papal infallibility become an *eidol* that is focused on with *latria*?

Many examples of authentic religion could be lifted up. Let me pick just one here that, in different ways, reflects all three of the Semitic religions. The Jew Rabbi Jesus from Nazareth, whom both Christians and Muslims call the Messiah, said that "it is not what goes into the mouth" (an external), but "what comes out" (an internal reflecting the *kavanah* in action) that makes a person good, or not, and elsewhere said, "For what you have *done* to the least ones…enter into the reward prepared for you."

Authentic religion is "within me, and between me and thee."

Comparative Religion and Interreligious Dialogue

For the most part, the study of religion was done from the perspective of the religion of the teacher/student. Thus, there was Christian theology, Muslim *kalam*, and so forth. After the eighteenth-century Enlightenment in the West and the subsequent development of the "critical" science of history, and then the various social sciences (sociology, anthropology, psychology, etc.) in the course of the nineteenth century, the "scientific" study of religion (*Religionswissenschaft*) was born—Max Müller being recognized as its "Father"—in its last quarter.

The study of religion largely continued in departments of theology, and the equivalent, in religiously related universities for the rest of the nineteenth century and more than half of the twentieth century. When religions other than the "home" religion were studied and taught, in the West it was almost inevitably by a Christian theologian. This began to change when Temple University became a state-related university, divested itself of its divinity school, and established its Department of Religion in 1964 (other state universities, for example, the University of Iowa, had developed various symbioses with religious bodies in the teaching about religion). Temple University's Department of Religion pioneered a new way to study and teach religion, namely, by gathering professors who had grown up in a particular religion, became critical scholars of it, and now taught about it, in addition to professors whose approach was more *Religionswissenschaft*. Thus, the world's religions were studied/taught by critical scholars who knew the religion from the inside and the outside.

One can begin here to discern the differences between the study of and teaching about religion via one of the various forms of *Religionswissenschaft* on the one hand, and the studying and perhaps experiencing of interreligious dialogue on the other. Interreligious dialogue occurs when religious insiders, that is, members of two or more religions, come together primarily to learn from each other what the other thinks/does and why.

The epistemological assumption underlying dialogue is that "Nobody knows everything about anything." That clearly includes that most complicated of all disciplines, religion, which purports to give an explanation of the *ultimate* meaning of life. Hence, the primary aim of interreligious dialogue is for the dialogue partners to learn something about the ultimate meaning of life that they did not know solely from their own religious perspective. Whether or not I agree with my dialogue partner's view of something, learning more about how and why s/he understands, and hence acts in, the world necessarily influences how I perceive, and therefore act in, the world. Thus, ultimately, the philosophy guiding interreligious dialogue can be said to be pragmatism: the participants in interreligious dialogue are interested in what William James and other pragmatists designated the "cash value" of the ideas discussed—what difference they make in how they see life and, hence, live it.

In the study of religion in higher education, interreligious dialogue *itself* occurs, as does also the study *about* it. There are a number of philosophical, social-scientific, and religious issues that underlie interreligious dialogue that need to be studied in order to understand it.[3] The results of this study, in turn, significantly influence the actual dialogues that occur, whether in a university setting or elsewhere.

Comparative religion engages in a historical cross-cultural study of religious phenomena with the emphasis being on comparison. Scholars "observe similar phenomena from religions laid side by side and draw conclusions from such comparison."[4] They examine concepts and categories for similarities and differences, at times hypothesizing about their origins—whether there was a historical connection or an independent origin of recurrent themes. Some scholars seek universal structures in concrete religions, while others reject this as an unwarranted imposition upon diverse religious phenomena. Comparative religion does not per se promote interreligious dialogue, but insights from it may be useful in dialogue.

Thus, comparative religion, or more broadly, *Religionswissenschaft*, makes invaluable contributions to our understanding of religion and its influences on human life. It provides helpful resources for interreligious dialogue, helping religious and nonreligious persons and groups understand themselves and others better, and consequently act with greater respect for one's own religious self and that of the Other. It is interreligious dialogue that in fact allows the religious insider to utilize these resources from *Religionswissenschaft* and elsewhere, to engage in that respectful, learning encounter with the religious Other—which is the very definition of interreligious dialogue. It is to dialogue that I now turn.

3

The Cosmic Dance of Dialogue: Dialogue of the Head, Hands, Heart, the Holy

The whole of reality is fundamentally dialogic—from the macro-level of matter and energy (e=mc^2), to the micro-level of electron-protron, the human body-spirit, male-female, individual-community, integrated into a whole, "holy" unity—thus creating a "Cosmic Dance of Dialogue" in which the human is the highest finite member.

"Nobody Knows Everything about Anything!"[1]

Now in the dawning "Age of Global Dialogue," we humans are increasingly aware that we cannot know everything about anything. This is true for the physical sciences: no one would claim that s/he knows everything about biology, physics, and so on. No one would claim that s/he knows everything about the human sciences, sociology, or anthropology, or, good heavens, economics (!), and each of these disciplines is endlessly complicated. To repeat, as a mantra: "Nobody knows Everything about Anything!"

However, when it comes to the most comprehensive, the most complicated, discipline of all—religion, which attempts to provide an explanation of not just part of reality as the various physical, social, and human sciences do, but of the *totality* of reality—billions of us still claim that we know all there is to know, and that whoever thinks differently is simply mistaken! But, if it is true that we always can only know partially in any limited study of reality, as in the physical, social, or human sciences, surely it is all the more true of religion, which is an "explanation of the *ultimate* meaning of life, and how to live accordingly, based on some notion and experience of the Transcendent."[2] We must then be even more modest in our claims of knowing better in this most comprehensive field of knowledge, religion, the *ultimate* meaning of life.

Because of the work of great thinkers like Bernard Lonergan (1904–1984),[3] Hans-Georg Gadamer (1900–2002),[4] and Paul Ricoeur (1913–2005),[5] we now also realize that no knowledge can ever be completely objective, for we the knower are an integral part of the process of knowing. In brief, all knowledge is interpreted knowledge. Even in its simplest form, whether I claim that the Bible is God's truth, or the Qur'an, or the Gita, or, indeed, the interpretation of the pope, Martin Luther, it is *I* who affirm that it is so. But, if neither I nor anyone else can know everything about anything, including most of all, the most complicated claim to truth, religion, how do I proceed to search for an ever fuller grasp of reality, of truth? The clear answer is dialogue.

In dialogue I talk with you primarily so that *I* can learn what I cannot perceive from my place in the world, with my personal lenses of knowing. Through your eyes I see what I cannot see from my side of the globe, and vice versa. Hence, dialogue is not just a way to gain more information. Dialogue is a whole new way of thinking. We are painfully leaving behind the "Age of Monologue" and are, with squinting eyes, entering the "Age of global Dialogue."

The Universe Is a Cosmic Dance of Dialogue

Dialogue—in its broadest meaning, the mutually beneficial interaction of differing components, is—at the very heart of the universe, of which we humans are the highest expression—from the basic interaction of matter and energy (in Albert Einstein's unforgettable formula: $E=mc^2$—energy equals mass times the square of the speed of light), to the creative interaction of protons and electrons in every atom, to the vital symbiosis of body and spirit in every human, through the creative dialogue between woman and man, to the dynamic relationship between individual and society. Thus, the very essence of our humanity is dialogical, and a fulfilled human life is the highest expression of the Cosmic Dance of Dialogue.

In the early millennia of the history of humanity as we spread outward from our starting point in central Africa, the forces of divergence were dominant. However, because we live on a globe, in our frenetic divergence we eventually began to encounter each other more and more frequently. Now the forces of stunning convergence are becoming increasingly dominant. In the past, during the Age of Divergence, we could live in isolation from each other; we could ignore each other. Now, in the Age of Convergence, we are forced to live in One World. We increasingly live in a global village. We cannot ignore the Other, the Different. Too often in the past we have tried to make over the Other into a likeness of ourselves, often by violence. But this is the very opposite of dialogue. This egocentric arrogance is in fundamental opposition to the Cosmic Dance of Dialogue. It is not creative; it is destructive.

Hence, we humans today have a stark choice: dialogue or death!

Dialogue of the Head, Hands, Heart, and Holiness

Because we humans are self-reflecting/correcting beings, we are capable of dialogue, self-transforming dialogue. There are for us four main dimensions to dialogue that correspond to the structure of our humanness: Dialogue of the Head, the Hands, the Heart, Holiness.

The Cognitive or Intellectual: Seeking the Truth

In the Dialogue of the Head, we mentally reach out to the Other to learn from those who think differently from us. We try to understand how they see the world and why they act as they do. The world is far too complicated for any of us to understand alone; we can increasingly understand reality only with the help of the Other in dialogue. This is vital, because how we understand the world, determines how we act in the world.

The Illative or Ethical: Seeking the Good

In the Dialogue of the Hands we join with Others to make the world a better place in which we all live together. Since we can no longer live separately, we must work jointly to make it not just a house but also a home for all of us to live in; we join hands with the Other to "heal the world" (Hebrew: *tikkun olam*). The world within us, and all around us, always is in need of healing, and our deepest wounds can be healed only together with the Other, only in dialogue.

The Affective or Aesthetic: Seeking the Beautiful, the Spiritual

In the Dialogue of the Heart we open ourselves to receive the beauty of the Other. Because we humans are body and spirit, or rather, body-spirit, we give bodily-spiritual expression in all the arts to our multifarious responses to life: joy, sorrow, gratitude, anger...and most of all, love. We try to express our inner feelings, which grasp reality in far deeper and higher ways than we are able to put into rational concepts and words; hence, we create poetry, music, dance, painting, architecture...the expressions of the Heart. All the world delights in beauty, and so it is here that we find the easiest encounter with the Other, the simplest door to dialogue; through the beauty of the Other we most easily enter into the Other. Here, too, is where the depth, and the spiritual and mystical dimension of the human spirit are given full rein. As seventeenth-century mathematician/philosopher Blaise Pascal said, "Le cœur a ses raisons que la raison ne connaît point." "The heart has its reasons, which reason knows not."

Holiness: Seeking the One

We humans cannot live a divided life. If we are even to survive, let alone flourish, we must "get it all together." We must not only dance the dialogues of the Head, Hands, and Heart, but also bring our various parts together in Harmony (a 4th "H") to live a *H*olistic (a 5th "H"), life, which is what religions mean when they say that we should be *H*oly (a 6th "H"—"Holy" comes from the Greek *H*olos, to be whole![6]). Hence, we are authentically *H*uman (a 7th "H") only when our manifold elements are in dialogue within one other, and we are in dialogue with the others around us. We must dance together the Cosmic Dance of Dialogue of the *H*ead, *H*ands, and *H*eart, *H*olistically,[7] in *H*armony within the *H*oly *H*uman.

4

What Is Dialogue?

"Nobody knows Everything about Anything!" Therefore, in order to know ever more, each person must open her-/himself to the Other, the one who experiences and thinks differently from her-/himself. Hence, Dialogue means to encounter the Other in order to learn more Truth (Dialogue of the Head), join together with the Other to heal the world (Dialogue of the Hands), embrace the beauty and "spirit/heart" of the Other (Dialogue of the Heart), and integrate all into a *Holos* (Dialogue of the Holy).

The Meaning of Dialogue

In the next pages (the first version of which I wrote in the 1970s, and which is deliberately only slightly modified here), I am not yet beginning to speak of Deep-Dialogue, but only of Dialogue as it slowly began to be increasingly discussed starting in the 1960s. Moreover, here I focus on just one of the dimensions of Dialogue, namely, the "Dialogue of the Head"—Seeking the Truth.

These days when we speak of dialogue between religions or ideologies, we mean something quite definite, namely, a two-way communication between persons; one-way lecturing or speaking is obviously not meant by this term. However, there are many different kinds of two-way communication, for example, fighting, wrangling, debating, and so on. Clearly none of these are meant by dialogue. On the other extreme is the communication between persons who hold precisely the same view on a particular subject. We also do not mean this when we use the term dialogue; rather, we might call that something like encouragement, reinforcement, but certainly not dialogue. Now, if we look at these two opposite kinds of two-way communication, which are *not* meant by the word dialogue, we can learn quite precisely what we do in fact mean when we use the term dialogue.

Looking at the last example first—the principle underlying "reinforcement" and so forth is the assumption that both sides have a total grasp on the truth of the subject and hence simply need to be supported in their commitment to it. Since this example, and the principle underlying it, are excluded from the meaning of dialogue, clearly dialogue must include the notion that neither side has a total grasp of the truth of the subject, but that both need to seek further.

The principle underlying "debating" and so on in the second example is the assumption that one side has all the truth concerning the subject and that the other side needs to be informed or persuaded of it. Since that example also, and its principle, are excluded from the meaning of dialogue, this clearly implies that dialogue means that no one side has a monopoly on the truth on the subject, but both need to seek further.

It may turn out in some instances, of course, that after a more or less extensive dialogue, it is learned that the two sides in fact agree completely on the subject discussed. Naturally, such a discovery does not mean that the encounter was a nondialogue, but rather that the dialogue was the means of learning the new truth, which was that both sides agreed on the subject. To continue from that point on, however, to speak only about the area of agreement would then be to move from dialogue to reinforcement. Hence, to express at least the initial part of the meaning of dialogue positively: dialogue is a two-way communication between persons who hold significantly differing views on a subject, with the purpose of learning more truth about that subject from the other person.

This analysis may to some seem obvious, and, hence, superfluous. But I do not believe it is. Dialogue has become a faddish term, and is sometimes, like charity, used to "cover a multitude of sins." Sometimes, for example, it is used by those who are quite convinced that they have all the truth on a subject, but feel that in today's climate in which "dialogue" is in vogue a less aggressive style would be more effective in communicating to the ignorant the truth that they already possess in full. Therefore, while their encounters with others still rely on the older nondialogue principle—that they have all the truth on a subject—their less importuning approach will now be *called* dialogue. This type of use would appear to be merely an opportunistic manipulation of the term dialogue.

Maybe some of those people, however, truly believe that they are engaging in dialogue when they employ such a "soft-sell" approach and encourage their interlocutors also to express their own views on the subject—even though it is known ahead of time, of course, that they are false—for such a dialogue may well make the ignorant person more open to receiving the truth, which the one side knows it already has. In that situation, the "truthholders" simply had a basic misunderstanding of the term dialogue and mistakenly termed their "convert-making" dialogue. Therefore, the above clarification is important.

We are, of course, in this context speaking about a particular kind of dialogue, namely, interreligious dialogue in the broadest sense, that is, dialogue on a religious subject by persons who understand themselves to be in different religious traditions and communities. If religion is understood as an "explanation of the ultimate meaning of life and how to live accordingly, based on some notion and experience of the transcendent," then that would include all such systems, even though they customarily would not be called religions, but rather, ideologies, such as, atheistic Humanism and Marxism. Hence, it is more accurate to speak of both interreligious and interideological dialogue.

Why Dialogue Arose

One can, of course, point to recent developments that have contributed to the rise of dialogue, for example, growth in mass education, communications, and travel, a world economy, the threat of global destruction. Nevertheless, a major underlying cause is a paradigm shift in the West in how we perceive and describe the world. A paradigm is simply the model, the cluster of assumptions, on the basis of which phenomena are perceived and explained. For example, the geocentric paradigm for explaining the movements of the planets; a shift to another paradigm—as to the heliocentric—will have a major impact. Such a paradigm shift has occurred and is still occurring in the Western understanding of truth statements, which has made dialogue not only possible but even necessary.

Whereas the understanding of truth in the West was largely absolute, static, monologic or exclusive up to the nineteenth century, it has subsequently become deabsolutized, dynamic, and dialogic—in a word: relational. This relatively "new" view of truth came about in at least six different but closely related ways:

0) Until the nineteenth century in Europe, truth, that is, a statement about reality, was conceived in an absolute, static, exclusivistic either-or manner. It was believed that if a statement was true at one time, it was always true, and not only in the sense of statements about empirical facts but also in the sense of statements about the meaning of things. Such is a *classicist* or *absolutist* view of truth.

1) **Historicism**: Then, in the nineteenth century, scholars came to perceive all statements about the truth of something as being partially products of their historical circumstances; only by placing truth statements in their historical *Sitz im Leben* (situation in life) could they be properly understood. A text could be understood only in *context*. Therefore, all statements about the meaning of things were seen to be deabsolutized in terms of time. Such is a *historical* view of truth.

2) **Intentionality**: Later on, it was noted that we ask questions so as to obtain knowledge, truth, according to which we want to live; this is a *praxis* or *intentional* view of truth. That is, a statement has to be understood in relationship to the action-oriented intention of the thinker who poses the question that is being answered, and is thereby further limited.

3) **Sociology of knowledge**: Just as statements of truth were seen by some thinkers to be historically deabsolutized in time (a text can be understood only in historical *context*), so too, starting in the twentieth century, scholars like Karl Mannheim, developed what he called the sociology of knowledge, which points out that every statement about the meaning of something is perspectival, for all reality is perceived, and spoken of, from the cultural, class, sexual, and so forth perspective of the perceiver. Such is a *perspectival* view of truth, thereby once more limiting a "truth," a statement about reality.

4) **Limitations of language**: A number of thinkers, and especially Ludwig Wittgenstein (1889–1951), uncovered the limitations of human language. Every description of reality is necessarily only partial, for although reality can be seen from a limitless number of perspectives, human language can express things from only one perspective at once. This partial and limited quality of all language is necessarily greatly intensified when one attempts to speak of the Transcendent, which by definition "goes beyond." Such is a *language-limited* view of truth.

5) **Hermeneutics**: The contemporary discipline of hermeneutics, led by Bernard Lonergan, Hans-Georg Gadamer, and Paul Riceour,[1] stresses that all knowledge is interpreted knowledge. This means that in all knowledge *I* come to know something; the object comes into me in a certain way, namely, through the lens that I use to perceive it. As Thomas Aquinas wrote, *Cognita sunt in cognoscente secundum modum cognoscentis*[2] (Things known are in the knower according to the mode of the knower). Such is an *interpretative* view of truth.

6) **Dialogue**: A further development of this basic insight is that I learn not by being merely passively open or receptive to, but by being *in dialogue* with, extramental reality. Reality can "speak" to me only with the language that I give it; the "answers" that I receive back from reality will always be in the language, the thought categories, of the questions I put to it. If the answers I receive are sometimes confused and unsatisfying, then I probably need to learn to speak a more appropriate language when I put questions to reality. For example, if I ask the question "How heavy is green?", of course I will receive a nonsense answer. Or, if I ask questions about living things in mechanical categories, I will receive confusing and unsatisfying answers. I will likewise receive confusing and unsatisfying answers to questions about human sexuality if I use categories that are solely physical-biological. (Witness the absurdity of the answer that birth control is forbidden by natural law—the question falsely assumes that the nature of humanity is merely physical-biological.) Such an understanding of truth is both necessarily limited and a *dialogic* understanding.

In brief, our understanding of truth and reality has been undergoing a radical shift. The new paradigm that is being born understands all statements about reality, especially about the meaning of things, to be historical, praxial or intentional, perspectival, language limited or partial, interpretive, and dialogic. Our understanding of truth statements, in short, has become "deabsolutized"—it has become relational. That is, all statements about reality are now seen to be *related* to the historical context, praxis intentionality, perspective, and so forth of the speaker, and in that sense no longer absolute. Therefore, if my perception and description of the world is true only in a limited sense, that is, only as seen from my place in the world, then if I wish to expand my grasp of reality I need to learn from others what they know of reality that they can perceive from their place in the world that I cannot see from mine. That, however, can happen only through dialogue.

Who Should Dialogue

One important question is, who can, who should, engage in interreligious, interideological dialogue? There is clearly a fundamental communal aspect to such a dialogue. For example, if a person is not either a Lutheran or a Jew, s/he could not engage in a specifically Lutheran-Jewish dialogue. Likewise, persons not belonging to any religious, or ideological, community could not, of course, engage in interreligious, interideological dialogue. They might, of course, engage in meaningful religious, ideological dialogue, but it simply would not be *inter*religious, *inter*ideological, between religions, or ideologies.

Who, then, would qualify as a member of a religious community? If the question is of the official representation of a community at a dialogue, then the clear answer is those who are appointed by the appropriate official body in that community: the congregation, *bet din*, roshi, bishop, Central Committee, or whoever. However, if it is not a case of official representation, then general reputation usually is looked to. Some persons' qualifications, however, can be challenged by elements within a community, even very important official elements. The Vatican Congregation for the Doctrine of the Faith, for example, has declared that Professors Hans Küng, Charles Curran, Roger Haight, Juan Segundo, and Peter Phan (all among the world's most respected Catholic theologians) were no longer to be considered Catholic theologians. In both the Küng and the Curran cases, however, hundreds of Catholic theologians later stated publicly in writing that both those professors were indeed still Catholic theologians (after a while— e.g., in the cases of Haight, Segundo, and Phan, the theological world simply tended to ignore the Vatican).

In the end, however, it seems best to follow the principle that each person should decide for her-/himself whether or not s/he is a member of a religious community. Extraordinary cases may at rare times present initial anomalies, but they inevitably will resolve themselves. Furthermore, it is important to be aware that, especially in the initial stages of any interreligious, interideological dialogue, it is very likely that the literally *eccentric* members of religious, ideological communities will be the ones who will ecchave the interest and ability to enter into dialogue; the more centrist persons will do so only after the dialogue has been proved safe for the mainline, official elements to venture into.

Likewise it is important to note that interreligious, interideological dialogue is not something to be limited to official representatives of communities. Actually, the great majority of the vast amount of such dialogues that has occurred throughout the world, particularly in recent decades, has not been carried on by official representatives, although that too has been happening with increasing frequency.

What is needed then is (a) an openness to learn from the other, (b) knowledge of one's own tradition, and (c) a similarly disposed and knowledgeable dialogue partner from the other tradition. This can happen on almost any level of knowledge and education. The key is the openness to learn from the other. Naturally no one's knowledge of her/his own tradition can ever be complete; each person must continually learn more about it. One merely needs to realize that one's knowledge is in fact limited and know where to turn to gain the information/wisdom needed. It is also important, however, that the dialogue partners be more or less equal in knowledge of their own traditions and so forth. The larger the asymmetry, the less the communication will be two-way, that is, dialogic.

Hence, it is important that interreligious, interideological dialogue *not* be limited to official representatives or even to the experts in the various traditions, although they both have their irreplaceable roles to play in the dialogue. Dialogue, rather, should involve every level of the religious, ideological communities, all the way down to the persons in the pews. Only in this way will the religious, ideological *communities* learn from each other and come to understand each other as they truly are.

The Catholic bishops of the world expressed this insight very clearly and vigorously at Vatican II when they "exhorted *all the Catholic faithful* to recognize the signs of the times and to take an active and intelligent part in the work of ecumenism [dialogue among the Christian churches, and in an extended understanding, dialogue among the religions and ideologies, as is made clear by other Vatican II documents and the establishment of permanent Vatican Secretariats for dialogue with Non-Christians and with Non-Believers]." Not being content with this exhortation, the bishops went on to say that, "in ecumenical work, [all] Catholics must... make the *first approaches* toward them [non-Catholics]." In case there were some opaque minds or recalcitrant wills out there, the bishops once more made it ringingly clear that ecumenism [interreligious, interideological dialogue] "involves the whole Church, faithful and clergy alike. It extends to everyone, according to the talent of each."[3] Certainly this insight is not to be limited to the 1,300,000,000 Catholics in the world— and the further billions they directly or indirectly influence—massive and important as that group may be.

However, what about the challenge of those who charge that dialogists are really elitists because they define dialogue in such a "liberal" manner that only like-minded liberals can join in? I will argue below in more detail that only those who have a deabsolutized understanding of truth will in fact be able to enter into dialogue. Put in other words, only those who understand all truth statements, that is, all statements about reality, to be always limited in a variety of ways, and in that sense not absolute, can enter into dialogue. This, however, is no elitist discrimination against absolutists, or fundamentalists, by not allowing them to engage in dialogue. Such a charge would simply be another case of not understanding what dialogue is: a two-way communication so that both sides can learn. If one partner grants that s/he has something to learn from the other, that admission presupposes that s/he has only a limited—a deabsolutized—grasp of truth concerning the subject. If one partner thinks that s/he has an absolute grasp of the truth concerning the subject, s/he obviously believes that s/he has nothing to learn from the other, and hence the encounter will not be a dialogue, but some kind of attempt at one-way teaching or a debate. Thus the partner with the absolutized view of truth will not only not be able to engage in dialogue, s/he will very much not want to—unless "dialogue" falls into the category either of harboring the earlier described misunderstanding of the meaning of dialogue, or the intention of an opportunistic manipulation of the term.

Kinds of Dialogue

In the question of what constitutes interreligious, interideological dialogue, it is important to notice that we normally mean a two-way communication in ideas and words. At times, however, we give the term an extended meaning of joint action or collaboration, and joint prayer or sharing of the spiritual or depth dimension of our tradition. While the intellectual and verbal communication is indeed the primary meaning of dialogue (Dialogue of the Head), if the results therefrom do not spill over into the other two areas of action (Dialogue of the Hands) and spirituality (Dialogue of the Heart), it will have proved sterile. Beyond that, it can lead to a kind of schizophrenia and even hypocrisy.

On the positive side, serious involvement in joint action and/or spirituality will tend to challenge the previously held intellectual positions and lead to dialogue in the cognitive field. Catholic and Protestant clergy, for example, who found themselves together in the concentration camp Dachau because of joint resistance to one or other Nazi antihuman action, began to ask each other why they did what they did and through dialogue were surprised to learn that they held many more positions in common than that separated them. In fact these encounters and others like them fostered the *Una Sancta* movement in Germany, which in turn was a major engine that moved the Catholic Church in the Second Vatican Council officially to embrace ecumenism and interreligious/interideological dialogue after many centuries of vigorous official rejection.

Because religion, as noted above, is not something just of the head and the hands, but also of the heart—of the whole human being—our encounter with our partner must also eventually include the aesthetic/spiritual dimension. This dimension engages our emotions, imagination, intuitive consciousness. If we do not come to know each other in this deepest dimension of our selves, our dialogue will remain relatively superficial. The technique that John Dunne called "crossing over" can help here. Through it we focus on a central image, or metaphor, from our partner's spiritual life and let it work on our imagination, our emotions, evoking whatever responses it may, leading us to different feelings. We then return to our own inner world enriched, expanded, with a deeper sympathy for, and sensitivity to our partner's inner world. Within this expanded inner dimension we will be prompted to look thereafter for new cognitive articulations adequate to reflect it, and we will be prompted to express our new awareness and understanding of our partner's religious reality in appropriate action.

Encountering our partner on just one or two levels will be authentic dialogue, but, given the integrative and comprehensive—holistic—nature of religion and ideology (Dialogue of the Holy), it is only natural that we be led from dialogue on one level to the others, and finally integrated into a holistic, "holy" *Way*. Only with dialogue in this full fashion on all four levels will our interreligious, interideological dialogue be complete.

Goals of Dialogue

The general goal of dialogue (of the Head) is for each side to learn, and to change accordingly. Naturally, if each side comes to the encounter primarily to learn from the other, then the other side must teach, and thus both learning and teaching occur. We know, however, that if each side comes to the encounter primarily to teach, both sides will tend to close up, and as a result neither teaching nor learning takes place.

We naturally gradually learn more and more about our partners in the dialogue and in the process shuck off the misinformation about them we may have had. However, we also learn something more—something even closer to home. Our dialogue partner likewise becomes for us a mirror in which we perceive ourselves in ways we could not otherwise. In the very process of responding to the questions of our partners, we look into our inner selves and into our traditions in ways that we perhaps never would otherwise, and thus come to know ourselves as we could not have outside of the dialogue.

In addition, in listening to our partners' perceptions of us, we learn much about "how we are in the world." Because no one is simply in her-/himself, but is always in relationship to others, how we are in the world, how we relate to and have an impact on others, is in fact part of our reality, is part of us. As an example, it is only by being in dialogue with another culture that we really come to know our own. I became aware of my particular American culture, for example, only because I lived in Europe for a number of years. I became conscious of American culture as such with its similarities to and differences from the European only in the mirror of my dialogue partner of European culture.

This expanded knowledge of ourselves and of the other that we gain in the dialogue cannot of course remain ineffective in our lives. As our self-understanding and understanding of those persons and things around us change, so too must our attitude toward ourselves and others change, and thus our behavior as well. Once again, to the extent that this inner and outer change, this transformation, does not take place, to that extent we tend toward schizophrenia and hypocrisy. Whether one wants to speak of dialogue and then of the subsequent transformation as "beyond dialogue," as John Cobb once did, or speak of transformation as an integral part of the continuing dialogue process, as Klaus Klostermeier has,[4] need not detain us here. What is important to see is that the chain dialogue—knowledge—change must not be broken. If the final link, change, falls away, the authenticity of the second, knowledge, and the first, dialogue, are called into question. To repeat: the goal of dialogue is that each side to learn and change accordingly.

There are also communal goals in interreligious/interideological dialogue. Some of them will be special to particular dialogue partners. Several Christian churches, for example, may enter into dialogue with the goal of structural union in mind. Such union goals, however, will be something particular to religious communities *within* one religion, that is, within Christianity, within Buddhism, within Islam, and so forth. Dialogue *between* different religions and ideologies, however, will not have this structural union goal. Rather, it will seek first of all to know the dialogue partners as accurately as possible and try to understand them as sympathetically as possible. Dialogue will seek to learn what the partners' commonalities are and what their differences are.

There is a simple technique to learn where the authentic commonalities and differences are between two religions or ideologies: attempt to agree with the dialogue partner as far as possible on a subject without violating one's own integrity. At the point where one can go no further, there is where the authentic difference is, and what has been shared up until that point are commonalities. Experience informs us that very often our true differences lie elsewhere than we had believed before the dialogue.

One communal goal in looking to learn the commonalities and differences that two religions hold is to bridge over antipathies and misunderstandings—to draw closer together in thought, feeling, and action on the basis of the commonalities that are shared. This goal, however, can be reached only if another principle is also observed: interreligious, interideological dialogue must be a two-sided dialogue—across the communal divide, and within it. We need to be in regular dialogue with our fellow religionists, sharing with them the results of our interreligious, interideological dialogue so that they too can enhance their understanding of what is held in common and where the differences truly are, for only thus can the whole communities grow in knowledge and inner and outer transformation, and thereby bridge over antipathies and draw closer. Further, if this two-sided dialogue is not maintained, the individual dialogue partners alone will grow in knowledge and experience the resultant transformation, thus slowly moving away from their unchanging community, thereby becoming a tertium quid (a third reality)—hardly the intended integrative goal of interreligious, interideological dialogue.

It is clear that it is important to learn as fully as possible the things we share in common with our dialogue partners, which most often will be much more extensive than we could have anticipated beforehand. We will thus be drawn together in greater harmony. Likewise, however, it is important that we learn more comprehensively what our differences are. Such differences may be (a) *complementary*, as for example, a stress on the prophetic rather than the mystical, (b) *analogous*, as for example, the notion of God is in the Semitic religions and *Sunyata* within Mahayana Buddhism, or (c) *contradictory*, where the acceptance of one entails the rejection of the other, as for example, the Judeo-Christian-Islamic notion of the inviolable dignity of each individual person and the now largely disappeared Hindu custom of *suttee*, widow burning. The issue of the third category of differences will be discussed below, but here we can note that the differences in the first two categories are not simply to be perceived and acknowledged; they should in fact be cherished and celebrated both for their own sakes and because by discerning them we have extended our own understanding of reality, and how to live accordingly—which is the main goal of dialogue.

The Means of Dialogue

A great variety of means and techniques of dialogue have been successfully used, and doubtless some are yet to be developed. The overall guiding principle in this issue, however, should be (a) to use our creative imaginations and our sensitivity for persons. Techniques that have already been utilized range from joint lectures and dialogues by experts from different traditions that are listened to by large audiences at one extreme, to personal conversations between rank-and-file individuals from different traditions at the other extreme. One important rule to keep in mind, however, whenever something more formal than the personal conversation is planned is that (b) all the traditions that are to be engaged in a dialogue should be involved in its initial planning. This is particularly true when different communities first begin to encounter each other. Then dialogue on the potential dialogue itself becomes an essential part of the dialogic encounter.

It is clear that in the first encounters between communities, (c) the most difficult points of difference should not be tackled. Rather, those subjects that show promise of highlighting commonalities should be treated so that mutual trust between the partners can be established and developed. For without mutual trust, there will be no dialogue.

Vital to the development of this needed mutual trust is that (d) each partner come to the dialogue with total sincerity and honesty. My partners in dialogue wish to learn to know me and my tradition as we truly are; this is impossible, however, if I am not totally sincere and honest. Of course, the same is true for my partners; I cannot learn to know them and their traditions truly if they are not completely sincere and honest. Likewise note: we must simultaneously presume total sincerity and honesty in our partners as well as practice these behaviors ourselves, otherwise there will be no trust—and without trust there will be no dialogue.

Care must also be taken in dialogue (e) to compare our ideals with our partner's ideals and our practices with our partner's practices. By comparing our ideals with our partner's practices we will always "win," but of course we will learn nothing—a total defeat of the purpose of dialogue. For example, the Hindu *practice* mentioned above, the burning of live widows, *suttee,* is not to be compared with the Christian *ideal* of a commitment to the dignity of each individual life, but to the Christian centuries-long practice (fortunately now, also like *suttee,* abandoned) of burning heretics and witches.

There has already been earlier mention of several other means of dialogue: (f) each partner in the dialogue must define her-/himself. Only a Muslim, for example, can know from the inside what is means to be a Muslim, and this self-understanding will change, grow, expand, deepen as the dialogue develops, and hence perforce can be accurately described only by the one experiencing the living, growing religious reality. (g) Each partner needs to come to the dialogue with no fixed assumptions as to where the authentic differences between the traditions are, but only after following the partner with sympathy and agreement as far as one can without violating one's own integrity will the true point of difference be determined. **(h)** Of course, only equal individuals can engage in full, authentic dialogue; the degree of inequality will determine the degree of two-way communication, that is, the degree of dialogue experienced.

An indispensable major means of dialogue is **(i)** a self-critical attitude toward our self and our tradition. If we are unwilling to look self-critically at our own, and *our tradition's*, position, the implication clearly is that we have nothing to learn from our partner—but if that is the case, we are not interested in dialogue, the primary purpose of which is to learn from our partner. To be sure, we come to the dialogue as a Buddhist, as a Christian, as a Muslim, and so on, with sincerity, honesty, and integrity. Self-criticism, however, does not mean a lack of sincerity, honesty, integrity. Indeed, a lack of self-criticism will mean there is no valid sincerity, no true honesty, no authentic integrity.

Finally, the most fundamental means to dialogue is **(j)** having a correct understanding of dialogue, which is a two-way communication so that both partners can learn from each other and change accordingly. If this basic goal is kept fixed in view and acted on with imagination, then creative, fruitful dialogue, and a growing transformation of each participant's life and that of her/his community will follow. (See the Dialogue Decalogue below.)

The Subject of Dialogue

I already spoke about choosing at first those subjects that promise to yield a high degree of common ground so as to establish and develop mutual trust, and about the three main areas of dialogue: the cognitive, active, aesthetic/spiritual—Dialogues of the Head, Hands, Heart, all integrated in the Dialogue of the Holy.

In some ways, the aesthetic/spiritual (Dialogue of the Heart) area, would seem the most attractive, especially to those with a more interior, mystical, psychological bent. Moreover, it promises a great degree of commonality: the mystics appear to all meet together on a high level of unity with the Ultimate Reality no matter how it is described, including even in the more philosophical systems, for example, Neoplatonism. For instance, the greatest of the Muslim sufis, Jewish kabbalists, Hindu bhaktas, Christian mystics, Buddhist bodhisattvas, and Platonist philosophers all seem to be at one in their striving for and experience of unity with the One, which in the West is called God, *Theos*. At times the image is projected of God as being the peak of the mountain that all humans are climbing by way of different paths. Each one has a different *way* (recall: *hodos* in Christian Greek; *halachah* in Jewish Hebrew; *shar'ia* in Muslim Arabic; *marga* in Hindu Sanskrit; *tao* in Chinese Taoism; *to* in Japanese Shinto) to reach *Theos—Brahman, Shang-Ti*—but all are centered on the one goal. Consequently, such an interpretation of religion or ideology can be called *theocentric*.

Attractive as theocentrism is, one must be cautious not to wave the varying understandings of God aside as if they were without importance. They can make a significant difference in human self-understanding, and hence how we behave toward ourselves, each other, the world around us, and the

Ultimate Source. Moreover, a theocentric approach has the disadvantage of not including nontheists in the dialogue. This would exclude not only atheistic Humanists and Marxists, but also nontheistic Theravada Buddhists, who do not deny the existence of God, but rather understand ultimate reality in a non-theistic, nonpersonal manner (theism posits a "personal" God, *Theos*). One alternative way to include these partners in the dialogue, even in this area of "spirituality," is to speak of the search for ultimate meaning in life, for "salvation" (recall: *salus* in Latin, meaning a salutary, whole, [w]holy life; similarly, *soteria* in Greek), however it is understood, as what all humans, theists and nontheists, have in common in the spiritual area. As a result, we can speak of a *soterio*-centrism.

In the *active* area (Dialogue of the Hands), dialogue has to take place in a fundamental way on the underlying principles for action that motivate each tradition. Once again, many similarities will be found, but also differences that will prove significant in determining the communities' differing stands on various issues of personal and social ethics. It is only by carefully and sensitively locating those underlying ethical principles for ethical decision-making (this is what a global ethics is—more about that below) that later misunderstandings and unwarranted frustrations on specific ethical issues can be avoided. Then specific ethical matters, such as sexual ethics, social ethics, ecological ethics, and medical ethics, can become the focus of interreligious, interideological dialogue—and ultimately joint action, where it has been found congruent with each tradition's principles and warranted in the concrete circumstances.

It is, however, in the *cognitive* (Dialogue of the Head) area where the range of possible subjects is greatest. It is almost unlimited—remembering the caution that the less difficult topics be chosen first and the more difficult later. That having been said, however, every dialogue group should nevertheless be encouraged to follow creatively its own inner instinct and interests. Some groups, of course, will start with more particular, concrete matters, and then be gradually drawn to discussing the underlying issues and principles. Others, on the other hand, will begin with more fundamental matters and eventually be drawn to reflect on more and more concrete implications of the basic principles already discovered. In any case, if proper preparation and sensitivity are provided, no subject should a priori be declared off limits.

Encouragement can be drawn here from a (for some perhaps unexpected) source, the Vatican Curia. The "Secretariat for Dialogue with Unbelievers" wrote that even "doctrinal dialogue should be initiated with courage and sincerity, with the greatest freedom and with reverence." It then continued with a statement that is mind-jarring in its liberality: "Doctrinal discussion requires perceptiveness, both in honestly setting out one's own opinion and in recognizing the truth everywhere, *even if the truth demolishes one so that one is forced to reconsider one's own position, in theory and in practice, at least in part.*" The Secretariat then stressed that "in discussion the truth will prevail by no other means than by the truth itself. Therefore, the liberty of the participants must be ensured by law and reverenced in practice."[5] These are dramatic words—which again should be applicable not only to the Catholics of the world, but in general.

When to Dialogue—and When Not

In principle, of course, we ought to be open to dialogue with all possible partners on all possible subjects. Normally this principle should be followed today and doubtless for many years to come because the world's religions and ideologies have stored up so much misinformation about, and hostility toward, each other that it is almost impossible for us to know ahead of time what our potential partner is truly like on any given subject. Consequently, we normally need first of all to enter into sincere dialogue with every potential partner, at least until we learn where our true differences lie.

In this matter of differences, however, we have to be very careful in the distinctions we make. As pointed out above, in the process of the dialogue we will often learn that what we thought were real differences in fact turn out to be only apparent differences; different words or misunderstandings merely hid commonly shared positions. When we enter dialogue, however, we have to allow for the possibility that we will ultimately learn that on some matters we will find not a commonality but an authentic difference. These differences may be, as suggested briefly above, (a) complementary, as for example, a stress on the prophetic rather than the mystical, (b) analogous, as for example, the notion of God in the Semitic religions and of *Sunyata* in Mahayana Buddhism, or (c) contradictory, where the acceptance of one entails the rejection of the other, as for example, the Judeo-Christian-Islamic notion of the dignity of each person and the Hindu custom of *suttee*. Complementary authentic differences will of course be true differences, but not such that only one could be valid. Furthermore, we know from our experience that the complementary differences will usually far outnumber the contradictory. Similarly, learning of these authentic but complementary differences will not only enhance our knowledge but also may very well lead to the desire to adapt one or more of our partner's complementary differences for ourself. As the very term indicates, the differences somehow complete each other, as the Chinese Taoist saying puts it, *Xiang fan xiang cheng* (Contraries complete each other).

Just as we must constantly be extremely cautious about "fixing" our differences a priori lest in acting precipitously we *misplace* them, so too, must we not too easily and quickly place our true differences in the contradictory category. Perhaps, for example, the Hindu *moksha*, the Zen Buddhist *satori*, the Christian "freedom of the children of God," and the Marxist "communist state" could be understood as different, but nevertheless analogous, descriptions of true human liberation. In speaking of true but analogous differences in beliefs or values here, we are no longer talking about discerning teachings or practices in our partner's tradition that we might then wish to appropriate for our own tradition. That of course does, and should at times, happen, but then we are speaking either of something that the two traditions ultimately held in common and that was perhaps atrophied or suppressed in one, or of something that is an authentic but complementary difference.

If this difference, however, is perceived as analogous rather than complementary or contradictory, it will be seen to operate within the total organic structure of the other religion-ideology, fulfilling its function properly only within it. It would not be able to have the same function, that is, relationship to the other parts, in our total organic structure, and hence would not be understood to be in direct opposition, in contradiction, to the "differing" element within our structure. At the same time, however, it must be recalled that these real but analogous differences in beliefs/values should be seen not as in conflict with one another, but as parallel in function, and in that sense analogous.

Nevertheless, at times we can find contradictory truth claims, value claims, presented by different religious-ideological traditions. That happens, of course, only when they cannot be seen as somehow ultimately different expressions of the same thing (a commonality) or as complementary, or analogous. When it happens, however, even though it be relatively rare, a profound and unavoidable problem faces the two communities: What should be their attitude and behavior toward each other? Should they remain in dialogue, tolerate each other, ignore each other, or oppose each other? This problem is especially pressing in matters of value judgments. What, for example, should the Christian (or Jew, Muslim, Marxist) have done in face of the now largely suppressed Hindu tradition of widow burning (*suttee*)? Should s/he try to learn its value, tolerate it, ignore it, oppose it (in what manner)? Or the Nazi tenet of killing all Jews? These, however, are relatively clear issues, but what of a religion-ideology that approves slavery, as Christianity, Judaism, and Islam did until a little more than a century ago? Maybe that is clear enough today, but what of sexism—or only a little sexism? Or the claim that only through capitalism—or socialism —human liberation can be gained? Making a decision on the proper stance becomes less and less clear cut.

Eventually it was clear to most nineteenth century non-Hindus that the proper attitude was not dialogue with Hinduism on *suttee*, but rather opposition. But apparently it was not so clear to all non-Nazis that opposition to Jewish genocide was the stance to take. Further, it took Christians almost 2,000 years to come to that conclusion concerning the rejection of slavery. Many religions/ideologies today stand in the midst of a battle over sexism, some even refusing to admit the existence of the issue. Lastly, no argument need be made to point out the controversial nature of the contemporary capitalism-socialism issue.

Clearly, important contradictory differences between religions-ideologies do exist and at times warrant not dialogue, but opposition. Individually, we rather frequently make critical judgments on the acceptability of positions within our personal lives, and within our own traditions—for example, I have worked strenuously for many decades against the authoritarian governance structure of my Catholic Church.[6]

But certainly this exercise of our critical faculties is not to be limited to ourselves and our tradition; this perhaps most human of faculties should be made available to all—with all the proper constraints and concerns for dialogue already detailed at length. Of course, it must first be determined on what grounds we can judge whether a religious-ideological difference is in fact contradictory, and then, if it is, whether it is of sufficient importance and of a nature to warrant active opposition.

Full Human Life

Because all religions and ideologies are attempts to explain the ultimate meaning of human life, and how to live accordingly, those doctrines and customs that are perceived as hostile to human life—whether in my own religious-ideological tradition or that of another—must be opposed, and that opposition should be proportional to the extent they threaten life. What is to be included in an authentically full human life then must be the measure against which all elements of all religions-ideologies must be tested as we make judgments about whether they are in harmony, complementarity, analogy, or contradiction, and then act accordingly.

Since human beings are by nature historical beings, what it means to be fully human is evolving. At bottom, everything human flows from what would seem to be acceptable to all as a description of the minimally essential human structure, that is, being an animal who can think abstractly and make free decisions. Humanity has only gradually come to the contemporary position that claims are made in favor of "human rights," that things are due to all humans specifically because they are human. This position, in fact, has not always and everywhere been held. Indeed, it was for the most part hardly conceived until recently.

Just a century-plus years ago, for example, slavery was still widely accepted and even vigorously defended and practiced by high Christian churchmen, not to speak of Christian, Jewish, and Muslim slave traders. And yet this radical violation of human rights has today been largely eliminated both in practice and law. Today no thinker or public leader would contemplate justifying slavery, at least in its directly named form of the past (see the *Universal Declaration of Human Rights* by the United Nations in 1948; art. 4). Here we have an obvious example of the historical evolution of the understanding of what it means to be fully human, that is, that human beings are by nature radically free.

What in the twentieth century was acknowledged as the foundation of being human is that human beings ought to be autonomous in their decisions, such decisions being directed by their own reason and limited only by the same rights of others: "All human beings are born free and equal in dignity and rights. They are endowed with reason and conscience and should act toward one another in a spirit of brotherhood" (*Universal Declaration* art. 1). In the ethical sphere, this autonomy, which Aquinas recognized already in the thirteenth century,[7] expanded into the social, political spheres in the eighteenth century—well capsulated in the slogan of the French Revolution: "Liberty, Equality, Fraternity" (contemporary consciousness of sexist language would lead to a substitute like "Solidarity" for "Fraternity"). With the term "liberty" is understood all personal and civil rights; with the term "equality" is understood political rights of participation in public decision-making; with the term "solidarity" is understood (in an expanded twentieth-century sense) social rights.

Although frequently resistant in the past, and too often still in the present, the great religious communities of the world have likewise often and in a variety of ways expressed a growing awareness of and commitment to many of the same notions of what it means to be fully human. Hence, through dialogue humanity is creeping painfully slowly toward a consensus on what is involved in an authentically full human life. The 1948 United Nations *Universal Declaration of Human Rights* was an important step in that direction. In September 1991, my friend Professor Hans Küng and I launched the Global Ethic Movement[8] (more on that below). Of course, much more consensus needs to be attained if interreligious, interideological dialogue is to reach its full potential.

Conclusion

The conclusion from these reflections, I believe, is clear: interreligious, interideological dialogue is absolutely necessary in our contemporary world. Again, every religion and ideology can make its own several official statements, from the Catholic Church about the necessity of dialogue, starting with Pope Paul VI in his first encyclical:

> *Dialogue* is *demanded* nowadays.... It is *demanded* by the dynamic course of action which is changing the face of modern society. It is *demanded* by the pluralism of society, and by the maturity man has reached in this day and age. Be he religious or not, his secular education has enabled him to think and speak, and to conduct a dialogue with dignity *(Ecclesiam suam,* no. 78).

To this the Vatican Curia later added:

> All Christians should do their best to promote dialogue between men of every class as a duty of fraternal charity suited to our progressive and adult age.... The willingness to engage in dialogue is the measure and the strength of that general renewal which must be carried out in the Church [read: in every religion and ideology].[9]

5

Deep-Dialogue/Critical-Thinking/Emotional-Intelligence/Competitive-Cooperation: The Most Authentic Way to Be Human

Deep-Dialogue opens one to the Other, and it needs to be matched by Critical-Thinking, meaning first of all, the three "W" questions: What precisely is meant by the terms used? Whence is the source of the claim made? Whither its implications? Emotional-Intelligence leads to self-knowledge, and how to relate to the Other, and Competitive-Cooperation (preferring win-win, both-and solutions over zero-sum, either-or), completes the circle of Perception-Reflection-Relation-Action.

As mentioned earlier, when I started down the path of dialogue over a half century ago in 1957, the term dialogue was very little used and had not been much meditated on as yet. After it received a huge boost at the Catholic Second Vatican Council (1962–1965), the term began to be used more broadly, and in the 1970s, I and others began to reflect on its deeper implications. Then, after the sudden end of the Cold War in 1989, it became so popular that, as briefly outlined above, I and my colleagues developed the term Deep-Dialogue to indicate that we were talking about this largely new, transformative, whole new way of thinking. At that time I also began to realize that Deep-Dialogue was, as it were, only one side of the coin of our humanity and the other side of the coin was Critical-Thinking. I developed the two as intimately connected, as reflected in my late-1990s online course (www.astro.temple.edu/~swidler/course/index.htm). Of course, our "humanity" could not be fully described by only thinking and talking, but needed to include action. I completed that dimension of my reflections in an editorial in the spring issue, 2012, of the *Journal of Ecumenical Studies*, and still later I added the further dimension of Emotional-Intelligence. I am inserting them here in their brief entirety, even though there is some repetition (again, recalling: *repetitio est mater studiorum!*)

All Knowledge Is Interpreted Knowledge

To begin, we humans as a group have in the last two centuries increasingly learned that "Nobody knows everything about anything!" We now know that all knowledge is interpreted knowledge. There is no "truth" out there. There is "reality" out there, but "truth" resides in our knowing capacities: senses, sensitivities, intellect, and so forth. Normally we use the words truth and true to refer to our *statements* about something. We would say that my statement "The door is closed" is true if we checked and found that the statement accurately described reality—in this case, that the door in fact is closed. At the same time, we can of course say many other true things about the door, for example, that it is so tall, so wide, is a particular color, made of such material, and on and on indefinitely. Our potential knowledge of that door is endless, except that it is limited by our "receptors." If I know little, for example, about chemistry, my knowing about the chemical makeup of the door is thereby limited.

If this is true about a simple physical object, how much more is it true about more complicated, abstract matters, such as are claimed in understandings of literature, political affairs, history—and especially that most comprehensive of all disciplines, religion/ideology ("An explanation of the *ultimate* meaning of life, and how to live accordingly"—if based on some notion/experience of the transcendent, however understood, then called "religion," if not, then called, perhaps, "ideology"). The all-encompassing meaning of claims in the Bible, the Qur'an, the Vedas... will necessarily be limited by my knowing capacities. If I am a believing Muslim, for example, the Qur'an will be completely without effect in my life until it has gotten into my knowing capacities, my senses, sensitivities, intellect. But, like liquid Jello being poured into its container, it—in this case, the meaning of the Qur'an—takes the shape of the container. The "truth" of the Qur'an will take the shape of my senses, sensitivities, intellect. Analogously, this is the case with all religious believers (or for whatever passes in a person's life as religion, or ideology). So, if I am the kind of Catholic who says, "Whatever the pope says is true," then *I* have decided that truth will take the shape of whatever the pope says, or analogously, *I* as a Muslim say, "Whatever the sheikh says the Qur'an says, I accept," or on the other hand, I say that *I* will decide for myself what is the ultimate meaning of life, or, or, or... There is no escape from the fact that *I* am intimately involved in *all* knowledge, that "All knowledge is interpreted knowledge."

Am I then trapped in a destructive solipsism (Latin: *solus*, alone; *ipsus*, myself), a Leonard Swidler bubble? No, for we humans can communicate with other knowers, who also necessarily perceive the world from their own vantage points, as a I do from mine. That gives us the possibility of learning about other facets of reality—seen from, for example, Mary Murphy's perspective, or from Mutombo Nkulu's perspective, or, or, or...—so that I can compare, analyze their knowledge, and aim at gaining an ever fuller—but never complete and never totally objective grasp of reality. In a word, the only way we can endlessly escape our "myself alone" bubble is by *Dialogue*. I need to come to know about reality as perceived and understood by, for example, a Chinese Buddhist woman, who clearly will perceive and understand facets of reality that I as an American Catholic man cannot perceive and understand from my experience of reality, and vice versa. In short we both need to be in dialogue with each other, and everyone else—endlessly! This is a far deeper, life-transforming understanding of Dialogue than the often now rather superficial common understanding. Hence, I increasingly use the expanded term Deep-Dialogue to get at this more profound, substantial, life-shaping meaning.

Dialogue Is the Very Foundation of the Cosmos

Dialogue—understood in its broadest sense as the mutually beneficial interaction of differing components—is at the very heart of the Universe, of which we humans are the highest expression: from the basic interaction of matter *and* energy (in Albert Einstein's unforgettable formula, $E = MC^2$; energy equals mass times the square of the speed of light), to the creative interaction of protons *and* electrons in every atom, to the vital symbiosis of body *and* spirit in every human, to the creative dialogue between woman *and* man, to the dynamic relationship between individual *and* society. Thus, the very essence of our humanity is dialogical, and a fulfilled human life is the highest expression of the Cosmic Dance of Dialogue.

In the early millennia of the history of humanity, as we spread outward from our starting point in central Africa, the forces of divergence were dominant. However, because we live on a globe, in our frenetic divergence we eventually began to encounter each other more and more frequently. Now the forces of stunning convergence are becoming increasingly dominant.

In the past, during the age of divergence, we could live in isolation from each other; we could ignore each other. Now, in the age of convergence, we are forced to live in one world. We increasingly live in a global village. We cannot ignore the Other, the different. Too often in the past we have tried to make over the Other into a likeness of ourselves, often by violence, but this is the very opposite of dialogue. This egocentric arrogance is in fundamental opposition to the Cosmic Dance of Dialogue. It is not creative; rather, it is destructive. Hence, we humans today have a stark choice: dialogue or death![1]

Dialogue of the Head, Hands, Heart in Holistic
Harmony of the Holy Human

For us humans, there are four main dimensions to dialogue, corresponding to the structure of our humanness: Dialogue of the Head, Hands, Heart in Holistic Harmony of the Holy Human.

The Cognitive or the Intellectual: Seeking the True

In the Dialogue of the Head, we reach out to those who think differently from us in order to understand how they see the world and why they act as they do. The world is too complicated for anyone to grasp alone; increasingly, we can understand reality only with the help of the other, in dialogue. This is important, because how we *understand* the world determines how we *act* in the world.

The Illative or Ethical: Seeking the Good

In the Dialogue of the Hands, we join with others to work to make the world a better place in which we all must live together. Since we can no longer live separately in this one world, we must work jointly to make it not just a house but a home for all of us to live in. In other words, we join hands with the other to heal the world—*Tikun olam*, in the Jewish tradition. The world within us and all around us is always in need of healing, and our deepest wounds can be healed only together with the other, only in dialogue.

The Affective or Aesthetic: Seeking the Beautiful, the Spiritual

In the Dialogue of the Heart, we open ourselves to receive the beauty of the other. Because we humans are body and spirit—or, rather, body-spirit—we give bodily-spiritual expression in all the arts to our multifarious responses to life: joy, sorrow, gratitude, anger, and, most of all, love. We try to express our inner feelings, which grasp reality in far deeper and higher ways than we are able to put into rational concepts and words; hence, we create poetry, music, dance, painting, architecture—the expressions of the heart. (Here, too, is where the depth, spiritual, mystical dimension of the human spirit is given full rein.) All the world delights in beauty, and so it is here that we find the easiest encounter with the Other, the simplest door to dialogue. As seventeenth-century mathematician/philosopher Blaise Pascal said, *Le cœur a ses raisons que la raison ne connaît point.* "The heart has its reasons, which reason knows not."

Holiness: Seeking the One

We humans cannot live a divided life. If we are to survive, let alone flourish, we must get it all together. We must not only dance the dialogues of the *H*ead, *H*ands, and *H*eart but also bring our various parts together in *H*armony (a fourth "H") to live a *H*olistic (a fifth "H"), life, which is what religions mean that we should be *H*oly (a sixth "H"). Hence, we are authentically *H*uman (a seventh "H") only when our manifold elements are in dialogue within each other and when we are in dialogue with the others around us. We must dance together the Cosmic Dance of Dialogue of the *H*ead, *H*ands, and *H*eart, *H*olistically,[2] in *H*armony within the *H*oly *H*uman.

Deep-Dialogue Entails Critical-Thinking

Meaning of Terms

If we reflect at all about the term dialogue, it will be clear that it is about think-ing.[3] The Greek prefix *dia* has a variety of meanings, including across, among, together. The Greek word *logos* is familiar to all speakers of Western languages in its many cognates, starting with "logic"—the science of thinking clearly. Further, all words ending in "logy," like geology, psychology, anthropology and so forth mean the systematic thinking about the *geos* (earth), the *psyche* (spirit), the *anthropos* (human) and so on. Thus, *dialogos* means thinking-across or thinking-together, which makes it clear that at the heart of *dialogos* is *thinking*, and not just any thinking, but systematic thinking, logical thinking, that is, Critical-Thinking.

Hence, if Dialogue is at the foundation of the whole cosmos, with the human as its conscious pinnacle, who is the lead Dancer of the "Cosmic Dance of Dialogue," it is also true that *logos*, thinking, is at the center of Dialogue, at the center of the cosmos (Greek: *cosmos*=order; *chaos* =confusion; we humans are constantly learning more and more about the *logos*, the "order," the *cosmos*—which persists even in the midst of, seemingly to us at times, *chaos*, confusion—that permeates all reality). If we are seriously to engage in dialogue, Deep-Dialogue, we necessar-ily must also engage in *logos*, logic, *denken*, thinking: Critical-Thinking.

The first thing to recognize about the term Critical-Thinking is that it does not mean negatively criticizing someone or something. Rather, the term "criti-cal" comes from the Greek *krinein*, "to make a judgment, a decision." However, we can make a judgment, a decision thoughtfully (with systematic *denken*, *logos*, logic) only if we have the data in front of us so that we can first analyze it (Greek: *ana*, up, *lysis*, break), that is, to break up the ideas, the information into their component parts to see how they fit together. Then we move to synthesis (Greek: *syn* together, *thesis*, to put), that is, after seeing how the component parts fit together, to explore the relations of the parts to other things, or at times to put the parts together in new ways.

The Three "W" Questions: What? Whence? Whither?

If analysis and synthesis are the fundamental ways we humans think, in order to think critically, to make a judgment, a decision on the basis of gathered data and systematic, analytic-synthetic thought, we must first address three basic "W" questions: What, Whence, Whither?

What? means that we need to develop the habit of striving to understand as precisely as possible what it is we are talking about. This principle is so obvi-ous that it tends, as so often in life, to be violated in proportion to its simplicity. Oftentimes it helps to ask what the etymological roots of the term in question are (as I have been doing here) to help us get a clear grasp of what we are talking about. Example: to believe means having faith in someone or something; faith comes from the Latin *fides*, having trust. Hence, believing something, having faith in something means affirming that something is true, not because we have proof of it, but because we trust the source of that information.

We also need to make sure that I and my interlocutors have precisely the same understanding of the idea or term being discussed; otherwise, we will simply be talking past each other. It is also especially vital that we keep precisely the same meaning of the term when we move from one statement to another. If we do not, we will end up with a four-term syllogism. A typical syllogism runs like this: A is E; E is C; therefore, A is C. We need to be certain that the meaning of the connecting term, "E," has precisely the same meaning in the second premise as in the first. If, however, deliberately or inadvertently, we change the meaning, however slightly, of the connecting term—E to e—while keeping the same sound, we will have a four-term syllogism: A is E; e is C; therefore...? Therefore, nothing (!) simply because we have four terms: A, E, e, and C. Hence, it is vital to know precisely What we are talking about.

In thinking, alone or with others, out loud or in writing, we start with an idea or term—and, as just noted, in answering the first question of What? we need to be clear about its precise meaning. Secondly, we then need to ask ourselves, Whence? Where does the basis for affirming this idea come from? Are we beginning by simply defining something to be the case? Is this idea an unexamined presupposition? Do we have factual evidence for it? Is it a valid, logical deduction from solidly proven data? Is it based on a trustworthy source? and so on. Any truthful results of thinking, alone or with others, will depend on the validity of the answer to this question: Whence the evidence for what we are talking about?

If we have been careful in understanding precisely What we are talking about, and have carefully tested the bases—the Whence—for our affirming the idea in question, then we need to ask ourselves where—Whither?—this idea leads to. What are its implications, for, if the idea is true, then we want to base our subsequent actions on it. In other words, ideas have consequences! Example: If the Golden Rule is judged to be a valid ethical principle, then I need to respect others, tell the truth to others, help others, and so on because I would want them to treat me the same way.

Secondly, it is important to follow these implications in order to learn whether or not they lead to a *reductio ad absurdum* (reduction to absurdity). If that turns out to be the case, then we will need to reinvestigate our databases and the whole line of reasoning from the beginning in order to find the flaw of fact or logic. Example: Some Christian theologians (e.g., St. Augustine, Martin Luther, John Calvin) argued that nothing can happen except that God *makes* it happen, including making humans commit sins that will condemn them to hell for all eternity—the doctrine of predestination. But for followers of Jesus, who depicted God as his loving Father who reaches out to all humans to lead them to himself, this is a clear contradiction, a *reductio ad absurdum*—a loving God deliberately creating humans not to lead them to God but to hell! This line of critical thinking led many Augustinians, Lutherans, and Calvinists to reject predestination.

Unconscious Presuppositions

A further fundamental move we must strive to make in order to engage in Critical-Thinking concerns our *Unconscious Presuppositions*. To be conscious of something is, of course, to be aware of it. Obviously unconscious means *not* to be aware of something. Also clearly, *pre* (Latin) means beforehand, and *supposition* (Latin: *sub positio* = under position) means something underlying. Hence, a presupposition is an idea that ahead of time *underlies* another idea or set of ideas. When we speak of an *unconscious presupposition*, it is one that we are *un*aware of; it is *un*conscious. Example: previously, and unfortunately still today, many men and women, thought that women were incapable of clear, rational thought. This was a presupposition, a prior underlying assumption, that prevented women from attending the university. For the most part it was unconscious, that is, most people did not think about it. They just assumed it without being aware that they were doing so.

So long as a presupposition remains uninvestigated, we cannot know that we are acting on the basis of a reality or a mirage. We cannot truthfully tell ourselves that we are acting thus in a rational manner. The situation is even vastly more devastating when the presupposition is unconscious. Then we are controlled totally by an idea that might be partially, or even totally, unwarranted—and we can do absolutely nothing about it (!), for we are powerless to analyze an idea, and change the consequent action, if we do not even know of the existence of the idea, which is the "motor" that secretly drives our mind and behavior.

We all have endless numbers of unconscious presuppositions that we need to seek out, bring to the conscious level, proceed to analyze, and judge (*krinein*) whether they are valid or not. This is an endless task, for all the information we gather is accepted into *our* cognitive faculties. That is, it is necessarily poured into our mental containers, our presuppositions, or, in a term frequently used today, into our paradigms. A typical example of a paradigm is: earlier all astronomical data was poured into the paradigm (presupposition) that the Earth was the center of the planetary system, rather than the later paradigm that the Sun was the center. But how do we find our unconscious presuppositions so that we may analyze and judge them? There is no sure way but through endless reflection and self-examination. However, one major help is to enter into ongoing dialogues, for when sufficient mutual trust is built, our dialogue partners will then be able to point out some of our unconscious presuppositions, which they can see but we cannot; our trusted dialogue partners become for us mirrors in which we can see how at least a part of the outside world perceives us.

Emotional-Intelligence

Since the latter decades of the twentieth century, increased attention has been paid to what is often referred to as Emotional-Intelligence. This is an important, but not crystal clear, field of investigation. Our emotions can lead us to do many wonderful, and not so wonderful, things. We often claim that we want to bring our actions out from under the sway of our emotions and under the guidance of our clear-thinking intellect. In general, such a goal appears desirable, but that is not the focus of the investigation of our Emotional-Intelligence.

Rather, the focus of Emotional-Intelligence is learning how we humans can effectively mature emotionally. Basically that means learning 1) to know and understand oneself, 2) to know and understand other persons, and 3) how appropriately to relate to each other. One may have learned to analyze a situation with impeccable syllogistic logic (Critical-Thinking), but be totally blind about how one or/and others, fits into the puzzle. An example of such an extreme disjunction might be that of a brilliant Critical-Thinker in the body of socially "clueless" person, a so-called idiot savant.

The goal of maturing our Emotional-Intelligence is not something new under the sun. St. Augustine of Hippo pointed to it when in the fifth century he uttered a prayer, asking "To know you O God, and myself!" Clearly our Emotional-Intelligence needs to be expanded in tandem with our Critical-Thinking, and then expressed in Competitive-Cooperation action—all of which clearly takes place within the all-encompassing embrace of Deep-Dialogue.

Closing the Loop: Competitive-Cooperation

If our actions are to be compatible with Deep-Dialogue and Critical-Thinking/Emotional-Intelligence, they must strive toward being Competitive-Cooperative. Let me explain this last, seemingly contradictory, term.

If the way we understand the world determines the way we act in the world, then action completes the circle of perception-thought-decision-action. We first perceive, then try to understand, in light of which we make a decision, and finally act, putting our perceptions, understanding, decisions into concrete behavioral form. If we have begun to engage the world in a deeply dialogical manner and have critically analyzed/synthesized our perceptions and thoughts, we will want to make decisions on their bases and carry out our actions in the world in an analogously dialogic/critical/emotional-intelligent manner. I am suggesting that the most appropriate way to describe such action is "Competitive-Cooperation."

The outcome of our Deep-Dialogue and Critical-Thinking/Emotional-Intelligence must be our free/responsible action because the core of being human is freedom and its corresponding responsibility. This freedom/responsibility core has always been the case since the emergence of *Homo sapiens* perhaps 100,000 years ago in central Africa, even though this core did not begin to be de facto widespread and recognized until around two hundred years ago with the Enlightenment. Our core human freedom/responsibility flows from our humanly developed rational intellect, which allows us to abstract (Latin: *ab*, "from" and *tractus*, "pulled," as in "tractor") from our myriad sense perceptions various concepts and possibilities, on the bases of which we can choose, decide to act one way or another. This is another way to say we "love," that is, we reach out to become one with what we perceive to be the "good"—for example, becoming one with the "good" ice cream, the "good" Mozart music, the "good" friend...each in its appropriate way.

Humans have long recognized that we are something unique in the cosmos (there may be other free beings we have not yet discovered—or perhaps never will) because of our radical freedom (despite its limitations, of which we are increasingly becoming aware) based on our rationality.

I have written extensively—and am very deliberately restressing here!—about how humanity has in the last two centuries increasingly come to realize that because all knowledge is necessarily limited, is interpreted by the knower— "Nobody knows Everything about Anything!"[4] Hence, we have no other intelligent choice but to reach out in dialogue, Deep-Dialogue, to those who think differently from us to learn increasingly/endlessly more about reality. I have also increasingly stressed the other side of our "coin of humanity," Critical-Thinking, wherein we constantly pose the critical Three "W" Questions: What precisely are we talking about? Whence comes the basis for affirming it? Whither do its implications lead—*reductio ad absurdam*, or not? Steven Pinker has most recently brilliantly shown that it is the increasing human rationality, in the sense of the increasing development of reasonable habits of mind, abstract thinking, and thence actions, that is leading to an increasingly peaceful human world (counterintuitive though that may at first blush seem!).[5] Even before him, in a more philosophical than social scientific manner, Bernard Lonergan also argued that increasing intelligence was a necessity for an increasingly ethical behavior.[6]

Since we humans are also bodies, our perceptions, reflections, decisions need to result in actions in the world. Through fostering our Critical-Thinking/Emotional-Intelligence and reaching out to increasingly expand our necessarily myopic view of reality through Deep-Dialogue, we will want to act in a manner that is a reflection of our "both-and" Deep-Dialogue/Critical-Thinking/Emotional-Intelligence: namely, through Competitive-Cooperation. The Cooperation half is relatively easy to understand. So long as the "Other" is not acting in a destructive manner, then we would want to act, at a minimum, not negatively toward the Other, but as much as possible in tandem, so as to create a win-win situation as much as possible.

But "Competitive"? That would seem necessarily to aim at a win-lose, a zero-sum approach. To a certain extent that is accurate. However, I am thinking first of all of this "Competition" as being with ourself, striving to be as effective, efficient, creative as possible—to borrow from Islam the initial meaning of *Jihad*, the Great *Jihad* (Arabic: struggle), the Competition, with ourself to live out our inner principles (placed there by God, according to Islam—and Judaism and Christianity as well). This *Creative* Competition may at times mean that one individual, one group, will get the contract, will be chosen to provide the requested product or service—win-lose, zero-sum in that sense. But the *Creative* Competition individual and group should thereby be led to create, develop new alternatives—as, for example, renewable energy sources as alternatives to fossil fuels, or President Barack Obama inviting Hilary Clinton into his cabinet. In the business field, an ever more human organization increasingly searches for the most creative, expansive, all-inclusive way of operating—a "both-and," a "win-win" for both the producers and users, reflecting the creative balance of Deep-Dialogue, "pro and con" Critical-Thinking/Emotional-Intelligence in a balance of Creative Competition and Cooperation.

A striking example of such thinking—and action—in the global corporate world was given by Ryuzaburo Kaku, Chairman of the Board of the Japanese multinational Canon, Inc. His vision in leading his company convinced me that what I in English terms describe as Competitive-Cooperation was in fact doable. He expressed his vision as the *Kyosei* principles: "Living and working together for the common good." He argued that this concept of *Kyosei* should be a creed that all corporations and nations follow, and outlined the progress of ethical companies through four stages, describing the fourth stage thus:

> The fourth type is the "corporation assuming global social responsibilities," a "truly global corporation." This type of company cares for all its direct stakeholders, including its local community—but it goes beyond: it strives to fulfill its corporate obligations on a global scale. Its social responsibilities transcend national boundaries.

Mr. Kaku was not a naive "do-gooder," but a creative business entrepreneur, insisting that constant innovation was the key to creating ever more wealth for humanity—and his company: "By creating new products and processes...the company will not only succeed financially, but will also have made the world a better place to live. That is what it means to be an ethical business leader!" He also wrote: "Competition is vital for efficiency, but it must be 'fair' competition, based on innovation, quality and efficiency," combining thereby competition with cooperation: "Innovative corporations with specialties in different areas can also work together in the spirit of *Kyosei* to produce outstanding products. In this way a synergy is created, and products can be produced that neither company alone could develop." Impressive as this vision is, Kaku later projected a stunningly challenging fifth stage:

> I have recently come to believe that a fifth category is needed in my analysis of companies as they evolve into ethical social institutions. This fifth type I see as a company that seeks to change the world for the better. Companies in the fifth stage also try to increase the number of like-minded partners that assume global social responsibilities and that are actively concerned with global problems. ... Companies in the fifth stage realize it is not right for the enormous number of corporations existing in the world to remain apathetic about the various perplexing problems emerging on our planet. They know it is not enough for a corporation to transform itself only into a fourth type of corporation and simply strive to correct imbalances—it knows it must go further.

Kaku would have *Kyosei* serve as a key principle in the new world order that emerged after the end of the Cold War. He insisted that democracy, human rights, and peace are indeed indispensable values, but alone they are not adequate. Said another way, they are necessary, but not sufficient causes of the common weal; *Kyosei* needs to augment them. In English terms for *Kyosei*, I offer Competitive-Cooperation.

In summary, Competitive-Cooperation, in putting into action in a manner in keeping with Deep-Dialogue/Critical-Thinking/Emotional-Intelligence:

1. is not satisfied with the passable, but reaches for the best;
2. strives to make decisions within broader frameworks;
3. is not satisfied with the standard, but stresses constant creativity;
4. as much as possible, avoids zero-sum, win-lose solutions, but seeks creatively win-win ones;
5. prefers not either-or, but both-and choices.

Therefore, I propose that our most authentic human way to be and act is Deep-Dialogue/Critical-Thinking/Emotional-Intelligence/Competitive-Cooperation.

6

The Dialogue Decalogue: Ground Rules for Interreligious, Interideological Dialogue

For over 30 years the Dialogue Decalogue—ten commonsense rules that, if followed, lead to true mutual learning, to Dialogue—have helped thousands, perhaps millions, of people of all religions, and beyond, open up and truly encounter the Other, thereby expanding themselves.

This is the "classical" version of the Dialogue Decalogue, written before the term Deep-Dialogue was invented.[1] Also, this document focuses on the "Dialogue of the Head":

> Dialogue is a conversation on a common subject between two or more persons with differing views, the *primary* purpose of which is for each participant to learn from the other so that s/he can change and grow. This very definition of dialogue embodies the first commandment of dialogue.

In the religious-ideological sphere in the past, we came together to discuss with those differing with us, for example, Catholics with Protestants, either to defeat an opponent or to learn about an opponent so as to deal more effectively with her or him, or at best to negotiate with her or him. If we faced each other at all, it was in confrontation—sometimes more openly polemically, sometimes more subtly—but always with the ultimate goal of defeating the other, because we were convinced that we alone had the absolute truth.

But dialogue is *not* debate. In dialogue, each partner must listen to the other as openly and sympathetically as s/he can in an attempt to understand the other's position as precisely and, as it were, as much from within, as possible. Such an attitude automatically includes the assumption that at any point we might find the partner's position so persuasive that, if we would act with integrity, we would have to change, and change can be disturbing.

We are here, of course, speaking of a specific kind of dialogue, an *inter*religious, *inter*ideological dialogue. To have such a dialogue, it is not sufficient that the dialogue partners discuss a religious-ideological subject, that is, the ultimate meaning of life and how to live accordingly. Rather, they must come to the dialogue as persons who somehow significantly identify with a religious or ideological community. If I were neither a Christian nor a Marxist, for example, I could not participate as a "partner" in Christian-Marxist dialogue, although I might listen in, ask some questions for information, and make some helpful comments.

It is obvious that interreligious, interideological dialogue is something new. We could not conceive of it, let alone do it in the past. How, then, can we effectively engage in this new practice? The following are some basic ground rules, or commandments, of interreligious, interideological dialogue that must be observed if dialogue is actually to take place. These are not theoretical rules, or commandments given from on high, but basic rules that have been learned from hard experience.

FIRST COMMANDMENT: The primary purpose of dialogue is to learn, that is, to change and grow in the perception and understanding of reality, and then to act accordingly. Minimally, the very fact that I learn that my dialogue partner believes "this" rather than "that" proportionally changes my attitude toward her, and a change in my attitude is a significant change in me. We enter into dialogue so that *we* can learn, change, and grow, not so we can force change on the *other*, as one hopes to do in debate—a hope realized in inverse proportion to the frequency and ferocity with which debate is entered into. On the other hand, because in dialogue *each* partner comes with the intention of learning and changing herself, one's partner in fact will also change. Thus the goal of debate, and much more, is accomplished far more effectively by dialogue.

SECOND COMMANDMENT: Interreligious, interideological dialogue must be a two-sided project—within each religious or ideological community and between religious or ideological communities. Because of the "communal" nature of interreligious dialogue, and because the primary goal of dialogue is that each partner learn and change himself, it is also necessary that each participant enter into dialogue not only with his partner across the faith line—the Lutheran with the Anglican, for example—but also with his coreligionists, with his fellow Lutherans, to share with them the fruits of the interreligious dialogue. Only thus can the whole community eventually learn and change, moving toward an ever more perceptive insight into reality.

THIRD COMMANDMENT: Each participant must come to the dialogue with complete honesty and sincerity. It should be made clear in what direction the major and minor thrusts of the tradition move, what the future shifts might be, and, if necessary, where the participant has difficulties with her own tradition. False fronts have no place in dialogue.

Conversely—each participant must assume that the other partners have a similar attitude of complete honesty and sincerity. Not only will the absence of sincerity prevent dialogue from happening, but the absence of the assumption of the partner's sincerity will do so as well. In brief: no trust, no dialogue.

FOURTH COMMANDMENT: In interreligious, interideological dialogue we must not compare our ideals with our partner's practice, but rather our ideals with our partner's ideals, our practice with our partner's practice. For example, compare the former Hindu practice of burning live widows (*suttee*) with the former Christian former practices of burning witches and auto-da-fés.

FIFTH COMMANDMENT: Each participant must define himself. Only the Jew, for example, can define what it means to be a Jew. The rest can only describe what it looks like from the outside. Moreover, because dialogue is a dynamic medium, as each participant learns, he will change and hence continually deepen, expand, and modify his self-definition as a Jew—being careful to remain in constant dialogue with fellow Jews. Thus it is mandatory that each dialogue partner define what it means to be an authentic member of his own tradition.

Conversely—the one who is interpreted must be able to recognize herself in the interpretation. This is the golden rule of interreligious hermeneutics, as has been often reiterated by the "apostle of interreligious dialogue," Raimundo Panikkar. For the sake of understanding, each dialogue participant will naturally attempt to express for herself what she thinks is the meaning of the partner's statement; the partner must be able to recognize herself in that expression. The advocate of a world theology, Wilfred Cantwell Smith, would add that the expression must also be verifiable by critical observers who are not involved.

SIXTH COMMANDMENT: Each participant must come to the dialogue with no hard-and-fast assumptions as to where the points of disagreement are. Rather, each partner should not only listen to the other partner with openness and sympathy but also attempt to agree with the dialogue partner as far as is possible, while still maintaining integrity with his own tradition. Where he absolutely can agree no further without violating his own integrity, precisely there is the real point of disagreement—which most often turns out to be different from the point of disagreement that was falsely assumed ahead of time.

SEVENTH COMMANDMENT: Dialogue can take place only between equals— both of them coming to learn, or *par cum pari,* as Vatican II put it. Both individuals must come to learn from each other. Therefore, if, for example, the Muslim views Hinduism as inferior, or if the Hindu views Islam as inferior, there will be no dialogue. If authentic interreligious, interideological dialogue between Muslims and Hindus is to occur, then both the Muslim and the Hindu must come mainly to learn from each other. Only then will the dialogue be equal with equal, *par cum pari.* This rule also indicates that is no one-way dialogue. For example, Jewish-Christian discussions that began in the 1960s were mainly only prolegomena to interreligious dialogue. Understandably and properly, Jews came to these exchanges only to teach Christians, although the Christians came mainly to learn. But, if authentic interreligious dialogue between Christians and Jews is to occur, then the Jews must also come mainly to learn. Only then will the dialogue too be *par cum pari.*

EIGHTH COMMANDMENT: Dialogue can take place only on the basis of mutual trust: approach first those issues most likely to provide common ground, thereby establishing human trust. Although interreligious, interideological dialogue must occur with some kind of "communal" dimension, that is, the participants must be involved as members of a religious or ideological community—for instance, as Marxists or Taoists—it is also fundamentally true that it is only *persons* who can enter into dialogue. But a dialogue among persons can be built only on personal trust. Hence it is wise not to tackle the most difficult problems in the beginning, but rather to approach first those issues most likely to provide some common ground, thereby establishing the basis of human trust. Then, gradually, as this personal trust deepens and expands, the more thorny matters can be undertaken. Thus, as in learning we move from the known to the unknown, so too in dialogue do we proceed from commonly held matters—which, given our mutual ignorance that has resulted from centuries of hostility, will take us quite some time to discover fully—to discuss matters of disagreement.

NINTH COMMANDMENT: Persons entering into interreligious, interideological dialogue must be at least minimally self-critical of both themselves and their own religious or ideological traditions. A lack of such self-criticism implies that one's own tradition already has all the correct answers. Such an attitude makes dialogue not only unnecessary but even impossible, since we enter into dialogue primarily so *we* can learn, which obviously is impossible if our tradition has never made a misstep, if it has all the right answers. To be sure, in interreligious, interideological dialogue one must stand within a religious or ideological tradition with integrity and conviction, but such integrity and conviction must include, not exclude, a healthy self-criticism. Without it there can be no dialogue—and, indeed, no integrity.

TENTH COMMANDMENT: Each participant eventually must attempt to experience the partner's religion or ideology "from within," for a religion or ideology is not merely something of the head, but also of the spirit, heart, and whole being, both individual and communal. John Dunne[2] here speaks of "passing over" into another's religious or ideological experience and then coming back enlightened, broadened, and deepened. While retaining our own religious integrity, we need to find ways of experiencing something of the emotional and spiritual power of the symbols and cultural vehicles of our partner's religion—and then come back to our own, enriched and expanded, having experienced at least a little bit of the affective side of our partner's religion or ideology.

Interreligious, interideological dialogue operates in four areas—the Dialogues of the Head, Hands, Heart and Holy: the practical (Dialogue of the Hands), where we collaborate to help humanity; the aesthetic/spiritual (Dialogue of the Heart), where we attempt to experience the partner's expressions of beauty and her/his religion or ideology "from within"; the cognitive (Dialogue of the Head), where we seek understanding and truth; and the integrative (Dialogue of the Holy).

Interreligious, interideological dialogue has three major phases (its more detailed Seven Stages are outlined below). In the first phase we unlearn misinformation about each other and begin to know each other as we truly are. In phase two we begin to discern values in the partner's tradition and wish to appropriate them into our own tradition. For example, in the Buddhist-Christian dialogue Christians might learn a greater appreciation of the meditative tradition, and Buddhists might learn a greater appreciation of the prophetic, social justice tradition—both values traditionally associated strongly, although not exclusively, with the other's community. If we are serious, persistent, and sensitive enough in the dialogue, we may at times enter into phase three. Here we together begin to explore new areas of reality, of meaning, and of truth, of which neither of us had even been aware before. We are brought face to face with this new, as-yet-unknown-to-us dimension of reality only because of questions, insights, probings produced in the dialogue. We may thus dare to say that patiently pursued dialogue can become an instrument of new revelation, a further unveiling of reality—on which we must then act.

There is something radically different about phase one on the one hand and phases two and three on the other. In the latter we do not simply add on quantitatively another truth or value from the partner's tradition. Instead, as we assimilate it within our own religious self-understanding, it will proportionately transform our self-understanding. Since our dialogue partner will be in a similar position, we will then be able to witness authentically to those elements of deep value in our own tradition that our partner's tradition may well be able to assimilate with self-transforming profit. All this of course will have to be done with complete integrity on each side, each partner remaining authentically true to the vital core of his/her own religious tradition. However, in significant ways that vital core will be perceived and experienced differently under the influence of the dialogue, but if the dialogue is carried on with both integrity and openness, the result will be that, for example, the Jew will be even more authentically Jewish and the Christian even more authentically Christian, *not despite* the fact that Judaism and/or Christianity have found and adapted something of deep value in the other tradition, *but because of it.* There can be no talk of a syncretism here, for syncretism in the pejorative sense means amalgamating various elements of different religions into some kind of a confused whole without concern for the integrity of the religions involved—which is not the case with authentic dialogue.

7

Dialogue Decalogue: Pastoral Applications[*]

It turns out that the principles of the Dialogue Decalogue are precisely the same basic insights that are taught as the foundation of effective pastoral psychology; in brief, to be a helpful pastor or counselor, one needs to follow the principles of dialogue. Concretely, this was found to be the case in both North and South America.

Ecumenism has been well served in the last few decades by pastoral education. A gradual consensus has been emerging with regard to what pastoral ministry is and how people should be prepared to do it.[1] This consensus, largely unarticulated *as* an ecumenical achievement, characterizes professional groups such as the Association of Clinical Pastoral Education, the American Association of Pastoral Counselors, and the Association for Theological Field Education. It is evidenced in the range of the membership and the operating criteria of the Association of Theological Schools. It permeates the content of programs such as clinical pastoral education and professional degrees such as the Master of Divinity and Doctor of Ministry.

A central focus of this consensus is the importance of dialogue in pastoral ministry. Most pastoral ministry revolves around conversation. Accordingly, the skills involved in listening, responding, and communicating are primary in any pastoral preparation program. In this regard pastoral education not only cuts across denominational lines for resources and techniques for use in training but it also enhances the possibilities of ecumenical dialogue by increasing the dialogue skills of future ministers.[2]

Given this situation, it is instructive to look at the recent Dialogue Decalogue (*JES* 20 [Winter, 1983]: 1–4) from a pastoral perspective. Such an overview can strengthen/clarify the ecumenical-pastoral connection, while reinforcing and perhaps advancing the ground rules for both.

General Observations

a. Ground rules should come from the ground up. The Decalogue's ground rules "are not theoretical rules or commandments given from on high," but ones that "have been learned from hard experience." This coincides with the basic approach of pastoral education. Experience, especially hard experience, is the starting point for any adequate pastoral learning.[3] By examining their own practice of ministry, students are able to see more clearly for themselves their operative principles and style of ministry. Initially this is a hard experience, but out of it students learn better how to listen, respond, communicate—dialogue.

b. The Decalogue distinguishes between debate and dialogue. In pastoral education the same important distinction appears as the difference between control and care.[4] In its most crass form, control attempts to bring others into line with the minister's goals and values. Another form is more manipulative—seeking to understand people in order to get them to do what the minister wants without their being aware of it. A third form of control is selective. A level of openness is manifested, but only on those matters or to the degree that the minister has decided is open for negotiation. As in a debate, pastoral control becomes a contest in which the stakes are win or lose. Corresponding to dialogue is pastoral care: mutual interaction initiated by either the one who cares or the one who is cared for. The goal of the encounter emerges from the communication itself; the style is relational. In the process, listening skills are key, even if what the pastoral agent hears is not comfortable or expected.

c. Authentic interreligious dialogue presupposes that the dialogue partners have some identification with the community for which they speak. Some level of commitment is necessary. On the pastoral side this is primarily a professional rather than a denominational identification. Because most of the skills and techniques used in pastoral work are also used in (and sometimes drawn from) other disciplines that do not have an explicit religious character, pastoral persons often struggle with their proper identity as pastoral counselors in relation to their professional peers.[5] These questions cannot always be answered easily or satisfactorily, yet the very effort of ministerial students to clarify and make explicit their pastoral identity deepens their sense of involvement in the distinctly pastoral dimension of the work and allows for a committed dialogue to take place with other professionals.

The Decalogue

a. The first and the tenth commandments relate to ultimate goals or hoped-for outcomes of dialogue. They are "to change and grow in the perception and understanding of reality and then to act accordingly" and eventually "to experience the partner's religion 'from within'." The very words used in formulating these rules make a pastoral person feel at home. To change, to grow, to experience are the primary goals in any pastoral encounter.

Both pastoral education and pastoral ministry are person centered, while persons are understood to be dynamic, open, relating agents. In a genuine pastoral encounter, all participants are drawn into the exchange and affected by it. The ideal ministry is mutual. One of the clearest indications of the person-centeredness of pastoral ministry is the primary dialogue partner in pastoral education—psychology and its cognate fields of application. Among the authors whose interpretations of the human person are available to pastoral educators, those most frequently used are those of developmental psychologists, whose view of the human person emphasizes growth, change, passage, openness, development.[6]

One of the lessons learned in pastoral education is that persons themselves are the prime resources for meaningful, growthful experience. They cannot stand apart from one another and expect to make any progress. They must enter each other's world, establish and build a relationship.[7] Another key lesson in pastoral education is that pastoral conversation and interpersonal relations are intended to facilitate action. Empathic relating and support are not narcissistic. The pastoral criterion is not simply how one feels in the relationship, but who one becomes in the relationship, which leads to a results from action taken on the basis of reflection and decision-making.[8] The action need not be a radical departure from one's previous practice or a totally new threshold of experience in one's life. Sometimes just choosing to do what one ordinarily does is a significant result, or being a little more assertive or clear about one's own needs or expectations is the action outcome. The action outcome is not predetermined, especially not by a pastoral person; rather, action emerges from the relationship. Personal decisions may be influenced, conditioned, supported by others (e.g., a minister), but ultimately they should be the free choices of individuals.

Regarding interreligious dialogue, such a pastoral perspective would affirm that each religious body and each religious person must decide what it will do as a result of dialogue. This outcome cannot be predetermined—even in defining the eventual goal of dialogue. Pastoral education would also affirm a wide range of possible action results, acknowledging that development is gradual and that each step forward should be celebrated.

b. The second and ninth commandments concern the dialoguer's attitude toward his/her own identity group. "Interreligious dialogue must be a two-sided project—within each religious community and between religious communities," & "persons entering into interreligious dialogue must be at least minimally self-critical of both themselves and their own religious traditions." The thrust behind this first injunction is to carry the results of interreligious dialogue back into one's own religious group, to raise critical questions and push one's "coreligionists" to carry out the implied actions. The point of the second is to avoid any tendency to assume that one's own group already has all the answers so that real dialogue (openness to mutual change) is not necessary for oneself.

In pastoral education, the need for the second commandment appears in the unfortunate gap between academic, scholarly theologians and professional, pastoral practitioners. The hybrid discipline of pastoral-practical theology tries to close the gap somewhat, but there is often a healthier and more productive exchange *between* pastoral agents and their secular counterparts than there is *within* the theological community by pastoral agents and their theologian counterparts.[9] Practitioners and scholars need each other. Schools of theology foster mutual contributions when academic and pastoral faculty teach together, serve together on degree boards, and help students integrate their experience in theological reflection seminars. There is still a long way to go. Each group needs to cultivate communication with the other. Although the general rules of dialogue help, the experience of pastoral education shows that communication increases best when people work together and experience each other together.

Regarding the ninth commandment, pastoral agents are sometimes *overly* self-critical. This appears in the anxiety (noted in the third general observation) over the exact meaning of pastoral. Because so many of the skills and even underlying theory used in pastoral work are taken over from other disciplines, there is a tendency to undervalue or miss altogether the contributions of the directly and distinctly pastoral experience.[10] The challenge is to be self-critical without abandoning one's pastoral commitment or assuming there is nothing but derivative value in it. This relates back to personal change and growth through another's perception (the first and tenth commandments).

In pastoral education the goal with students is to help them claim their identity as it appears in concrete circumstances—their field placement or their peer reflection group. In these settings a person's strengths and limitations come out through interaction and dialogue. Identity is thus affirmed in the context of actual ministerial relationships rather than in the context of generic ideals and definitions of ministry. The contribution of pastoral education to interreligious dialogue in this regard is that persons entering into such dialogue can best be self-critical in relation to specific issues/questions rather than generic descriptions of their traditions.

c. The third, fourth, sixth, and eighth commandments address essential presuppositions for dialogue. "Each participant must come to the dialogue with complete honestly and sincerity," "must assume a similar complete honesty and sincerity in the other partners," and "must come to dialogue with no hard and fast conceptions as to where points of disagreement are," and "dialogue can take place only on the basis of mutual trust." The difference between honesty/sincerity and trust is that the former frees persons to acknowledge where their particular tradition is going and how they feel about that direction, while the latter acknowledges that persons are able to dialogue freely when they trust each other. Trust has to be built gradually. In interreligious dialogue this is fostered by beginning with issues that are likely to provide common ground, and then, as mutual trust grows, moving to more disputed issues. These same principles are presupposed in pastoral education, but there is also a recognition that completely honest and sincere dialogue is hard to come by. There are many hidden factors that prevent people from being as honest as they want to be or think they are. A key pastoral technique for dealing with this is confrontation.[11]

Confrontation is distinguished from conflict. Conflict implies disagreement because opposing positions have already been taken. Confrontation is direct inquiry into another's position to determine whether conflict exists. The confronter is responsible for putting out his or her perception of the other person; the confronted is the expert, however, who decides the accuracy of the perception. In conflict, the locus of the judgment is reversed. It is hard at times to keep confrontation from becoming personal or from being interpreted as a personal attack, because there is usually an emotional edge to confrontation.

However, confrontation basically is direct communication for the purpose of clarification.[12]

Pastoral education would certainly affirm the value and need for honesty in interreligious dialogue, but it would recall that honesty is not always easy to express. To try to insure honesty, confrontation is needed and should be focused on clarifying a position rather than judging persons. At the same time, pastoral educators are alert for a person's growing edges or issues. These are usually the most alive parts of a person. Sensitivity is needed in order not to pry, although most of the time students are willing to share themselves when invited to do so and when they sense the educator is willing to accompany them as they explore tensions with their own tradition or identity or role.[13]

The pastoral parallel to the eighth commandment is the connection that occurs in counseling and supervision between the presenting problem and the real problem. The presenting problem is one that covers familiar ground, where trust can be presumed, but meanwhile a person is testing to see whether it is safe to breach deeper issues. The real problem is often perceived by the person as too unusual or intimate or complex to claim the help of another, so trust must be developed. There is usually a connection between the presenting and the real problem, just as there is a connection between common ground and disputed areas in interreligious dialogue.[14] Pastoral education has learned to recognize and value the movement from initial testing to trust, which allows deeper issues to emerge and be dealt with. There can be no bypassing this first step, no rushing into trust. Interreligious dialogue, like pastoral conversation, *must* move gradually, step by step.

d. The fifth commandment requires that "each participant must define himself." The corollary is that "the one interpreted must be able to recognize herself in the interpretation." There is an implied responsibility here for each dialogue partner to keep monitoring his or her own developing identity. In one sense interreligious dialogue can help a person do just this. As others' interpretations are given of one's own tradition, these interpretations can actually shed new light on one's own experience of the tradition, or can open new challenges and opportunities to appropriate or evaluate the tradition. In any event, it is the responsibility of each individual to say yes or no to the interpretation of one's own tradition.

The key pastoral parallel is accurate empathy,[15] a process of constantly restating how one perceives what the other is sharing. It is not merely repeating or even paraphrasing what another has said, but one's own formulation of how the world looks as one attends empathically to what the other is sharing. Stating one's perception invites the other person to confirm, modify, replace, or disagree with that perception. The goal is to test one's own perception of another's world to see whether one is accurately understanding, grasping, and feeling, because one assumes congruence rather than potential conflict. The quest for accuracy is aided by a commitment to clarification. Questions are asked and reinterpretations offered to help persons enter each other's world. This implies that each person's world is a valuable place that is accessible only through a sincere and steady effort to perceive it accurately from the one who is the true expert, the person her- or himself.

In making an empathic response, however, one does not assume control. The other person always retains the authority to say whether his or her perception and expression are accurate, at least in terms of how the person feels her- or himself to be. One may be clinically correct in an interpretation, but if the other person does not experience that interpretation as accurate, one cannot proceed and must continue dialoguing. Patience and creativity are needed: patience to arrive at a mutually agreeable interpretation or expression, and creativity to find alternative and more acceptable ways of expressing what is perceived or of perceiving more accurately what is really there. This value is concretely realized in pastoral education in that final evaluations of a student's work are jointly discussed and then signed. As a permanent record of the person's performance, such evaluations reflect accurately what has been experienced by both parties and insure that "each participant defines herself" at least by affirming the pastoral educator's definition.[16]

Sometimes discrepancies appear between a person's self-definition and actual practice. Such discrepancies are valuable clues to how a person really identifies herself. For this reason pastoral educators usually have persons perform definite actions (field placement or a practicum) or react to certain situations (role play), in order to observe how they really function. The pastoral conclusion for interreligious dialogue is that the locus of control is with each participant. At the same time, a person's stated self-perception and actual behaviors are closely observed. When discrepancies appear, these are prime resources for exploring the accuracy of a person's self-interpretation or the interpretation of other dialogue partners.

e. The seventh commandment respects the various levels of interreligious dialogue: "dialogue can take place only between equals." Equality refers to the training, competence, and skill of participants, and also to an openness to speak and listen, to teach and learn equally. Equality aims at a sufficient similarity to get on with the project. Too great a gap in competence or openness dooms the enterprise from the outset and may erroneously suggest that interreligious dialogue cannot work or is not worth the effort.

The chief pastoral parallel has already been mentioned: inequality between trained specialists (a theologian or professional counselor) and the general practitioner, or the inequality between the theoretician and the hands-on minister. The tendency in pastoral education has been to allow the two to remain separate and out of dialogue with each other. This results in unfortunate gaps, misperceptions of each other's value, and wasted energy defending one's own legitimacy or belittling the other's contribution.

To overcome this separation, a type of bridge role is evolving in pastoral education, often referred to as a theological reflector or more traditionally as a pastoral theologian. The person in this role is expected to have both specialized, theoretical training and direct experience with hands-on ministry and practice. Sufficiently familiar with both arenas, a theological reflector helps persons on both sides communicate better with each other.[17] Another, more conventional way of overcoming inequalities is referral. Usually referral goes from the generalist to the specialist, from the volunteer to the professional. Sometimes this tendency betrays a misplaced feeling of inadequacy on the part of the generalist, as if any really serious problem brought to him or her must be referred. The reverse also occasionally occurs, whereby a specialist will refer clients to a generalist, especially in the area of faith questions, spiritual direction, and support groups or faith community.

Conclusion

In summary, the Dialogue Decalogue reverberates with principles, values, and goals that are congruent with those of pastoral education. The fact that there is such compatibility is itself an ecumenical statement worth making. Beyond that, the pastoral experience in these same areas can further stimulate interreligious dialogue.

Specifically, pastoral education reaffirms the importance of learning from experience. Awareness of the forms of pastoral control can alert one to subtle types of debate rather than dialogue. Clarifications of one's religious/pastoral identity emerge best in dialogue rather than prior, unilateral definitions.

Further, relationship is key to dialogue and leads to action of many kinds—but is always determined by the participants in dialogue, not by outsiders. Internal dialogue is aided by mutual projects and specific experiences together. Confrontation fosters honesty, which occurs gradually as one moves from initial, safe issues to hidden, more complex issues. Accurate empathy fosters clarification, while leaving each person in charge of his or her own position. Some type of intermediary role or referral system may help bridge inequalities between potential dialogue partners.

These few parallels suggest a fuller correspondence and contribution between pastoral education and ecumenical dialogue. If the parallels are pursued, the Decalogue may be enriched and, more importantly, dialogue will be too.

8

The Deep-Dialogue Decalogue: Ground Rules of Personal/ Communal Deep-Dialogue/ Critical-Thinking/Emotional- Intelligence/Competitive- Cooperation

Here are the same ten principles of the Dialogue Decalogue rearticulated later in different language, now using the term Deep-Dialogue in order to stress the profound, transformative effect of dialogue, of Deep-Dialogue.

Prologue

The term dialogue had become so popular that, as noted earlier, Ashok Gangadean and I came up with the term Deep-Dialogue to indicate that I/we are talking about something much deeper than only Dialogue of the Head, but that is life transforming, for the whole of the cosmos is ultimately a Dance of Dialogue. The nature of, not just the human mind or the human being in totality, but—as laid out earlier—the very structure of the entire cosmos from the micro to the macro levels is dialogical, Deep-Dialogical! The earlier described four dimensions of human Deep-Dialogue are also recalled here—Dialogue of the Head, the Hands, the Heart, the Holy—although the focus here is mainly on the Dialogue of the Head. Here is a slightly reworked version of my earlier Dialogue Decalogue as Ashok Gangadean and I rearticulated it in the middle 1990s, and I have modified it still further here.

Deep-Dialogue is a conversation between individual persons—and through them, two or more communities or groups—with differing views, the *primary* purpose of which is for each participant to learn from the other so that s/he can change and grow—and thereby the respective groups or communities as well. The very definition of Deep-Dialogue embodies the first Ground-Rule of Deep-Dialogue.

At the same time, to open oneself to Deep-Dialogue, it is also necessary to develop the skills of thinking carefully and clearly, the skills of Critical-Thinking (critical, from the Greek, *krinein*, to choose, to judge—Critical-Thinking will be treated more thoroughly below, and hence, only briefly here). We need to understand what we, and others, really mean when we say something and why we say it, so as to "choose," to "judge" where we believe the truth lies and what the implications are. In brief, we must answer three questions: What? Whence? Whither?

Critical-Thinking, in addition to answering those three questions, entails at least this: first, that we raise our presuppositions from the unconscious to the conscious level. Only then can we deal with them rationally, deciding for, against, or partly for/partly against them; second, that we realize that *our* view of reality is *a* view, and therefore not absolute but perspectival, shaped by the lenses of our experience, through which we experience and interpret all reality; third, that we learn to understand all statements in *their* context. That is, a text can be correctly understood in *its* context—only then will we be able to translate the original core of the statements/texts into *our* context. This process of Critical-Thinking, then, entails a dialogue within our own mind. Hence, at its root Critical-Thinking is dialogic. In turn, Deep-Dialogue at its root entails clear, critical thought—they are two sides of the coin of humanity.

However, we cannot stop at Deep-Dialogue and Critical-Thinking, but must deepen the latter to include Emotional-Intelligence, and then on those bases we must act in Competitive-Cooperation, as outlined above. It is not sufficient to describe an authentic human life as a two-sided coin; rather, a full human life is four-dimensional, embracing Critical-Thinking, Deep-Dialogue, Emotional Intelligence, and Competitive-Cooperation. The first three of these must issue in action, and in keeping with their essence and orientation, the consequent action must reflect both the "soft" openness and reaching out to the Other of Deep-Dialogue, and at the same time the "sharp-edge"quality of Critical-Thinking and the relational appropriateness of Emotional-Intelligence. The resultant Competitive-Cooperation action strives toward a maximum of creative win-win results, although at time they will be on different "levels" and/or timetables, as suggested above.

Because Deep-Dialogue, Critical-Thinking, Emotional-Intelligence, and Competitive-Cooperation are in fact necessarily four dimensions of one reality, whenever I speak of Deep-Dialogue, I automatically mean to include Critical-Thinking, Emotional-Intelligence, and Competitive-Cooperation.

In the past, we encountered those who differ from us, for example, Muslims from Hindus, Catholics from Protestants, either to defeat our opponents or, at best, to negotiate with them. If we faced each other at all, it usually was in confrontation—sometimes more openly polemically, sometimes more subtly so, but nearly always with the goal of defeating the other, because we were convinced that we alone had the "truth."

But Deep-Dialogue is not debate, or even negotiation. In Deep-Dialogue each partner listens to the other as openly and sympathetically as s/he can in an attempt to understand the other's position as precisely and, as it were, as much from within, as possible. This also clearly entails internal and external critical thinking. Such an attitude automatically includes the assumption that at any point we might find the partner's position so persuasive that, if we were to act with integrity, we would have to change. Obviously, then, through such Deep-Dialogue/Critical-Thinking/Emotional-Intelligence/Competitive-Cooperation and change we will move closer to a deeper, richer understanding of "truth," of the way things really are in the world.

We are here speaking not of superficial dialogue or merely techniques of dialogue, helpful though they may be. Rather, we are speaking of Deep-Dialogue, its counterparts Critical-Thinking/Emotional-Intelligence, and consequent action Competitive-Cooperation. Deep-Dialogue/Critical-Thinking/Emotional-Intelligence Competitive-Cooperation must become a Virtue, a Way of encountering and understanding oneself, others, and the world at the deepest levels. This opens up possibilities of grasping the fundamental meanings of life, individually and corporately, and its various dimensions—which in turn transforms the Way we deal with ourselves, others, and the world. Deep-Dialogue on a broad, communal scale, is thus a whole new Way of thinking, of understanding the world—and bearing in mind, in addition, the Dialogues of the *Heart*, *Hands*, and the *Holy*, of living more deeply both within and without. It was understood and practiced in the past by a number of great spiritual geniuses of humankind—Socrates, Jesus, Gautama, the Sufis, Gandhi, and so forth—but it never before reached into communal consciousness. Now, applying the insights and experiences of prior giants, it is beginning to. In that vital sense, it *is* something new under the sun.

The following are basic ground rules of Deep-Dialogue that must be observed if authentic dialogue is actually to take place. These are not theoretical rules given from "on high," but ones that have been learned from hard experience. To the extent they are observed, to that degree, Deep-Dialogue/Critical-Thinking/Emotional-Intelligence/Competitive-Cooperation with all their benefits, will occur. To the extent they are *not* observed...

First Ground Rule

Be Open Within!

Be open to our dialogue partner to learn, that is, to grow/change in our perception/understanding of reality, and then act accordingly—a self-critical-thinking, intrapersonal move.

We enter into Deep-Dialogue so that we can learn, change, and grow, that is, so as to promote self-critical-thinking/emotional-intelligence and consequent competitive-cooperation, not so that we can force change on the *other*, as one hopes to do in debate—a hope realized in inverse proportion to the frequency and fierceness with which debate is entered into. On the other hand, because in Deep-Dialogue each partner comes with the intention of learning and changing herself by self-critical-thinking/emotional-intelligence, and consequently acting in competitive-cooperation, our partner will in fact also change. Thus the goal of debate, and more, is accomplished far more effectively by Deep-Dialogue, self-Critical-Thinking, Emotional-Intelligence, and Competitive-Cooperation.

Second Ground Rule

Attend!

Be fully present both to our self and our partner in a Critical-Thinking mode, and in subsequent Emotional-Intelligence and Competitive-Cooperation; respond to our partner rather than make our favorite speech.

Since we engage in dialogue so that *we* can *learn* from our partner, it is imperative that *we* be fully present, that is, to be conscious of ourselves and our presuppositions, and of our partner—Critical-Thinking/Emotional-Intelligence (and then act consequently in Competitive-Cooperation). Otherwise, how can *we* learn? Also, to learn we must focus on our *partner,* from whom we hope to learn. Again, otherwise, how can we *learn*? Further, because dialogue is a two-way project, we need to respond to what our partner has said, rather than deliver a pat lecture. Otherwise, we are attending only to ourselves within the framework of our unconscious presuppositions.

Third Ground Rule

Be Open Between!

Make dialogue a two-sided project—within each community as well as between communities—a Critical-Thinking, Emotional-Intelligence, Competitive-Cooperation intercommunal move.

Because of the "corporate" nature of community or group Deep-Dialogue, and because the primary goal of Deep-Dialogue is that each partner learn and change her- or himself, it is also necessary that each of us enter into Deep-Dialogue not only with our partner across the community or group line—Muslim with Hindu, Lutheran with Anglican, for example—but also with our own community, with our fellow Muslims or fellow Lutherans, to share with them the fruits of the Deep-Dialogue. Only thus can the whole community or group eventually learn and change, moving toward an ever truer, deeper insight into reality—a kind of communal Critical-Thinking, Emotional-Intelligence, and subsequent Competitive-Cooperation.

Fourth Ground Rule

Be Honest and Trusting!

Come to the dialogue with honesty and sincerity, that is, in a Critical-Thinking/Emotional-Intelligence mode.

Each of us should attempt to make clear in what direction the major and minor thrusts of our community or group move, what the future shifts might be, and, if needed, where we have difficulties with our community or group. We must make a serious effort to engage in Critical-Thinking/Emotional-Intelligence. No false fronts have any place in Deep-Dialogue.

Conversely, we must assume a similar honesty, sincerity—Critical-Thinking/Emotional-Intelligence—in our partner. Not only will the absence of sincerity and Critical-Thinking/Emotional-Intelligence prevent dialogue from happening but the absence of the assumption of our partner's sincerity will do so as well. In brief: no trust, no Deep-Dialogue, nor subsequent Competitive-Cooperation.

Fifth Ground Rule

Cultivate Personal Trust!

Cultivate personal trust by searching first for commonalities, since Deep-Dialogue can take place only on the basis of mutual trust.

If we engage in a communal Deep-Dialogue, there will be some kind of corporate dimension, that is, we will be involved as members of a community—for example as Jews, as Confucians, Buddhists, and so forth. Nevertheless, it is fundamentally true that only *persons* can enter into Deep-Dialogue. However, since a Deep-Dialogue among persons can be built only on personal trust, it is wise not to tackle the most difficult problems in the beginning, but rather to approach first those issues most likely to provide some common ground, thereby establishing the basis of human trust. Then, gradually, as this personal trust deepens and expands, the more thorny matters can be confronted.

Thus, as in learning we move from the known to the unknown, so too in Deep-Dialogue do we proceed from commonly held matters—which, given our mutual ignorance, will often take us quite some time to discover fully—to discuss matters of likely disagreement. This is Critical-Thinking/Emotional-Intelligence par excellence, that is, raising our presuppositions from the unconscious to the conscious level, then judging them, and then acting in Competitive-Cooperation.

Sixth Ground Rule

Don't Prejudge; Compare Fairly!

Come to the Deep-Dialogue with no hard-and-fast assumptions as to where the points of agreement and disagreement are.

Each of us should not only listen to the other with openness and sympathy but also attempt to agree as far as possible, while still maintaining integrity with our own community or tradition. Where we absolutely can agree no further without violating our own integrity, precisely *there* is where agreement ends and disagreement really begins—a point that often turns out to be different from what was falsely assumed ahead of time. Again, Critical-Thinking/Emotional-Intelligence is implemented, and is followed by Competitive-Cooperation in action.

At the same time, we should compare our ideals with our partner's ideals, our practice with our partner's practice. For example, compare the old Hindu practice of widow burning with the old Christian practice of witch burning, not with the Christian ideal of loving one's neighbor as oneself. In fact, that ideal of the Golden Rule is found in most religious and ethical traditions, including Confucian, Hindu, Buddhist, Jewish, Christian, Muslim, Aboriginal and Secular.

Seventh Ground Rule

Define Yourself—In Dialogue!

We and our partner define ourselves in dialogue.

Only the Jew, for example, can define what it means to be a Jew, or a Christian what it means to be a Christian—although our dialogue partner can contribute to that self-definition. Because Deep-Dialogue is a dynamic medium, as each of us learns from the other, we will change and thus continually deepen, expand, and modify our self-definition—Critical-Thinking/Emotional-Intelligence, followed by Competitive-Cooperation in action, as a Jew, as a Christian, and so forth, being careful to remain in constant Deep-Dialogue with our fellow Jews, fellow Christians, and so on. Thus it is mandatory that each us define what it means to be an authentic member of our own community/tradition, but do so in dialogic openness to our fellow members and our partner.

Eighth Ground Rule

Treat Others as Equals!

Treat our partner as an equal, for Deep-Dialogue, self-Critical-Thinking, Emotional-Intelligence, and *Competitive-Cooperation can take place only between equals.*

Both of us as partners must come to dialogue to learn from each other. Therefore, if, for example, Christians and Jews do not respect each other, or the Muslim views Hinduism as inferior, or the Hindu views Islam as inferior, there will be no Deep-Dialogue. If authentic Deep-Dialogue is to occur, both Jews and Christians, Muslims and Hindus must come together mainly to learn from each other. All participants, regardless of prior status, must enter into a "safe space" of equality if authentic Deep-Dialogue, Critical-Thinking, Emotional-Intelligence, and Competitive-Cooperation are to be attained. Deep-Dialogue/ Critical-Thinking/Emotional-Intelligence/Competitive-Cooperation, however, not only require but also tend to produce equal empowerment between partners.   Deep-Dialogue/Critical-Thinking/Emotional-Intelligence/Competitive-Cooperation foster a "virtuous circle." There can be no such thing as a one-way Deep-Dialogue/Critical-Thinking/Emotional-Intelligence/Competitive-Cooperation.

Ninth Ground Rule

Be Healthily Self-Critical!

Be healthily self-critical of our self and our group or community; only then can we be compassionately critical of our partner.

A lack of self-criticism implies that we and our own community have all the correct answers. Such an attitude makes Deep-Dialogue/Critical-thinking/Emotional-Intelligence not only unnecessary but even impossible, since we enter Deep-Dialogue/Critical-Thinking/Emotional-Intelligence primarily so we can learn—which is impossible if we have never made a misstep, if we have all the right answers. To be sure, in communal Deep-Dialogue/Critical-Thinking/Emotional-Intelligence we must stand within a community/tradition with integrity and conviction, but such integrity and conviction must include, not exclude, healthy self-criticism. Without it there can be no Deep-Dialogue/Critical-Thinking/Emotional-Intelligence—indeed, no integrity! Once we have shown our self to be seriously self-critical, our partner will be open to a compassionate, constructive critique of her position. Thus, again, a "virtuous circle" is fostered through Deep-Dialogue/Critical-Thinking/Emotional-Intelligence and consequent Competitive-Cooperation.

Tenth Ground Rule

Reach out, Pass over and Return!

Reach out to work together, pass over and experience our partner's community or tradition "from within," and then return to our own, enriched.

A community or tradition is not merely something of the mind (Dialogue of the *H*ead), but also of the *H*ands (Dialogue of Cooperation), *H*eart (Dialogue of Beauty and Spirit), and "Whole Being" (Dialogue of the *H*oly), individual and communal. Hence, in Deep-Dialogue/Critical-Thinking/Emotional-Intelligence we join hands to work together for the good, and to "pass over" into our partner's "interior" world and experience something of its emotional and symbolic impact. Then we return to our own world, enlightened and enriched, bringing something of the Other that is now within us. This edging toward engaging in the "spiritual" dimension of the Dialogue of the Heart, reminds us that we also need to engage our dialogue partner in the "beauty" dimension as well, along with the Dialogue of the Hands—Competitive-Cooperation—and finally the integrating Dialogue of the *H*oly.

In summary: Deep-Dialogue among individuals/communities operates in *four areas*:

1. The intellectual, where we seek understanding—Dialogue of the *H*ead

2. The practical, where we collaborate to help humanity—Dialogue of the *H*ands

3. The aesthetic and/or spiritual dimensions, where we enjoy the beauty produced by our partner, and/or experience something of the partner's emotional and meaning-of-life/spiritual resources "from within"—Dialogue of the *H*eart

4. The integrating coalescence of all the dimensions of a *H*armonious *H*uman—Dialogue of the *H*oly

Deep-Dialogue among individuals and communities has *four phases*:

1. In the first phase we unlearn misinformation about each other and come to know each other as we truly are.

2. In phase two we begin to discern values in our partner's community or tradition and may wish to adapt them to our own. For example, in an East-West interreligious dialogue, the Abrahamic religions may come to appreciate more deeply the Asian meditative practices, and the Asian religions may come to appreciate the "prophetic" virtues of challenging and changing world structures.

3. If we are serious and persistent in Deep-Dialogue/Critical-Thinking/Emotional-Intelligence/Competitive-Cooperation, we may at times enter into phase three. Here we together begin to explore new areas of reality and new ways of acting, new insights into meaning—none of which either of us had previously even been aware of. We are brought face to face with this new, until-then-unknown-to-us dimension of reality and possibility of action, insight into meaning, only because of the questions, insights, probings produced in Deep-Dialogue and Critical-Thinking.

4. If we experience phase three in more than one Deep-Dialogue, we will be propelled into phase four, in which we begin to perceive deeply—along with an increasing appreciation of diversity—the oneness of all people and our unity with nature. Thus, as it says on the US penny: *E pluribus unum* ("One from many"). This is Deep-Dialogue/Critical-Thinking/Emotional-Intelligence Competitive-Cooperation—par excellence.

Theoretical Background

Dialogue, Deep-Dialogue, and its companion foundational structural components of human reality—Critical-Thinking, Emotional-Intelligence, Competitive-Cooperation—as well as the background to, and the theory underlying, ten further principles, three facets, a global way, seven stages, and, finally, an online course for all are here laid out and explored.

Part II

Theoretical Background

Introduction to the Basic Documents of Deep-Dialogue/ Critical-Thinking/Emotional-Intelligence/Competitive-Cooperation

The elements of the theoretical background documents of Deep-Dialogue/ Critical-Thinking/Emotional-Intelligence/Competitive-Cooperation are here delineated and their interrelationship is shown.

Deep-Dialogue/Critical-Thinking/Emotional-Intelligence/Competitive-Cooperation is applicable to all human situations. We live within perspectives, worldviews, some form of interpretation. All our experience both forms and depends upon our interpretation and world making. Our inner lives and interpersonal relations are shaped by our habits of thinking. Deep-Dialogue/Critical-Thinking/Emotional-Intelligence/Competitive-Cooperation helps us in the full spectrum of life: from our personal relations at home, to our professional relations at work, to our social and political lives in the culture at large, to our religious/spiritual lives, to relations with our surroundings, that is, our "ecology" in the largest sense.

Since Deep-Dialogue/Critical-Thinking/Emotional-Intelligence/ Competitive-Cooperation operates at the base of human interchange, it provides tools for solving the ongoing problems of prejudice, ethnic conflict, ideological gridlock, tribal thinking, and other human ruptures. It is thus the basis for many intergroup techniques, such as diversity training, tolerance education, conflict management/resolution, nonviolent training, peace making, negotiation and arbitration, and so forth. Deep-Dialogue/Critical-Thinking/ Emotional-Intelligence/Competitive-Cooperation sets the framework within which each of these "applied techniques" can work to its maximum effect—in a lasting *Way*.

The Way of Deep-Dialogue/Critical-Thinking/Emotional-Intelligence/ Competitive-Cooperation is an integral process with diverse dimensions. The following documents form a whole and should be so read. Each is designed to amplify and enrich the other. There are many contexts in which this process may be used—seminars, retreats, workshops, courses, and the like. These documents are designed both for training leaders in various fields and grassroots practitioners at all levels. They are foundational reflections on which a larger body of material of all forms is constantly being constructed and adapted.

1. The Background of the Way of
   Deep-Dialogue/Critical-Thinking/Emotional-Intelligence/Competitive-Cooperation

2. Theory Underlying
   Deep-Dialogue/Critical-Thinking/Emotional-Intelligence/Competitive-Cooperation

3. Ten Principles Articulating
   Deep-Dialogue/Critical-Thinking/Emotional-Intelligence/Competitive-Cooperation

4. Three Facets of
   Deep-Dialogue/Critical-Thinking/Emotional-Intelligence/Competitive-Cooperation

5. The Global Way of
   Deep-Dialogue/Critical-Thinking/Emotional-Intelligence/Competitive-Cooperation

6. Seven Stages of
   Deep-Dialogue/Critical-Thinking/Emotional-Intelligence/Competitive-Cooperation

7. Online Course in
   Deep-Dialogue/Critical-Thinking/Emotional-Intelligence/Competitive-Cooperation

10

The Background of the "Way" of Deep-Dialogue/Critical-Thinking/Emotional-Intelligence/ Competitive-Cooperation

Most of the great world religions have at their center the idea and term "the Way," rather than the Western term "religion." This profound term is briefly laid here out in its manifold usages.

Here I discuss the background to the Virtue, the Way of Dialogue—Deep-Dialogue—with its "deep" life-transforming quality that true dialogue is meant to provide. At the same time, as noted earlier, the other side of the coin of our authentic humanity must be Critical-Thinking/Emotional-Intelligence, followed by the consequent action of Competitive-Cooperation. These reflections help the reader understand Deep-Dialogue/Critical-Thinking/Emotional-Intelligence/ Competitive-Cooperation more deeply so as to enter into the processes and practices designed to foster the Virtue of the Way of Deep-Dialogue/Critical-Thinking/Competitive-Cooperation.

I use the term W*ay* because (as noted above, and repeated here: *repetitio est mater studiorum*!) it is another ancient and widespread term referring to what Western civilization named "religion." Already from before the founding of the first civilizations in the third millennium BCE, humans sought to develop effective ways to live authentic lives. The central term in all major world religions has been the Way. For example, in the three "Semitic/Abrahamic" religions— Judaism, Christianity, and Islam—all the following terms mean the Way:

Central to Judaism, the Hebrew word *Halacha*, the *Way*, has come to mean the Rabbinic teachings, the legal decisions to be followed, in order to lead a life according to the Torah, that is, as instructed by God (the Hebrew word *Torah* means "instruction").

At the beginning of Christianity, the followers of Jesus (*Yeshua*, in Hebrew) were not called Christians, but followers of "the Way" (*Hodos*, in New Testament Greek[1]) that "Rabbi" Yeshua taught and exemplified.

In Islam, the traditional way to live a correct life was to follow the *shari'a*, an Arabic term for the Way—specifically the path to find water in the desert. It also came to mean, analogous to *Halacha* in Judaism, the myriad "legal" decisions that should be followed by the devout Muslim.

Much the same is also true for the major religions that come out of India— Hinduism and Buddhism:

In Hinduism, there are three major Ways, *Margas* in Sanskrit, to attain the goal in life: *Moksha* (Sanskrit for "liberation"), namely, the Way or *Marga* of knowledge (*Jnana*), the *Marga* of works (*Karma*), and the *Marga* of devotion (*Bhakti*).

In Buddhism, the key term meaning Way is *Magga*, in Pali, which refers to the Noble Eightfold *Path* (the 4th of Gautama's fundamental Four Noble Truths) to be followed in order to reach nirvana, the goal of life. Moreover, Gautama himself in his first, fundamental sermon, and Buddhism after him, described his way as the *Middle Way* (*Majjhima Pati-pada* in Pali) between harsh asceticism and loose sensuality that will lead to the goal of life.

For religions of the Far East too, the term the Way was central: the very name of Chinese Taoism places the Way, Tao, at the center, the foundation of the entire religion, the goal of which was to discern the Tao of the universe and live in harmony with it.

This notion of the Way, the Tao, was also central to the doctrine of Confucius, who taught that "The Way of Humanity" (*Ren-Tao*) is to follow the "Way of Heaven" (*T'ien-Tao*). For Confucius, Heaven, *T'ien*, was largely "personal," *Theos*, although eventually, and especially for the neo-Confucians of the Song Dynasty (960–1279 CE) and afterwards, *T'ien* became largely nonpersonal.

Japan's native religion, Shinto, likewise has embedded in its very name the term the Way, namely, *To*, "the Way of the Gods," *Shin-To*. The term was taken from the Chinese with the same meaning, *Shen-Tao*, to distinguish the original Japanese religion (which in pure Japanese was called the "Way of the *Kami* or Gods," *Kami-no Michi*) from that religion of India, Buddhism, which came to Japan by way of China through Korea, also known in Chinese as "the Way of Buddha," *Butsu-Tao*.

The very fact that there were several Ways made it likely that when the different Ways encountered each other, the reaction would be violent. The response to the challenge of these violent negative Ways-Encounters is to develop the Virtue of the Way of Deep-Dialogue/Critical-Thinking/Emotional-Intelligence/ Competitive-Cooperation.

The Development of the Way of Deep-Dialogue/Critical-Thinking/ Emotional-Intelligence/Competitive-Cooperation

Deep-Dialogue/Critical-Thinking/Emotional-Intelligence/Competitive-Cooperation is a Way of encountering and understanding Oneself, the Other, and the World at the deepest levels, grasping the fundamental meaning of life, individually and communally. This in turn transforms the Way we deal with Ourselves, Others, and the World. Deep-Dialogue/Critical-Thinking/Emotional-Intelligence/

Competitive-Cooperation has recently slowly begun to emerge from the centuries of largely negative Ways-Encounters. The increasingly positive Ways-Encounters are leading us to see that there is a deeper common ground out of which various Ways rise, namely, our very humanness, our body-spirit, which, against the background of the massive cosmos, fragilely, almost wraith-like, sways within the whole Cosmic Dance of Dialogue.

One of many well-known places where this underlying Deep-Dialogue is spelled out is at the beginning of the Bible (Gen 1:26): "And God made humans in God's image [*Imago Dei* in St. Jerome's Latin translation]." One part of us is our amazing, but nevertheless earthly limited body. "And God took some *adamah* [Hebrew for "earth"] and breathed his spirit [*ruach*] into it and created *ha adam* [literally the 'earthling'—not the 'male']." The other part of us is our limitless spirit (God's *ruach*). The Bible had it universally correct here, that every human is an *Imago Dei* in that we are God-like, limit-*less*, *in*-finite in our spirit (*ruach*), always reaching beyond! As we today gain ever more access to this deeper source of all cultural life and experience, it becomes increasingly evident that we humans are in the midst of a profound self-transformation, maturation of our very humanness—which, as noted above, is a work in progress.

We humans are centrally involved in shaping our own experience, in how we perceive, and then act accordingly in the world. We are shaped by our cultures, but we also in turn shape our cultures by how we think about our experience. A great lesson in global evolution is that our cultural realities are directly affected by our thought. We are slowly learning that if we remain turned only inward, we will be trapped in our own limited egos. When we then encounter persons from other cultures, we are likely to react with violence toward the Other—and all will suffer.

At the same time, this insight shows that the more we self-transform and awaken to   Deep-Dialogue/Critical-Thinking/Emotional-Intelli-gence/Competitive-Cooperation Ways of thinking and living, the more we flourish in our personal and communal lives. It is gradually becoming clear that we have been in a painful struggle of maturation out of *mono*logical into *dia*logical critical-thinking, emotionally-intelligent Ways of being. All the great religious, spiritual, rational, scientific, moral,[2] and political advances in the cultural evolution of the past can now be seen as part of the maturation from a monological mindset and practice toward the virtue of a Deep-Dialogue/Critical-Thinking/Emotional-Intelligence/Competitive-Cooperation Way of living.

Deep-Dialogue/Critical-Thinking/Emotional-Intelligence/Competitive-Cooperation is a Way of life that helps persons and communities flourish by self-transforming from a monological mindset to the Virtue of a Deep-Dialogue/Critical-Thinking/Emotional-Intelligence/Competitive-Cooperation Way of life through creative, positive Ways-Encounters.

Critical-Thinking, the *Obverse* of Deep-Dialogue

It cannot be too strongly stressed—or repeated—that in order to open ourselves to Deep-Dialogue we must also develop the skill of thinking clearly and carefully, the Virtue of Critical-Thinking (recall: *critical*, from the Greek, *krinein*, to judge, to choose). We need to

1. understand what we (and others) *really* mean when we say something,
2. understand why we say it, so as to "judge," to "decide" where we think truth is, and
3. understand what the implications are.

In brief, we must answer the three questions: What? Whence? Whither?

It might seem overly obvious to state in number 1 that we need to understand precisely what we mean when we say or hear something. However, it is most often here at the very beginning that the greatest confusion arises. A vast amount of time and energy is wasted and confusion is spread abroad because we often do not know precisely what a term or phrase means when we or another person uses it, or because we use the same term but understand it differently, without noticing that we are doing so. It is even more deleterious when we so often inadvertently slip into four-term syllogisms, and thus confuse ourselves and our listeners/readers. We use a word in an initial statement, and then when using it in a second statement, without noticing it, give it a greater or lesser different meaning, and then attempt to draw a conclusion therefrom! It is as if want to say:

A is **B**
B is C
Therefore
A is C
But in fact what are saying is:
A is **B**
b is C
Therefore....
Therefore nothing!

In addition to addressing the three questions above, Critical-Thinking entails at least these additional points:

4. that we raise our *pre*suppositions from the *un*conscious to the conscious level—only then can we deal with them rationally, deciding for, against, or part for/part against;
5. that we realize that our view of reality is *a* view, that although it shares much with others' views of reality, it is also partially shaped by our personal lenses through which we experience and interpret reality, and hence is not absolute but perspectival;
6. that we learn to understand all statements in their context. That is, a text can be correctly understood only in *its* context—only then will we be able to translate the original core of the statements/texts into *our* context.

This process of Critical-Thinking, then, entails a dialogue within our own minds. Hence, at its root Critical-Thinking is dialogic, and Deep-Dialogue at its root entails clear, critical thought—two sides of the coin of humanity.

Expanding Critical-Thinking to Include Emotional-Intelligence

Here I repeat what I outlined above about expanding my reflections concerning Critical-Thinking with the more recently developed thought about Emotional-Intelligence. I do so, as I promised at the beginning, first, so that the various sections of this volume may stand alone if a reader might wish to copy it for separate use. Second, *repetitio est mater studiorum* is good for one's mental health!

Since the latter decades of the twentieth century, increased attention has been paid to what is often referred to as Emotional-Intelligence. This is an important, but not crystal clear, field of investigation. Our emotions can lead us to do many wonderful, and not so wonderful, things. We often claim that we want to bring our actions out from under the sway of our emotions and under the guidance of our clear-thinking intellect. In general, such a goal appears desirable, but that is not the focus of the investigation of our Emotional-Intelligence.

Rather, the focus of Emotional-Intelligence is learning how we humans can effectively mature "emotionally." Basically that means learning 1) to know and understand oneself, 2) to know and understand other persons, and 3) how appropriately to relate to each other. One may have learned to analyze a situation with impeccable syllogistic logic (Critical-Thinking), but be totally blind about how oneself, or/and others, fit into the puzzle. An example of such an extreme disjunction might be that of a brilliant Critical-Thinker in the body of a socially clueless person, a so-called idiot savant.

The goal of maturing our Emotional-Intelligence is not something new. St. Augustine of Hippo pointed to it when in the fifth century he uttered a prayer, asking "To know you O God, and myself!" Clearly our Emotional-Intelligence needs to be expanded in tandem with our Critical-Thinking, and then expressed in Competitive-Cooperation action—all of which clearly takes place within the all-encompassing embrace of Deep-Dialogue.

Putting Deep-Dialogue/Critical-Thinking/Emotional-Intelligence into Consequent Action: Competitive-Cooperation

If our actions are to be compatible with Deep-Dialogue and Critical-Thinking/ Emotional-Intelligence, they must strive toward being Competitive-Cooperative. Let me explain this last, seemingly contradictory, double term.

If the way we understand the world determines the way we act in the world, then action completes the circle of perception-thought-decision-action. We first perceive, then try to understand, in light of which we make a decision, and finally act, putting our perceptions, understanding, decisions into concrete behavioral form. If we have begun to engage the world in a deeply dialogical manner and critically analyzed/synthesized our perceptions and thoughts, we will want to make decisions on their bases, and carry out our actions in the world in an analogously dialogic/critical manner. I am suggesting that the most appropriate way to describe such action is Competitive-Cooperation.

The outcome of our Deep-Dialogue and Critical-Thinking/Emotional-Intelligence must be our free/responsible action because the core of being human is freedom and its corresponding responsibility. This freedom/responsibility core has always been the case since the emergence of Homo sapiens perhaps 100,000 years ago in central Africa, even though this core did not begin to be de facto widespread and recognized until around two hundred years ago with the Enlightenment. Our core human freedom/responsibility flows from our humanly developed rational intellect, which allows us to abstract (Latin: *ab*, "from" and *tractus*, "pulled," as in "tractor") from our myriad sense perceptions various concepts and possibilities, on the bases of which we can choose, decide to act one way or another. This is another way to say we "love," that is, we reach out to become one with what we perceive to be the good—for example, becoming one with the good ice cream, the good Mozart music, the good friend...each in its appropriate way.

Humans have long recognized that we are something unique in the cosmos (there may be other free beings whom we have not yet discovered—or perhaps never will) because of our radical freedom (despite its limitations, of which we are increasingly becoming aware) based on our rationality.

I have written extensively—and am very deliberately stressing this again here!—about how humanity has in the last two centuries increasingly come to realize that because all knowledge is necessarily limited, it is interpreted by the knower—"Nobody knows Everything about Anything!"[3] Hence, we have no other intelligent choice but to reach out in dialogue, Deep-Dialogue, to those who think differently from us in order to learn increasingly/endlessly more about reality. I have also increasingly stressed the other side of our "coin of humanity," Critical-Thinking, wherein we constantly pose the critical Three "W" Questions: What precisely are we talking about? Whence comes the basis for affirming it? Whither do its implications lead—*reductio ad absurdum*, or not? Steven Pinker has most recently brilliantly shown that it is the increasing human rationality, in the sense of the increasing development of reasonable habits of mind, abstract thinking, and thence actions, that is leading to an increasingly peaceful human world (counterintuitive though that may at first blush seem!).[4] Even before him, in a more philosophical than social scientific manner, Bernard Lonergan also argued that increasing intelligence was a necessity for an increasingly ethical behavior.[5]

Since we humans are also bodies, our perceptions, reflections, decisions need to result in actions in the world. Through fostering our Critical-Thinking and reaching out to increasingly expand our necessarily myopic view of reality through Deep-Dialogue, we will want to act in a manner which is a reflection of our "both-and" Deep-Dialogue/Critical-Thinking/Emotional-Intelligence: namely through Competitive-Cooperation. The "Cooperation" half is relatively easy to understand. So long as the "Other" is not acting in a destructive manner, then we would want to act, at a minimum, not negatively toward the Other, but as much as possible in tandem, so as to create a win-win situation as much as possible.

But "Competitive"? That would seem necessarily to aim at a win-lose, a zero-sum approach. To a certain extent that is accurate. However, I am thinking first of all of this "Competition" as being with ourself, striving to be as effective, efficient, creative as possible—to borrow from Islam the initial meaning of jihad, the Great *Jihad*: (Arabic: struggle), the Competition, with ourself to live out our inner principles (placed there by God, according to Islam—and Judaism and Christianity as well). This Creative Competition may at times mean that one individual, one group will get the contract, will be chosen to provide the requested product or service—win-lose, zero-sum in that sense. But the Creative Competition individual and group should thereby be led to create, develop new alternatives—as, for example, renewable energy sources as alternatives to fossil fuels, or President Obama inviting Hilary Clinton into his cabinet. In the business field, an ever more human organization increasingly searches for the most creative, expansive, all-inclusive way of operating—a "both-and," a "win-win" for both the producers and users, reflecting the creative balance of Deep-Dialogue, "pro-and-con" Critical-Thinking/Emotional-Intelligence in a balance of Creative Competition and Cooperation.

A striking example of such thinking—and action—in the global corporate world was given by Ryuzaburo Kaku, Chairman of the Board of the Japanese multinational, Canon, Inc. His vision in leading his company convinced me that what I in English terms describe as Competitive-Cooperation was in fact doable. He expressed his vision as the *Kyosei* principles: "Living and working together for the common good." He argued that this concept of *Kyosei* should be a creed that all corporations and nations follow and outlined the progress of ethical companies through four stages, describing the fourth stage thus:

> The fourth type is the "corporation assuming global social responsibilities," a "truly global corporation." This type of company cares for all its direct stakeholders, including its local community—but it goes beyond: it strives to fulfill its corporate obligations on a global scale. Its social responsibilities transcend national boundaries.

Mr. Kaku was not a naive "do-gooder," but a creative business entrepreneur, insisting that constant innovation was the key to creating ever more wealth for humanity—and his company: "By creating new products and processes…the company will not only succeed financially, but will also have made the world a better place to live. That is what it means to be an ethical business leader!" He also wrote: "Competition is vital for efficiency, but it must be 'fair' competition, based on innovation, quality and efficiency," combining thereby "competition" with "cooperation": "Innovative corporations with specialties in different areas can also work together in the spirit of *Kyosei* to produce outstanding products. In this way a synergy is created and products can be produced that neither company alone could develop." Impressive as this vision is, Kaku later projected a stunningly challenging fifth stage:

> I have recently come to believe that a fifth category is needed in my analysis of companies as they evolve into ethical social institutions. This fifth type I see as a company that seeks to change the world for the better. Companies in the fifth stage also try to increase the number of like-minded partners that assume global social responsibilities and that are actively concerned with global problems.…Companies

in the fifth stage realize it is not right for the enormous number of corporations existing in the world to remain apathetic about the various perplexing problems emerging on our planet. They know it is it not enough for a corporation to transform itself only into a fourth type of corporation and simply strive to correct imbalances—it knows it must go further.

Kaku would have *Kyosei* serve as a key principle in the new world order emerging after the end of the Cold War. He insisted that democracy, human rights, peace are indeed indispensable values, but alone they are not adequate. Said other: they are necessary, but not sufficient causes of the common weal; *Kyosei* needs to augment them. In English terms for *Kyosei*, I offer Competitive-Cooperation.

In summary, Competitive-Cooperation, in putting into action in a manner in keeping with Deep-Dialogue/Critical-Thinking/Emotional-Intelligence: 1. Is not satisfied with the passable, but reaches for the best; 2. Strives to make decisions within broader frameworks; 3. Is not satisfied with the standard, but stresses constant creativity; 4. As much as possible, avoids zero-sum, win-lose solutions, but seeks creatively win-win ones; 5. Prefers not either-or, but both-and choices.

Therefore, I propose that our most Authentic Human Way to Be and Act is: Deep-Dialogue/Critical-Thinking/Emotional-Intelligence/Competitive-Cooperation.

What Is Unique in the Way of Deep-Dialogue/Critical-Thinking/ Emotional-Intelligence/Competitive-Cooperation

Deep-Dialogue/Critical-Thinking/Emotional-Intelligence/Competitive-Cooperation is a universal Way of life since it rises from the foundation of authentic human reason (which the Greeks called *logos*—more of that below) which is at the base of all experience and human life. By tapping into this universal essence of authentic human reason and consequent action, Deep-Dialogue/Critical-Thinking/Emotional-Intelligence/Competitive-Cooperation helps us fulfill the deepest yearnings of our philosophical, spiritual, religious, civic, and scientific goals. It is able to be impartial, not privileging any one cultural or religious worldview or secular ideology.

Religious worldviews have contended with each other for millennia. Scientific worldviews have confronted religious/spiritual worldviews, and secular cultures have been frustrated in seeking to open civic space in which multiple worldviews and ideologies may flourish together in civilized nonviolent dialogue and cooperation. Destructive divisions continue to pervade contemporary cultures—and too often our personal inner lives reflect this fragmentation, alienation, and disintegration.

The Virtue, the Way of Deep-Dialogue/Critical-Thinking/Emotional-Intelligence/Competitive-Cooperation, however, addresses these problems at their source by opening a Deep-Dialogue-Critical-Thinking/Emotional-Intelligence/Competitive-Cooperation space in which all can attain individual and communal well-being. It helps persons realize their deepest individuality, while coexisting in unity.

Introducing the Way of Deep-Dialogue/Critical-Thinking/ Emotional-Intelligence/Competitive-Cooperation

Several practices that will help further the Deep-Dialogue/Critical-Thinking/ Emotional-Intelligence/Competitive-Cooperation Way have been developed through Way encounters. The basis of process of Deep-Dialogue/Critical-Thinking/Emotional-Intelligence/Competitive-Cooperation is the recognition that when individuals flourish, the communities in which they live and work improve in quality of life and productivity. However, it is also recognized that there are real interpersonal forces in our shared corporate lives that must also be awakened and transformed. Hence, the Way of Deep-Dialogue/Critical-Thinking/Emotional-Intelligence/Competitive-Cooperation aims to transform both individual persons as well as institutions and communities.

A key to understanding Deep-Dialogue/Critical-Thinking/Emotional-Intelligence/Competitive-Cooperation is to recall that it all turns on opening oneself to authentically positive Way encounters, on standing back critically from our innermost habit of interpretation and world making, by transporting ourselves into other lifeworlds. This is vital in the dialogical-critical awakening. By reaching beyond our world we are more in touch with the common ground that is the source of our own world and that of others. This is why Deep-Dialogue is global dialogue. In this dialogical-critical turn as we encounter Others we become more fully our authentic selves—and this profound, challenging transformation continues over a lifetime.

II

Theory Underlying Deep-Dialogue/Critical-Thinking/Emotional-Intelligence/Competitive-Cooperation

This is the most abstract portion of the book, laying out the arguments for the naming of the Primal Principle, the *Ur-Prinzip*, of all reality: *Dia-Logos*—as well as the heart of each of the four core elements of being fully human: Deep-Dialogue/Critical-Thinking/Emotional-Intelligence/Competitive-Cooperation, and their interrelationships.

To recapitulate: Deep-Dialogue is something far beyond mere conversation between two or more persons. Together with its counterparts Critical-Thinking/Emotional-Intelligence/Competitive-Cooperation, it comprises a whole new way of thinking and acting, and flowing from that, a Virtue, a whole Way of life. To open oneself to Deep-Dialogue, then, it is necessary to also develop the skills of thinking carefully and clearly, of Critical-Thinking, Emotional-Intelligence, and consequently acting with Competitive-Cooperation.

A further word at this point about "virtue": with the third millennium's growing commitment to full equality for women and the consequent sensitivity to our generally male-dominant sexist languages, it must be noted that the very positive English term (and those of all the Romance languages as well) "virtue" suffers from male sexist bias. The word stems from the Latin *vir*, male human. So, to be "*vir*tuous" literally means to be "manly"—as William Shakespeare wrote, "play the man!" (Incidentally, German does not have this bias; its term for "virtue" is *Tugend*, coming from *tun*, to do.) The happier Greek term for a good human habit to be cultivated, stemming mainly from Aristotle, is *eudaimonia*, literally "good spirit." I am not, however, advocating dropping the English Latin-rooted term virtue. Fortunately/unfortunately, the vast majority of English speakers do not know any Latin—and hence are unaware of this sexist bias: *Quieta non movere!* (for non-Latinists, "Leave sleeping dogs lie!").

During the Axial Period—800–200 BCE—seminal thinkers such as Confucius, Mencius, Plato, and Aristotle spelled out for their cultures what they thought it meant to be an authentic human being. In the West, Plato, and particularly

Aristotle, were predominant in this effort. Aristotle and other Western thinkers, such as Cicero, St. Augustine, and St. Thomas Aquinas, reflected extensively on the various virtues that needed to be cultivated in order to become an authentic, whole, "holy" (recall, holy literally means whole—more about that below) human being.

After Aristotelian thought fell out of favor in the Renaissance, the focus in ethics was subsequently on questioning whether specific actions were "good" or "bad," leading to the development of ethical systems such as consequentialism[1] (actions are judged good or bad, depending on the consequences they have) and deontology[2] (actions are said to be inherently good or bad, and hence "rules" must always be followed). The related, although not exactly the same, notion of natural law had been articulated by Greek philosophers, preeminently Aristotle and the Stoics. The founder of Catholic canon law, Gratian, in the twelfth century, and then most of all, St. Thomas Aquinas in the thirteenth, promoted the idea that there is a certain structure or nature (Latin, *natus*, born) with which every human is born, and therefore every human ought to follow this "natural law" that is built into us.[3] This thinking has had an immense influence on all Western ethical and legal systems, and, indeed, on the global level as well. It is the basis for the now almost universally accepted (but often honored in the breach!) notion of human rights. What is not yet sufficiently recognized by the official Catholic teaching— although it is by many Catholic philosophers and theologians—is that the very nature of humanity is dynamic, changing; it is a work in progress. The ancient Greeks and medieval Christians did not, for example, hold a notion of human rights or the equality of women. Today practically all affirm human rights, and a rapidly increasing number affirm the equality of women.

Starting in the third quarter of the twentieth century, the Aristotelian and subsequent ethical tradition has made a strong comeback under the name of virtue ethics,[4] stressing the need to focus on the positive, the virtues that an authentic, holy human must develop. Here, the argument is that persons should be led to develop a positively virtuous character—courageous, honest, compassionate. Such a virtuous person will then know how to act ethically in all different situations. One is reminded of St. Augustine's remark: *Ama, et fac quod vis!* "Love and do what you will!" Viewed in a long-term pedagogical perspective, this approach has much to recommend it.

Hence, virtue in the dynamic sense of leading to the development of an authentic, holy human Way of life is what needs to be focused on not only in youth education but also throughout life.

Further, as noted at the beginning of this volume, even beyond being a whole new human Way of thinking, Deep-Dialogue/Critical-Thinking/Emotional-Intelligence/Competitive-Cooperation is at the very basis of *all* reality. At the foundation of the whole cosmos from the macro to the micro levels, there operates a Deep-Dialogue, which somehow is also at base Intelligence/Information, which at our human level is Critical-Thinking and Emotional-Intelligence, followed by consequent Competitive-Cooperation. Here are laid out the underlying theoretical principles of virtue, the Way of Deep-Dialogue/Critical-Thinking/Emotional-Intelligence/Competitive-Cooperation in as clear a manner as possible.

As seen already, Deep-Dialogue/Critical-Thinking/Emotional-Intelligence/ Competitive-Cooperation is grounded in the cosmos itself. Since the beginning of civilization five thousand years ago, the greatest minds have sought to grasp and name the *Ur-Prinzip*, the Primal Principle of existence. In modern science, Albert Einstein and his many followers have been tirelessly searching for the elusive "theory of all" in mathematical form. Many alternative, profound strategies have been developed through millennia, each recognizing in one way or another that our thinking is central in authentically encountering this primal principle. The diverse explanations of "what is first" made it impossible for the different worldviews to agree on an authentically global name, a universal explanation of all reality. Nevertheless, people have been convinced that there must be one *or*iginating (*ur*) principle underlying all realities, all worldviews, all evolution, whether philosophically, theologically, or mathematically articulated. This intuition of a primal and global first principle has persisted across almost all worldviews, especially worldviews of the physical sciences, insisting that there must be an *Ur-Prinzip*, a Primal Principle as the source of all unity and diversity, a unifying force that both generates and holds together all diverse realities.

There are, of course, those individuals, for example, deconstructionists, postmoderns—"atomists"—who claim that there is only multiplicity, that any unity we perceive is precisely that, merely *our* perception of unity. As Immanuel Kant (1724–1804) put it, we can never get beyond our perception of the Phenomena to the *Ding an sich*, the Thing in Itself. In a very real sense, this insight, however, is not really new, for the Greek philosophers—Aristotle and others—and consequent medieval Christian theologians—Thomas Aquinas and others—also did not claim that they could grasp, understand, the Ultimate, the Unmoved Mover, God. They were, however, persuaded that all the evidence, the Phenomena, pointed to its reality. That is, Aquinas in his famous *Quinque viae*, "Five Ways" that aimed to prove the existence of God, listed the multiple Phenomena that pointed to an *Ur-Prinzip*, a Primal Principle—the *Ding an sich*—which is the source of all the Phenomena. The intellectually consistent ancient philosophers and theologians did not think that they could understand or describe the *Ur-Prinzip*, but that it must *be* (e.g., Aquinas's name for the Unmoved Mover, God, was *Ipsum Esse Subsistens*, Self-Subsisting Being Itself), on the two principles that "something cannot come from nothing," and its variant, the "principle of sufficient reason." The position of the naysayers to the consistency of reality would seem to be merely yet another attempt at finding and naming the source of ultimate unity by claiming that it is each of us individually. A major problem with this multiple solipsistic position is that it does not square with our everyday experience; nobody *really* thinks that all of you are just projections of my mind, or that I am a projection of yours! Despite all our profound cultural and other differences, there is at least sufficient commonality for all of us to claim that we are different. For to be different, there must be *some* commonality from which we differ! Hence, the query: whence the commonality and difference? To which the response is: There is an *Ur-Prinzip*, a Primal Principle.

However, precisely because of the widely variant languages of experience, an authentically global name for the *Ur-Prinzip*, Primal Principle, is only now emerging as a result of the development of the dialogic/critical mentality. Only now is the dialogic form of consciousness and of the Way of thinking beginning to mature globally, making it possible to conceive, experience, name, and articulate in an appropriately limited human manner the reality of this unlimited, infinite origin. This new, deeper form of thinking moves beyond the older narrower habits of thought that localized, and hence both obstructed and deformed, access to the Primal Principle. Our thought patterns, language, and world making had first to break from inward-gazing habits and evolve into a more open space for language, thought, and experience, to become truly dialogical/critical and global.

This fundamental advance in human consciousness, which opens access to the Primal Principle, comes with the growth of the Virtue, the Way of Deep-Dialogue/Critical-Thinking, and constituts the dialogical/critical turn in human evolution. It opens the Way to a global consciousness that reaches the common ground between worldviews. This awakened global dialogical/critical perspective between worlds is a profound revolution in how we experience and process reality in all dimensions of our cultural life. It gives us the capacity to hold widely variant worldviews together in creative tension. This shift in thinking discloses deeper global dialogical/critical patterns of reality that could not be detected in the narrower pattern of thinking. We can now begin to see a global world that places all worldviews within the dialogical/critical universe. Humanity hereby is starting down the Way of consciously getting in sync with the Cosmic Dance of Dialogue!

Since antiquity, there has been a drive to name the *Ur-Prinzip*, the Primal Principle, as can be seen from the primal names presented by the great traditions. For example, in China, the Taoist and Confucian tradition wrote of *Tao*, the Way; in India, the Hindu tradition wrote of *Om*, the Infinite Word, and the Buddhist tradition talked of *Sunyata*, the Void; in the Near East, the Jewish spoke of *Hohmah*, Wisdom; in Europe, the Greeks wrote of *Logos*, Reason/Word; Christians also spoke of *Logos* (*en archē hēn ho logos*, "In the beginning was the Reason/Word," John 1:1); and contemporary science speaks of a *field of energy/matter*. All these are understood as the source or the ultimate principle (which etymologically literally means the "Final First").

In developing a global perspective, it becomes more urgent than ever at this moment in history to recognize that these limitless alternative primal names coarise from the same infinite source and coexpress the same universal origin, which, because it is seen from variant cultural perspectives, gives rise to the various names. This intuition follows immediately from rigorous reflection on the nature of the infinite ultimate principle. Such a principle must be infinitely unitive, and also infinitely numerative.

Karen Armstrong, in her widely read book *A History of God*, makes the same point when she writes,

> It seems that when human beings contemplate the absolute, they have very similar ideas and experiences. The sense of presence, ecstasy and dread in the presence of

a reality—called Nirvana, the One, Brahman or God—seems to be a state of mind and a perception that are natural and endlessly sought by human beings.[5]

No universal name has until now emerged that can embrace the entire spectrum of worldviews of primal names, both allowing their nuanced differences and uniting in their common foundation. Now at the beginning of the third millennium as the process of globalization is exploding with exponential rapidity, it becomes vital that a way be found to express the ultimate principle thatwill draw all peoples together, rather than split them into their cultural individualities.

In this spirit, I (nourished by earlier discssions and articulations with my friend Ashok Gangadean) nominate the concept *Dia-Logos* (Greek: thinking/word-between) as a global expression of the ultimate principle. Hence, when speaking English or other Indo-European languages, I will use the term *Dia-Logos*. It does not signify an absolute, but rather open-ended relationality.

We know today from subatomic physics, through astronomical cosmology, to the inner- and interworkings of humanity, that all reality is not static (Greek: *stasis*—standing still), but dynamic (Greek: *dynamis*—movement, energy). Hence, at the foundation of all reality is not just *Logos*, as expressed in the specific Greek and Christian cultural languages, but that on a global intercultural, interlanguage level it is *Dia-Logos*: "Thinking-Between." *Dia-Logos* also exquisitely links together Deep-Dialogue with Critical-Thinking (*Logos* = Thinking!) in the multiple and at the same time linked term: *Dia-Logos*.

The term *Dia-Logos* of course can draw on the rich heritage of the Greek/Christian term *Logos* and help us global humans unite by recognizing our common ground. To begin, its cognate, "logic," helps us to realize that there is a deep logic, an *onto*logic, of this ultimate principle, this *Ur-Prinzip*. Further, the myriad words ending in "-logy": geology, technology, psychology, sociology, ecology, biology, theology, and so on, carry the classical force of thinking, of giving an account, of a rigorous discipline or science, which also can help us enter a rigorous path with ecumenical power across diverse worldviews—Critical-Thinking.

However, it is vital here to recall again that as a global name for "what is first," *Dia-Logos*, does not displace the many primal names that have emerged over time and space. Rather, the global force of *Dia-Logos* keeps us mindful that the *Ur-Prinzip*, the Primal/Ultimate Principle, inherently generates alternative primal names, each of which has a unique creative force. Thus *Dia-Logos* must resonate: *Tao, Om, Sunyata, Hohmah, Logos,* Field of Energy/Matter...the unlimited range of historical primal names. Nor does this suggest that these diverse primal names for the Ultimate Principle are synonymous or equivalent in any naive or uncritical sense. For the deep logic of *Dia-Logos* provides for profound multiplicity and diversity—which nevertheless coarise in Unity. This is the power of *Dia-Logos*. It is Relational.

As we enter the global dialogical/critical way of thinking and speaking, we gain deeper access to the common ground between worlds. Deep-Dialogue/

Critical-Thinking/Emotional-Intelligence has helped expand our thought to the global level and led us to encounter in an open way the various primal names: *Logos, Tao, Hohmah*. At the same time it took the clarifying power of the individual primal names, *Logos, Tao, Hohmah,* to move us into effective *Dia-Logos*, into Deep-Dialogue/Critical-Thinking/Emotional-Intelligence with, and beyond, all of them. In this natural evolutionary circularity, we can look back and see that the rise in recent decades of a dialogical/critical consciousness, of an awareness of *Logos, Tao, Hohmah*, and with and beyond all of them, to *Dia-Logos* has in fact been thousands of years in process. This breakthrough in thinking to a globalized dialogical way of being has been a long evolutionary process. Deep-Dialogue/Critical-Thinking brings us to encounter the global, universal *Ur-Prinzip*, the Ultimate Principle of *Dia-Logos*. Looking back now, we see that humanity has been in intercultural interaction since the beginning of civilization, but now the globalizing dynamic of Ways-Encounters has so accelerated that it is precipitating an explosive chain reaction, leading thereby to the beginning of a global disclosure of the all-embracing/all-enabling *Dia-Logos*.

Ten Principles Articulating Deep-Dialogue/Critical-Thinking/Emotional-Intelligence/ Competitive-Cooperation

Here are laid out ten principles underlying Deep-Dialogue/Critical-Thinking/ Emotional Intelligence/Competitive-Cooperation: 1. The Continuum Principle, 2. The Dialogue-On-Dialogue Principle, 3. The Reality-Is-Dialogic Principle, 4. The Integrative Principle, 5. The Critical-Thinking-Is-the-Obverse of Deep-Dialogue Principle, 6. The Knowing-Is-Dialogic-Integrative Principle, 7. The Dialogue-Is-Communion Principle, 8. The Pluralizing-Authenticating Principle, 9. The Wholeness-as-Inner-/Inter-Dialogue Principle, 10. The Dialogue-as-Ontology-of-Goodness Principle.

Underlying all reality are at least ten theoretical dialogic/critical principles, which also underlie the *Virtue*, the *Way* of Deep-Dialogue/Critical-Thinking/ Competitive-Cooperation—*Dia-Logos*. Obviously there can be alternative formulations of principles of Deep-Dialogue/Critical-Thinking/Emotional-Intelligence/Competitive-Cooperation—*Dia-Logos*—which would stress and articulate other aspects not explicated here. Nor in this initial experimental formulation am I seeking to be comprehensive or conclusive. In the spirit of Deep-Dialogue/Critical-Thinking/Emotional-Intelligence/Competitive-Cooperation, *Dia-Logos* remains under revision and subject to ongoing amendment.

The Continuum Principle

All reality is dialogic/critical, operating on a continuum:

Destructive Dialogue →	Disinterested Dialogue	→ Dialogical Dialogue	→ Deep-Dialogue
Elements are polarized against each other	Elements are tolerant of each other	Elements learn from each other	Elements are mutually transformed

The Dialogue-On-Dialogue Principle

A primary way, a "Royal Road," to the dialogical/critical awakening is an extended dialogue on Deep-Dialogue/Critical-Thinking/Emotional-Intelligence/Competitive-Cooperation—*Dia-Logos* itself. Such an intense dialogue lays bare all the underlying issues—religious, philosophical, psychological, and so forth—which, when resolved, when integrated, will together serve as a *logo*motive, pulling forward all other issues submitted to dialogue.

The Reality-Is-Dialogic Principle

All reality is interactive, mutual, "dialogic." This dialogic structure is present from the subatomic to the cosmic (where on both levels, matter and energy are convertible; further, a growing number of thinkers believe that the binary structure of computers—that is, an endless series of 1's and 0's in "dialogue" with each other—is reflective of the fundamental nature of all reality), through the *intra*personal to the *inter*personal, still further to the intercommunal, and ultimately the global—and beyond to the Source and Goal of all reality.

The Integrative Principle

Not only is all reality "dialogic," it is also *integrative*. This "dialogue" of all reality oscillates in polar tension between the destructive and the integrative. For example, when the dialogic relationship between the electrons, protons, neutrons, and other particles and waves in an atom is not integrated, when the centrifugal and centripetal forces are not balanced in creative polar tension, the atom will disintegrate into either a black hole or a nuclear explosion. As matter becomes ever more complex, the integration of the dialogue becomes more and more that of a delicately balanced network, which makes a qualitative leap when it reaches living matter, and a still greater leap when it arrives at reflexive, rational/intuitive, affective, spiritual human beings.

Critical-Thinking Is the Obverse of the Deep-Dialogue Principle

In order to open oneself to Deep-Dialogue it is vital to likewise develop the skills of thinking carefully and clearly, that is, of Critical-Thinking—expressed as *Dia-Logos*—linking together essentially together dynamically Dialogue and Thinking. We need to learn how to understand what we, and others, really mean when we say something, why we say it, in order to choose, to judge where we believe the truth lies, and what the implications are—What? Whence? Whither? Critical-Thinking also entails at least these four additional elements:

a. We work to raise our presuppostions from the unconscious level—where by definition they reside—to the conscious level. Only then can we deal with them fully humanly, that is, rationally reflect on and decide for, against, or partly-partly concerning them.

b. We realize that *our* view of reality is *a* view of reality, that although it shares much with others' views of reality, it is also partially shaped by our personal lenses through which we experience and interpret reality, and hence is not absolute but perspectival.

c. We learn to understand all statements, whether from ourselves or others, in *their* context. That is, a text can be correctly understood only in *its* context. Only then will we be able to translate the original core of the statements/texts into *our* context.

d. We learn to probe with great precision *every* statement, first of our own, but also of all others, to learn *precisely* what they *really* mean. This is particularly important to do concerning simple statements, terms, and clichés because very often unconscious presuppositions lie beneath them.

This process of Critical-Thinking obviously entails a mental dialogue within our own mind. Thus, at its root Critical-Thinking is dialogic—and Deep-Dialogue at its root entails clear, critical thought—followed by consequent Competitive-Cooperation! However, we cannot stop at Deep-Dialogue and Critical-Thinking, but must deepen the latter to include Emotional-Intelligence, and then on the bases of those, act in Competitive-Cooperation, as outlined above. It is not sufficient to describe an authentic human life as a two-sided coin; rather, a full human life is four-dimensional, embracing Critical-Thinking, Deep-Dialogue, Emotional-Intelligence, and Competitive-Cooperation. They are the four dimensions of authentic humanity: They must become Virtues, habits of mind, spirit, and action.

The Knowing-Is-Dialogic-Integrative Principle

All knowing is both interactive, mutual, dialogic, *and* integrative between the known and the knower, for knowing is a kind of unifying of the object and the subject—a kind of integration. Example: the surface of a table becomes one with, integrated with, the surface of my fingers. The interactive, mutual, unifying, dialogic-integrative character is doubly true when the knower is also the known, as in my learning about what it means to be human. This is especially true when I learn what it means for me to be human. That dialogic-integrative character, then, is endlessly, infinitely true of all knowing, from

a. when the known and the knower are separate object and subject, through

b. when the known and knower are interpersonal, further through

c. when the known and knower are communities of persons, to ultimately

d. when they embrace the whole globe—and

e. beyond to the Source and Goal of all reality.

The Dialogue-Is-Communion Principle

Dialogue is a "coming together," a "conversation" with those who think differently from us primarily so we can learn. Because all reality is mutual, in a full dialogue *both* participants must come *primarily* to learn. Hence, secondarily, but essentially, our partners must also teach if we are to learn, and vice versa. When Destructive Dialogue moves toward integration, it becomes the attitudinally indifferent Disinterested Dialogue, and then progresses toward learning Dialogical Dialogue, and ultimately reaches Deep-Dialogue when the learning from each other attains the level that transforms our consciousness.

The Pluralizing-Authenticating Principle

Dialogue *can* occur when I realize that my view of reality is a view, not the view. Dialogue will occur when I perceive persons with views different from mine who are living what I (and obviously they) think are authentic human lives—I will then necessarily want to know how they do it!

The Wholeness-as-Inner-/Inter-Dialogue Principle

Dialogue engages the whole person: mind, emotions, action. It spills over from the cognitive to the affective area of life, and thence to the practical area— Competitive-Cooperation—both on the interpersonal and the communal, and then on the intercommunal, levels. This naturally leads to networking, alliances, and cooperative activities, which are dialogue-integration in action. Thus Dialogue heals, makes whole (holy!), persons and *polis*.

The Dialogue-as-Ontology-of-Goodness Principle

When one successfully experiences dialogue, Deep-Dialogue, it feels right. We feel integrated. Deep-Dialogue feels right, integrated, because human dialogue is in sync with not only our whole humanity, body and spirit, but also with the whole of reality from the subatomic through the cosmic to Ultimate Reality, Which/Who is in dialogue-integration with the world. We embrace, and are embraced by, the Cosmic Dance of *Dia-Logos*!

13

Three Facets of Deep-Dialogue/ Critical-Thinking/Emotional-Intelligence/Competitive- Cooperation

Three facets of Deep-Dialogue/Critical-Thinking/Emotional Intelligence/ Competitive-Cooperation are here laid out here: 1. The Reality Facet, 2. The Mutuality Facet, 3. The Reflexive-Awakening Facet.

It should be apparent that the ten principles articulated above are deeply integral to one another in the living praxis of Deep-Dialogue/Critical-Thinking/ Emotional-Intelligence/Competitive-Cooperation. In the following articulation of three fundamental Facets of Deep-Dialogue/Critical-Thinking/Emotional-Intelligence/Competitive-Cooperation, we shall see that the diverse principles actually arise together and cooperate in the living process of Deep-Dialogue/ Critical-Thinking/Emotional-Intelligence/Competitive-Cooperation—*Dia-Logos*.

The Reality Facet

Deep-Dialogue/Critical-Thinking/Emotional-Intelligence/Competitive-Cooperation is the human art of life grounded in the cosmos itself. It fundamentally is the art of being, of conducting our minds and actions in harmony with the Cosmic Dance of Dialogue. This awakening of awareness to a deeper encounter with reality is itself a natural evolution of our human condition. In light of the *Dia-Logos Ur-Prinzip*, we see how and why objective reality is a dynamic dialogic/critical or interactive process in which all existence is in a limitless, evolving interplay. Thus, the very fabric of reality is a dynamic drama of relations held together by the unifying power of *Dia-Logos*. All life is an unfolding dialogic/critical process. Nature unfolds in dialogue, and so we speak of "natural dialogue."

The Mutuality Facet

The "magic" and mystery of dialogue are that as the natural pulse of *Dia-Logos* they are at once the binding force that holds diverse things together in primal relationship and the differential force that generates and encourages multiplicity and differentiation. In brief: the primal force of existence is dialogic/critical—that is, the primal force is relational in that it allows things to be limitlessly differentiated, and yet unified in an integral whole. This is why all things essentially arise out of dialogical/critical force, out of *Dia-Logos*, how they find their identity and inner integrity in and through this strength, and are held together in a binding force that forms an integrating *continuum*, an integrity. The very *pulse* of existence is a natural dialogic/critical process. This *Dia-Logos* force, then, is why existence is a *continuum* of boundlessly differentiated beings, each evolving in inner unity and integrity.

The Reflexive-Awakening Facet

Human evolution has arisen out of the natural developing dialogue in which consciousness moves increasingly in a dialogic/critical awakening—a self-reflection in which life becomes self-aware of the dialogic/critical principle of *Dia-Logos* itself. This is the driving logomotive of human life and of Deep-Dialogue/Critical-Thinking/Emotional-Intelligence/Competitive-Cooperation. The awakening life process is the dialogic/critical impulse and imperative, awakening us to the living of the *Dia-Logos*. Thus, there is a deep circularity in the dynamic of Deep-Dialogue/Critical-Thinking/Emotional-Intelligence/Competitive-Cooperation. It takes Deep-Dialogue/Critical-Thinking/Emotional-Intelligence/Competitive-Cooperation for us to awaken to the moving force of life, which is realized in the reflexive awareness of Deep-Dialogue/Critical-Thinking/Emotional-Intelligence/Competitive-Cooperation.

The Global Way of Deep-Dialogue/Critical-Thinking/ Emotional-Intelligence/ Competitive-Cooperation

Here all the fundamental points already made are reiterated and integrated within a global context.

Here I wish to reiterate several of the most important points I already expressed at least once, but in a somewhat different way—on the principle that *Repetitio est mater studiorum*!

Deep-Dialogue/Critical-Thinking/Emotional-Intelligence/Competitive-Cooperation is a Way that translates the creativity generated by intercultural, interreligious dialogue at the global/local level into the culture-shaping elements of society. There are the four areas of dialogue: Head, Hands, Heart, Holy. Recall:

Deep-Dialogue of the Head is a Way of encountering oneself, others, and the world at the deepest levels, which opens up possibilities of grasping individually and communally the meaning of life. It is an encounter with those whose view of the world is significantly other than our own—a Ways encounter. The primary purpose of this opening out is for each person to gain a new insight into reality. Such a dialogical encounter enables us to view ourselves, others, and the world, as well as our understanding of it, from a new perspective, more "objectively," enriched through the eyes of others. This new Way of understanding reality, which is opening up and being made increasingly explicit at the beginning of the third millennium, provides each of us the opportunity to probe the inner depth of the meaning of life as we face it in the different dimensions of our experience: individually, with others, at work, in the family, on the several levels of community up to the global level, and amid the world around us. However, even beyond this, Deep-Dialogue is at the very foundation of the cosmos, at the macro- and micro levels, so that if we would be in sync with all reality and its source and goal, however understood, we all need to join this Cosmic Dance of Deep-Dialogue.

The converse of Deep-Dialogue is Critical-Thinking: to open oneself to Deep-Dialogue it is necessary also to develop the skills of thinking carefully and clearly, of Critical-Thinking (to repeat, *critical*, from the Greek, *krinein*, to choose, to judge). We need to understand what we and others really mean when we say something, why we say it, so as to "choose," "judge," where we believe the truth lies, and what the implications are: What? Whence? Whither? Critical-Thinking entails at least these further four: first, that we raise our pre-suppositions from the unconscious to the conscious level—only then can we deal with them rationally, deciding for, against, or part for/part against them; second, that we realize that our view of reality is *a* view, and therefore not abso-lute but perspectival, shaped by the lenses of our experience, through which we experience and interpret all reality; third, that we learn to understand all statements in *their* context, that is, a text can be correctly understood only in *its* context—only then will we be able to translate the original core of the state-ments/texts into *our* context.

This process of Critical-Thinking, then, entails a dialogue within our own mind. Hence, at its root Critical-Thinking is dialogic, and Deep-Dialogue at its root entails clear, critical thought—two sides of the coin of humanity.

Deep-Dialogue of the Hands: ethics. Ethics is the set of principles that each of us develops by which we decide how to act both in general and in particular situations. Because of the fluidity of modern society it is especially vital both for individuals and for communities to develop integrated, holistic ways of ethical behavior. At the same time, it is essential that we enter respectfully into Deep-Dialogue/Critical-Thinking/Emotional-Intelligence/Competitive-Cooperation with those whose ethical principles appear to be grounded differently than ours are. That is, we need to experience Ways Encounters, both to seek out what is held in common and to discern true differences. In the end, it is necessary for human survival that such individual and group commitment to integrated ethical living in a dialogical context expand to the fullest, aiming at the joint discovery of a global ethic.

Globality: Globalization on the physical level is accelerating at such a rapid rate that intellectually and emotionally we humans need to focus our full atten-tion on this reality if we are to survive on all three levels, intellectual, emo-tional and even physical—let alone flourish. However, globalization is likewise an incredible opportunity to overcome the "divisive dualisms" that have plagued humankind from the beginning: body-spirit, men-women, black-white, rich-poor, labor-management, religious-secular, Catholic-Protestant, Jewish-Christian, nation-nation, East-West. A humane globalization cannot succeed by way of dominance. Rather, it can be attained only by Deep-Dialogue/Critical-Thinking/Emotional-Intelligence/Competitive-Cooperation: within persons, among individuals, among groups, and onto the global level—issuing in a "global ethic," that is, the basic ethical principles discovered to be actually held worldwide, arrived at by consensus, brought about through Deep-Dialogue/Critical-Thinking/Competitive-Cooperation (more on a global ethic below)

Dialogue of the Heart: Spirituality is a term with a long use, but it has become more prominent of late in distinction to religion, with familiar statements such as

"I am not religious, but I am spiritual." Whence the word spiritual? It comes from the Latin *spiritus*, which means "breath" or "wind." Ancient humans noticed that if there was no breath in a human body, it was dead, that breath was a reality that could not be seen, that was within, and that obviously was literally vital to human life. Thus, spirituality refers to the interior, the internal, as distinct from the exterior, the external. It is that latter that the popular phrase means when it rejects religion. It understands religion as referring to externals, and spirituality to the interior life.

Actually, seeing religion as merely dealing with externals is a quite reductionist view of religion, as the earlier discussion made clear. Recall also from the earlier discussion that regardless of how we understand, or misunderstand, the term religion, it is clear that spirituality refers to the interior meaning of our humanity. Thus, when we speak of the spirituality of something, we are trying to get at the interior meaning of whatever we are talking about. We are talking about the internal significance of some external thing or actions. Spirituality refers to the way each individual and group inwardly understands the meaning of life and then outwardly gives it expression. Thus, spirituality underlies all aspects of everyday life—including every specific religion or ideology, each of which is a particular crystallization of that perception of the meaning of life and how to manifest it.

As persons mature, they enter into a kind of Deep-Dialogue/Critical-Thinking/Emotional-Intelligence/Competitive-Cooperation within themselves, thereby giving shape to their personal understanding of the meaning of life—their spirituality. Although this has often been done within the context of a religious tradition, today many people are discovering spiritual meaning in alternative ways. Hence, spirituality provides the basis from which ethics, the principles of behavior, springs. So too, because of the shifting quality of contemporary society, it is vital that each of us develops integrated, holistic ways of fusing our spirituality and everyday life: in the family, at work, in our communities, up to the global level, and in relation to the world around us. At the same time, it is essential that we enter Deep-Dialogue/Critical-Thinking/Emotional-Intelligence/Competitive-Cooperation with those whose spirituality is different from ours, both to seek what is common and to discern true differences.

In my personal working out of this spirituality, I also created a community, the Dialogue Institute. Besides helping me develop a Deep-Dialogue Way, it also serves to lead individuals and groups through the Seven Stages with the aid of the Dialogue Decalogue, Eleven-Step Program, and an Online Course on Deep-Dialogue/Critical-Thinking/Emotional-Intelligence/Competitive-Cooperation to the Virtue of Deep-Dialogue/Critical-Thinking/Emotional-Intelligence Competitive-Cooperation Way and helps them apply the results to their specific settings. It is to those Seven Stages of Deep-Dialogue/Critical-Thinking/Emotional-Intelligence/Competitive-Cooperation that I now turn.

15

Seven Stages of Deep-Dialogue/ Critical-Thinking/Emotional-Intelligence/Competitive-Cooperation

There can be discerned seven transformative stages through which a maturing person and community will grow, if not blocked, from a self-centered to an all-embracing humanity. These stages and their implications are described here.

The following are Seven Stages of Deep-Dialogue/Critical-Thinking/ Emotional-Intelligence/Competitive Cooperation that a person can go through if s/he persists in this project. The initial draft was drawn up by my colleague Ashok Gangadean, substantively revised by the two of us in dialogue, and further developed and modified by myself. The photos created by Professor Ingrid Shafer at astro.temple.edu/~swidler/course/index.htm are visualizations of the characteristics of each stage.

Stage One   Radical Encountering of Difference

Self Faces the Other

This first encounter comes with a certain shock, with a realization of an Other, a different way of life, a different worldview, an alien Other who resists, interrupts, disrupts my settled way of interpretation. With this initial encounter there is a new realization that my habits of thinking cannot make sense of this Other. This radical encounter with Difference—a different world, a different way of making sense of and experiencing the world—is disconcerting, sometimes threatening, and evokes a vulnerability to this alien presence. I have a new sense of delimitation, and I feel challenged to change, to revise my way of relating to this Other. I realize now that my habit of translating the Other into *my* pattern of thinking, of appropriating the Other to *my* worldview, is dysfunctional. I am forced toward a *self*-critical Deep-Dialogue/Critical-Thinking/Emotional-Intelligence and consequent Competitive-Cooperation. So I face a sudden silence, pause, opening—an open horizon of uncertainty and risk. I must make a decision to move forward—or draw back.

Stage Two   Crossing Over, Letting Go, and Entering the World of the Other

Self Transformed through Empathy

After the initial shock and realization that I now face an alien world, a world-view very different from mine, I feel challenged to inquire, investigate, engage enter this new world—to engage in reflective Deep-Dialogue/Critical-Thinking/Emotional-Intelligence/Competitive-Cooperation. As I open my Self to this Other, I realize that I need to stand back and distance myself from my former habits and patterns of perceiving the world. I begin to realize that this other world organizes and processes the world very differently from my way. I realize that I must learn new habits and ways of interpretation to make sense of this different world. I must learn a "new language." Indeed, I must translate myself into a different form of life that sees the world differently. This involves bracketing my assumptions.

Stage Three   Inhabiting and Experiencing the World of the Other

Self Transformed into the Other

I begin to feel a new and deep empathy for my new habitat; I want to let myself go—free myself to enter, experiment, learn, and grow in this new way of being—to embrace Deep-Dialogue/Critical-Thinking/Emotional-Intelligence/Competitive-Cooperation. I hold on to my prior views as much as I can, but I advance in a conservative fashion. Still, I experience an excitement in discovering, in inhabiting a new and different worldview. I have a new realization of an-Other, an alternative reality and form of life. But in the end I realize this is not really my home.

Stage Four   Crossing Back with Expanded Vision

Self Returns Home with New Knowledge

I now cross back, return, to my own world, bringing back new knowledge of how to think and act—self-reflective Deep-Dialogue/Critical-Thinking/Emotional-Intelligence/Competitive-Cooperation—and may even wish to adopt/adapt some of it for myself. As a result of this encounter with the world of the Other, I now realize that there are other ways of understanding reality. I am therefore open to rethinking how I see myself, others, and the world. I encounter my Self and culture anew, with a newly opened mind. My encounter with radical difference now challenges my former identity, and everything begins to appear in a new light. There now begins a dramatic deepening of my sense of my self, my identity, my ethnicity, my lifeworld, my religion, my culture. There is no return to my former unilateral way of thinking.

Stage Five   The Dialogical/Critical Awakening: A Radical Paradigm Shift

Self Inwardly Transformed

As a result of this new encounter with Self, when I cross back from my deep encounter with an Other, I begin to experience a profound shift in all aspects of my world—my inner experience, my encounter with others, my relating to the world. I begin to realize that my encounter with the Other has shaken the foundation of my former worldview, my former identity. Now that I am aware of the living reality of other worlds, other perspectives, I can no longer return to my former identity and forget this living presence of the Other. Indeed, I now begin to realize that there are many other worlds, other forms of life, other perspectives that surround me. I now open to a plurality of other worlds and perspectives, and this irrevocably changes my sense of Self. I feel transformed to a deeper sense of relation and connection with my surroundings, my "ecology." I feel more deeply rooted in this experience of relationality and community. I now see that my true identity is essentially connected with this expansive network of relations with Others. This is the ignition of the Deep-Dialogue/Critical-Thinking/Emotional-Intelligence/Competitive-Cooperation Awakening.

Stage Six   The Global Awakening: The Paradigm Shift Matures

Self Related to Self, Others, the World

In my transformed Deep-Dialogue/Critical-Thinking/Emotional-Intelligence/Competitive-Cooperation Awakening, I discover a deeper common ground among the multiple worlds and perspectives that surround me. I have a new sense that Self and Others are inseparably bound together in a limitless interrelational web. I realize that multiplicity and diversity enriches my Self and my world. I now see that all worlds are situated in a common ground of reality and that radical differences are nevertheless also situated in a field of unity. I experience three related dimensions of Global Deep-Dialogue/Critical-Thinking/Emotional-Intelligence/Competitive-Cooperation "Awakening":

a) An ever deepening discovery of Self: I become aware of a deep inner Deep-Dialogue/Critical-Thinking/Emotional-Intelligence/Competitive-Cooperation/within my Self. I discover a rich multiplicity and diversity of perspectives within my own inner world. In this inner Deep-Dialogue/Critical-Thinking/Emotional-Intelligence/Competitive-Cooperation, I feel increasingly more deeply rooted and grounded in my world. My identity is enriched with multiplicity, and I experience a more powerful sense of my uniqueness as I celebrate my expanded world of relationality with Others and with my surroundings, my "ecology."

b) A dynamic dialogue opens with Others in my Community: As my new inner Deep-Dialogue/Critical-Thinking/Emotional-Intelligence/Competitive-Cooperation evolves, I find myself in a new and transformed relation with others who share my world, tradition, religion, culture. This new phase of relations with my peers can be disorienting and disconcerting, for as I now grow more deeply in my identity, I find myself at an estranged distance from many of my peers, even as I discover a deeper affinity and embrace of my community. I face a new turbulence—miscommunication and misunderstanding with my colleagues—and a challenging and dialogue unfolds.

c) A global awakening emerges in all aspects of my life: As this inner and outer Deep-Dialogue/Critical-Thinking/Emotional-Intelligence/Competitive-Cooperation matures, I realize that my understanding of my world is suffused with a new "global" light: I realize that I am surrounded with many worldviews. I enter a global horizon and a global consciousness in which interreligious, intercultural, interideological, interdisciplinary, interpersonal dialogues abound in all directions. I now have a new globalized sense of reality—a Deep-Dialogue/Critical-Thinking/Emotional-Intelligence/Competitive-Cooperation domain in which multiple alternative worlds are situated in dynamic ever-deepening relations. With this understanding comes a new attitude toward life and to ethics.

Stage Seven   Personal/Global Transforming of Life and Behavior

*Self Lives and Acts in a New Global Deep-Dialogue/Critical-Thinking/
Emotional-Intelligence/Competitive-Cooperation Consciousness*

As this paradigm shift matures, I realize that there is a deep change in all aspects of my life—a new moral consciousness and practice. As my new Deep-Dialogue/Critical-Thinking/Emotional-Intelligence/Competitive-Cooperation consciousness becomes a habit, a virtue, it deepens into a Way of life, and I find that my behavior and my disposition to Self and Others have been utterly transformed. I feel a new sense of communion with my Self, with Others, and with my surroundings, my "ecology." I realize that the deepest care for my Self essentially involves my care for Others and the "environment." I have a deeper sense of belonging to my world, to my community, and with this a limitless sense of responsibility in all my conduct. I now realize that I am transformed in the deepest habits of mind and behavior. I find a deeper sense of Self-realization, fulfillment, and meaning in my life and my relations with others and the world around me, and its Source and Goal, however understood. I embrace, and am embraced by the Virtue, the Way of Deep-Dialogue/Critical-Thinking/Emotional-Intelligence/Competitive-Cooperation—*Dia-Logos*!

16

Online Course in Deep-Dialogue/ Critical-Thinking/Emotional- Intelligence/Competitive- Cooperation

It is one thing to grasp the meaning and implications of Deep-Dialogue/Critical-Thinking/Emotional-Intelligence/Competitive-Cooperation, but vastly more demanding to put them into action. Here is an online course designed to lead individuals and groups to integrate these practices into their lives.

Introduction

My core ideas and those of the Dialogue Institute: Interreligious, Intercultural, International on Deep-Dialogue/Critical-Thinking/Emotional-Intelligence/Competitive-Cooperation are online at astro.temple.edu/~swidler/course/index.htm, as a course to be taken either at specified times with a director, or alone anytime. It will provide a number of exercises to lead the participants to understand deeply their meaning, with the ultimate aim of so imbuing the participants with the mentality of the Way of Deep-Dialogue, Critical-Thinking, Emotional-Intelligence, and Competitive-Cooperation that they will tend to become "second nature" to the participants—the very definition of being a Virtue. Because these skills are so fundamental, they will necessarily also pervade the processes of this core course, as well as all subsequent training modules, in, for example, "Training of Teachers," and "Dialogue and Ethics for Corporate Business."

Although it is clear that Competitive-Cooperation is the final goal, it is very difficult to say which of the prior two, Deep-Dialogue or Critical-Thinking (and, to a lesser extent, Emotional-Intelligence), has priority, but—as in the love of one person for another, although both persons are essential, the love must start from the *(primus) ego* and move to the *alter ego*—one must first begin to think critically oneself. However, immediately then—as in the movement of love from the *ego* to the *alter*—one must engage the critical thinking of the partner in dialogue in order to make one's own thinking ever more fully critical.

Consequently, these exercises will focus first on understanding and practicing critical thinking—although of course they will be done in dialogue with the instructor and with other participants.

Introductory Exercise

(1) To begin, read all the way through slowly and carefully the following description of the essential elements of Deep-Dialogue, Critical-Thinking, Emotional-Intelligence, Competitive-Cooperation, and their relationships, stopping to write down any questions along the way.

(2) Then, read the description a second time, section by section, and see whether the questions have been answered (write the answers alongside the questions). Report to the instructor, or other participants in the e-group, your questions and subsequent answers, or lack thereof.

What Is Deep-Dialogue/Critical-Thinking/Emotional-Intelligence/Competitive-Cooperation?

A. To begin, very simply put, Deep-Dialogue means to
1. reach out in openness to the Other in the search for Truth and Goodness;
2. be open to the Other primarily so we can learn, find Truth and Goodness;
3. perceive that for us to learn, to find the good, the Others must teach and open themselves—and vice versa;
4. recognize, because Dialogue is a two-way project, and then both learn and share the good;
5. learn there are Other ways of understanding, of embracing the world than our own;
6. learn to recognize our commonalities and differences—and value both;
7. learn to move between different worlds and integrate them in care;
8. learn that Deep-Dialogue thus gradually transforms our inner selves—and our shared lives.

B. Very simply put, Critical-Thinking means to
1. (a) raise our unconscious presuppositions to the conscious level, and
   (b) after reflection, make a reasoned judgment ("critical," Greek *krinein* to judge) about them;
2. think analytically (Greek: *ana* up, *lysis* break), that is, break ideas into their component parts to see how they fit together;
3. think synthetically (Greek: *syn* together, *thesis* to put), that is, put components of different ideas together in new ways;

4. understand and use very precisely each word and phrase so that our deliberations and decisions are informed with clarity and grounded in reality;

5. understand all statements/texts in their contexts, and only then apply them to our contexts;

6. (a) recognize that our view of reality is *one* view, shaped by our experience, becoming aware, thereby, of multiple worldviews, and
   (b) see that each worldview is a new meaning network;
   (c) understand that only then can we reasonably appreciate/critique them.

7. In sum: Address the three W questions: **What? Whence? Whither?**
   What precisely does what we are talking about mean?
   Whence comes the evidence for what we are talking about?
   Whither do the implications of what we are talking about lead?

C. Very simply put, Emotional-Intelligence means learning to
   1. know and understand oneself;
   2. know and understand other persons, and
   3. know how appropriately to relate to each other.

D. Very simply put, Competitive-Cooperation means to
   1. not be satisfied with the passable, but reach for the best;
   2. strive to make decisions within broader frameworks;
   3. not be satisfied with the standard, but stress constant creativity;
   4. as much as possible, avoid zero-sum, win-lose solutions, but rather seek creatively positive-sum, win-win ones;
   5. prefer not either-or, but both-and choices.

E. Deep-Dialogue/Critical-Thinking/Emotional-Intelligence/Competitive-Cooperation relationship:
   1. Deep-Dialogue/Critical-Thinking/Emotional-Intelligence/Competitive-Cooperation are four facets of the one human reality.
   2. Deep-Dialogue entails at its root clear, reflective, critical thought.
   3. Critical-Thinking entails a dialogue within our own minds and lives—and hence, at its root is dialogic.
   4. Emotional-Intelligence entails a dialogue with our feelings and the feelings of others—and hence, at its root is dialogic.
   5. The consequent action flowing from Deep-Dialogue/Critical-Thinking/Emotional-Intelligence is Competitive-Cooperation.
   6. Deep-Dialogue/Critical-Thinking/Emotional-Intelligence/Competitive-Cooperation are thus four sides of our humanity.
   7. Deep-Dialogue/Critical-Thinking/Emotional-Intelligence/Competitive-Cooperation eventually must become a habit of mind, and action, traditionally known as a virtue—a new basic mentality, and consequent practice, that is, a Way of life.

Multiple Dimensions of Deep-Dialogue/Critical-Thinking/ Emotional-Intelligence/Competitive-Cooperation in Life/Education, from Cradle to Grave

1. Rational thinking at its very core is critical and dialogic.
2. The scientific method essentially is an endless critical dialogue between the scientist and the observed data.
3. Our language is the dialogic ability to express to others what is within; we should strive to be as critically clear, as precise as possible.
4. Our imagination is the dialogic ability to move out of our world into that of others, to which we should be open critically.
5. Our emotions move us dialogically from where we are to another place; they should be fostered under the critical reflection of reason.
6. Our aesthetic ability leads us dialogically and critically to find beauty in a world within and outside ourselves.
7. Our body should be encouraged to a constant critically reflective dialogue with itself, our spirit, our mind, other persons, and world about us.
8. Interpersonal relations need to be fostered in a dialogic win-win, though clear-headed, critical manner.
9. Our moral sensibilities must be developed in the critically reflective dialogue of loving the Other as ourselves.
10. Our actions should compete and cooperate to match our knowledge/ wisdom reached through dialogue and critical thought
11. We humans should heighten our ecological sensitivity through a critically, emotionally intelligent reflective dialogue between our selves and nature, which we are a part of, not apart from.

Exercise: Critical-Thinking

Principle: Critical-Thinking, Principle 1 (a) is

1. (a) Raise our unconscious presuppositions to the conscious level.

Explanation: To be conscious of something is, of course, to be aware of it. Obviously, unconscious means to *not* be aware of something. Also, clearly, *pre* (Latin) means beforehand, and *supposition* (Latin: *sub positio*) means something *underlying*. Hence, a presupposition is an idea that ahead of time underlies another idea or set of ideas, and in the case at hand, this presupposition is something we are unaware of; it is unconscious. Example: In the past, and unfortunately still today, many men, and women, thought that women were incapable of clear, rational thought. This was a presupposition that prevented women from attending the university, for instance. For the most part, it was unconscious, that is, most did not think about it, they just assumed it without being aware that they were doing so.

1. Exercise: (1) Describe in separate paragraphs several unconscious presuppositions (they need not be only negative examples—e.g., "strong men do not cry") from the past or present, and at least some of the consequences thereof.

(2) Send them to the instructor or e-group, and participate in the ensuing dialogue.

Principle: Critical-Thinking Principle 1 (b) is

> *1 (b). After reflection make a reasoned judgment ("critical,"*
> *Greek* krinein *to judge) about them.*

Explanation: So long as a presupposition remains uninvestigated, we cannot know with any certainty that we are acting on the basis of reality or a mirage. We cannot truthfully tell ourselves that we are acting thus in a rational manner. The situation is even vastly more devastating when the presupposition is unconscious. Then we are controlled totally in the concerned area by an idea that might be partially, or even totally, unwarranted—and we can do absolutely nothing about it (!), for we are powerless to analyze an idea and change the consequent action if we do not even know of the existence of the "motor" that secretly runs our mind and behavior.

2. Exercise: (1) Analyze in separate paragraphs your examples of unconscious presuppositions that you gave above, and indicate what rational judgments (*krinein*) you might make consequently along with matching actions, and suggest what differences in a person's life such analyses, judgments, and actions might make.

(2) Send them to the instructor or e-group, and participate in the ensuing dialogue.

Principle: Critical-Thinking Principle 2 is

> *2. Think analytically (Greek:* ana *up,* lysis *break), that is, break ideas into their*
> *component parts to see how they fit together.*

Explanation: When something is simple, it has no parts, but is only a single-part object. Almost nothing is truly simple. Even the smallest particles we have discovered so far in nuclear physics are not what they are except as in relationship to other things. For example, to speak of a proton does not make sense except in relationship to the electron. Negative has no meaning except as distinct from positive. So, even such a "simple" object as an electron is what it is only because it is related to a proton. Conclusion: practically everything is made up of parts.

Consequently, if we are to understand something, whether an object or an idea, we will need to know what the parts are that make it up and how they are related to each other. Example: how can we correctly care for or repair an automobile engine if we do not know what the parts and their functions are that make up the engine and how they interrelate? We can't. Again, how can we know that we are fostering a democratic society if we do not know what the essential parts and their functions are that make a democracy and how they interrelate? We can't.

3. Exercise: (1) In separate paragraphs, choose five or more *ideas* to analyze. Feel free to make abundant use of a good *American College* dictionary in the process, for the roots of words, as we have seen already, are often keys to unlocking their fundamental meaning. For example, "democracy" comes from the Greek: *demos,* people, *kratein* to rule. This might be a beginning of an analysis of the idea of democracy—but only a beginning, for one would have to decide what questions need to be asked and answered if one is to understand the parts and interaction thereof of democracy. One might ask questions like: Why should the people rule? What are the means to bring the people to rule? What are the consequences? Clearly there are many valid ways to analyze an idea.

(2) Send in each paragraph as it is completed to either the instructor or the e-group, and participate in the ensuing dialogue.

Principle: Critical-Thinking Principle 3 is

> *3. Think synthetically (Greek: syn together, thesis putting),*
> *that is, put components of different ideas together in new ways.*

Explanation: Aristotle, and Thomas Aquinas after him, noted that, "Nihil in intellectu quod non prius in sensu" ("Nothing is in the intellect which was not first in the senses"). All our ideas are made up of various parts that we absorbed in some way first through our senses. That is, we saw something, heard, touched, tasted, or smelled something. From those sensory experiences we "abstracted" general concepts or ideas. For example, after seeing and feeling numerous chairs of various shapes we came to abstract (Latin: *ab trahere,* to pull from—as in our English word "tractor") the general form or concept of a chair as "something to sit on." While in analytic thinking we break ideas into their parts, in synthetic thinking we do the opposite: We either take the component parts of an idea and put them together (*synthesize*) in a way different from how we found them in the original idea, thereby forming a new idea, or we take parts from more than one idea and put them together, thus forming a new idea. Hence, synthetic thinking can also be called creative thinking or imaginative thinking.

4. Exercise: (1) In separate paragraphs take the component parts of the above analyzed five ideas and by relating them differently, synthesize *new* ideas. For example: if you had analyzed the ideas of *democracy* and *business,* you might synthesize, that is, combine, parts of both and develop a more democratically organized business corporation, rather than a traditionally authoritarian one.

(2) Send in each paragraph as it is completed to either the instructor or the e-group, and participate in the ensuing dialogue.

Principle: Critical-Thinking Principle 4 is

*4. Understand and use very precisely each word and phrase
so that our deliberations and decisions are informed with
clarity and grounded in reality.*

Explanation: The most frequent reason for disagreement in discussions or even arguments is that, although the disputants are using the same central term, they in fact understand it differently. In every beginning philosophy class, the students are taught the three **D**'s: "**D**efine your terms, and **D**isagreements **D**isappear!"

Example one: Ivan claims that A is the biggest city in the United States, but Mirjam counters that, no, B is the largest city! Question one: Do both Ivan and Mirjam understand "city" to mean the strict legal city limits, or the "greater" city limits? Question two: Do Mirjam and Ivan both understand "biggest" to mean in area, or population, or...?

Example two: In 1970, West Germany, which was called the Federal Republic of Germany, claimed that it was a democracy and a republic, and that East Germany, even though it had named itself the German Democratic Republic, was in fact neither a democracy nor a republic. How could one decide which, if either, was correct? One could simply define what was meant by the terms "democracy" and "republic," and then compare that with the facts on the ground. Of course, in this example most East Germans knew perfectly well that their government was lying, as proved by the fact that at the first opportunity the people chose to abandon their Democratic Republic.

5. Exercise: (1) Write two short dialogues among three persons wherein there is a disagreement because they have not used a key term or two precisely, not having the same understanding of the term(s). Send in each dialogue as it is completed to either the instructor or the e-group, and participate in the ensuing dialogue.

(2) In a short paragraph for each dialogue, show how precise use of language would have avoided the disagreement, or at least brought the participants to understand where their *real* difference of opinion was.

(3) Send in each paragraph as it is completed to either the instructor or the e-group, and participate in the ensuing dialogue.

Principle: Critical-Thinking Principle 5 is

*5. Understand all statements/texts in their contexts, and only
then apply them to our contexts.*

Explanation: Every statement, every text can be properly understood only within *its* original context, that is, knowing where, when, why, by whom, to whom, under what circumstances, using what kind of language the statement was first made. To explain the meaning of a text is called "*ex*-egesis"—Greek: *ex* (out of) *egesmai* (to lead), meaning: to "lead out of" the text what is in it. The wrong-headed direction is "*eis*-egesis"—Greek: *eis* (into) *egesmai* (to lead), meaning: to put something into the text that was not there, but came from outside. This is very similar to an unconscious presupposition, where we do not see the facts in front of us, but unconsciously read *into* them what we mistakenly think are the facts in front of us. In reading texts, the greatest danger that we must be on the alert for is mistakenly doing *un*conscious *eis*egesis—instead of *ex*egesis.

Only after we have found out what the author meant to say in the original situation can we accurately apply that meaning to *our* context, if we judge it appropriate. If we don't first learn what the text originally meant, we are not able to apply it to ourselves. We will simply be applying our own or somebody else's, imagined meaning.

6. Exercise: (1) Choose two relatively brief texts from a sacred scripture (e.g., Bible, Qur'an, etc.) or other public document (e.g., the American Declaration of Independence or the French Declaration des Droits des Hommes et Citoyens) and write in one paragraph each what might be a typical *eis*egesis of each. Then send in each paragraph as it is completed to either the instructor or the e-group, and participate in the ensuing dialogue.

(2) Then write in two separate paragraphs what you think are correct *ex*egeses of each and

(3) send them to either the instructor or the e-group, and participate in the ensuing dialogue.

Principle: Critical-Thinking Principle 6 (a) is

> *6 (a). Recognize that* our *view of reality is* one *view, shaped by* our *experience, becoming aware, thereby, of multiple worldviews.*

Explanation: If in fact all data in our minds arrive there initially through our five senses, then obviously the capabilities of our senses will affect our view of reality. If we are color-blind, our view of reality will perhaps be in shades of grey rather than in the colors of the spectrum—just as in the difference between the "silver screen" and "technicolor" in the movies. *All* of our perceptions of reality necessarily come through the "lens" of our various knowing capacities. Thus, on a "higher" level, if we are socialized to think that diseases come as punishment for our past sins, or because someone has bewitched us, or from bacteria and other biological negativities, our views of reality will be shaped accordingly.

When we become aware of this fact, we will then begin to become aware that there are many differing views of reality, many even held in a stressful tension within ourselves. We then become ready for Dialogue.

7. Exercise: (1) In a total of six paragraphs, describe three situations as perceived in substantially different ways flowing from different sets of experience or socializations.

(2) Send in each pair of paragraph as they are completed to either the instructor or the e-group, and participate in the ensuing dialogue.

Principle: Critical-Thinking Principle 6 (b) is

6 (b). See that each worldview is a new meaning network.

Explanation: Nuclear physicists (micro level), cosmologists (macro level), and other physical scientists have known for a long time that *everything* is connected with everything else. They tell the proverbial story of a butterfly flapping its wings in Asia, and through a myriad of causes and effects months later a hurricane erupts in the Caribbean—and the two events are connected! So too it is with the mind of *each* person. Each of us has a unique view of the world that we create through our senses and mind within our particular communal context. Our views of the world share many things with those of many others. And yet, each worldview is unique, like each snowflake. Both Judaism and Islam make that clear in their sacred writings: "To whomever saves a single soul [Self] it is reckoned as if s/he saved the whole world.... To whomever destroys a single soul [Self] it is reckoned as if s/he destroyed the whole world.... From this you learn that one human is worth the whole of creation." (*Mishnah*: Aboth Rabbi Nathan 31); "Whoever kills an innocent human being, it shall be as if he has killed all humankind, and whoever saves the life of one, it shall be as if he had saved the life of all humankind" (*Qur'an*: 5:32). (Note the near identity in these two religions' "revelations"!)

8. Exercise: (1) Describe the world from the point of view of your own worldview, referring to at least ten items (e.g., **a.** how the natural world works, **b.** humans' place in it, **c.** the relationship between the individual and the community, **d.** the male-female relationship, **e.** the function of work, **f.** leisure, **g.** money, etc. These are *only* suggestions.)

(2) Then put yourself in a substantially different worldview and describe the world, referring to the same prior list of items.

(3) Write a paragraph reflecting on the similarity and difference between the two, and then, most importantly, reflect on the implications thereof. Share all three with your instructor or e-group and participate in the ensuing dialogue.

Principle: Critical-Thinking Principle 6 (c) is

6 (c). Only then can we reasonably appreciate/critique them.

Explanation: If we do not have some basic understanding of another's worldview, there is clearly no way that we can intelligently say yes or no to any or all of it. That would be tantamount to reviewing a book simply by looking at its cover. Imagine how fairly/unfairly judged you would feel if a book you authored were thus reviewed! However, once we have gained a substantive insight into another worldview—in any subject—we will then be able to glean the good from it that we might not have found elsewhere, or find reinforcement of the good we have known from our own, or yet other, worldviews. The same is true of what we could judge the shortcomings of a view that is different from ours; only when we have learned what the other view *really* is can we critique it fairly. Until then we have merely indulged in **pre**judicial polemics.

9. Exercise: (1) Take your examples from Principle 6 (b) and describe what you might find of positive value in the other worldview, and why.

(2) Take your examples from Principle 6 (b) and describe what you might find somehow defective in the other worldview, and why.

(3) Share both with your instructor or e-group and participate in the ensuing dialogue.

Principle: Critical-Thinking Principle 7 (a) is

7. In sum: Address the three "W" questions: What? Whence? Whither?

(a) What precisely does what we are talking about mean?
Explanation: To pursue clear, critical thinking we basically must adequately address three questions: What? Whence? Whither. *What* means that we need to develop the habit of striving to understand as precisely as possible what it is we are talking about. This principle is so obvious that it tends, as so often in life, to be violated in proportion to its simplicity. Oftentimes it helps to ask what the etymological roots of the term or idea in question are to help us get a clear grasp of what we are talking about. Example: *to believe* means having *faith* in someone or something; "Faith" comes from the Latin *fides*, having trust. Hence, believing something, having faith in something, means affirming that something is true, not because you have proof of it, but because you trust the source of that information.

We also need to make sure that I and my interlocutors have precisely the same understanding of the idea or term being discussed; otherwise we will simply be talking past each other. It is also especially vital that we keep precisely the same meaning of the term when we move from one statement to another. If we don't, we will end up with a four-term syllogism. A typical syllogism runs like this: A is B, B is C. Therefore, A is C. We need to be certain that the meaning of the connecting term, "B," has precisely the same meaning in second premise as in the first. If, however, deliberately or inadvertently, we change the meaning, however slightly, of the connecting term—B to b—while keeping the same sound and spelling, we will have a 4-term syllogism: A is B. b is C. Therefore.... therefore, nothing (!) simply because we have four terms: A, B, b, and C. Hence, it is vital to know precisely *What* you are talking about.

10. Exercise: (1) Pick three terms and look up their etymological derivation in a good dictionary and show how such analysis can help in understanding the terms better in various uses.

(2) Describe a line of reasoning which leads to a *reductio ad absurdum* (Latin, "reduction to absurdity"), and where the flaw is found.

(3) Share both with your instructor or e-group and participate in the ensuing dialogue.

Principle: Critical-Thinking Principle 7 (b) is:

7(b). "Whence comes the evidence for what we are talking about?."

Explanation: In thinking, whether alone or out loud with others, we start with an idea or term—and, as noted in the previous principle, we need to be clear about its precise meaning. Secondly, we need then to ask ourselves, *Whence?* Where does the basis for affirming this idea come from? Are we beginning by simply defining something to be the case? Is this idea an unexamined presupposition? Do we have factual evidence for it? Is it a valid, logical deduction from solidly proven data? Is it based on trust of a trustworthy source? and so forth. Any truthful results of thinking, alone or with others, will depend on the validity of the answer to this question: *Whence* the evidence for what we are talking about?

11. Exercise: (1) Choose three ideas—for example, "Jesus is God and Man," "Democracy is the best form of human government," "the sun rises in the East".... —and then spell out the bases—for example, told by someone, logical deduction, personal observation.... —for affirming those ideas; judge how sound they are.

(2) Share these with your instructor or e-group and participate in the ensuing dialogue.

Principle: Critical-Thinking Principle 7 (c) is:

7(c). "Whither do the implications of what we are talking about lead?"

Explanation: If we have been careful in understanding precisely what we are talking about, and have carefully tested the bases for our affirming the idea in question, then we need to ask ourselves where—whither?—this idea leads to. What are its implications, for if the idea is true, then we want to base out subsequent actions on it—otherwise we would deliberately be living a lie! In other words, ideas have consequences! Example: If the "Golden Rule" is judged to be a valid ethical principle, then I need to respect others, tell the truth to others, help others....

Secondly, it is important to follow out these implications to learn whether or not they lead to a *reductio ad absurdum*. In that case, we will need to reinvestigate our data bases and whole line of reasoning from the beginning in order to find the flaw of fact or logic. Example: Some Christian theologians (e.g., Augustine, Luther, Calvin) argued that nothing can happen except that God *makes* it happen, including humans (hence, no human truly free will) committing sins that will condemn them to hell for all eternity—the doctrine of "predestination." But for followers of Jesus, who depicted God as a loving Father who reaches out to humans to lead them to himself, this is a clear contradiction, a *reductio ad absurdum*—a loving God leading humans not to God but to hell! This line of critical-thinking led many Augustinians, Lutherans, and Calvinists to reject predestination.

12. Exercise: (1) Give three examples you hold to be true, and then spell out the implications for your life actions.

(2) Share these with your instructor or e-group and participate in the ensuing dialogue.

(3) Devise a line of thought that *prima facie* (Latin, "at first face") appears plausible, but when its implications are drawn out runs into a *reductio ad absurdum*—and then what you should do about it.

(4) Share these with your instructor or e-group and participate in the ensuing dialogue.

Partial Summary

13. Summary Exercise: (1) Write a five hundred word essay summing up the most important things learned about Critical-Thinking.

(2) Share it with your instructor or e-group and participate in the ensuing dialogue.

Exercise: Deep-Dialogue

Principle: Deep-Dialogue Principle 1 is

1. Reach out in openness to the Other in the search for Truth and Goodness.

Explanation: The presupposition to reaching out in the search for Truth and Goodness to those who think and value differently from us, to those who are Other, is that we do not know everything about, do not possess all goodness and value in, the matter at hand. Though we are convinced that what we know is true and the values we hold are good, we recognize that we must endlessly seek more truth, goodness, and value—beyond ourselves.

14. Exercise: (1) Write statements that you hold as true about: a. life, b. humanity, c. ethics. Examples: "Life refers to a physical body which is capable of assimilation, growth, reproduction, and death." "Humanity is a collection of animals capable of abstract thought and free choice/love." "Ethics are the principles of behavior that flow from a person's or group's explanation of the ultimate meaning of life." Share them with your instructor or e-group and participate in the ensuing dialogue.

(2) Write statements about these three topics that you would *not* have affirmed, but could imagine others affirming. Examples: "Life is valuable so long as it serves a higher goal—the community." "Humanity is the ultimate arbiter of what is right and wrong." "Ethics are the pious lies we tell ourselves in order to do what we want." Share them with your instructor or e-group and participate in the ensuing dialogue.

(3) Write the three *questions* that your statements are in fact answers to. Example: "What is the definition of physical life?"

(4) Do the same for the statements in number (2). Example: "What is the value of life?"

(5) Write a paragraph or more comparing the questions to the two sets of statements, and then write a 200-word reflection on the implications thereof. Share them all with your instructor or e-group and participate in the ensuing dialogue.

Principle: Deep-Dialogue Principle 1 is:

> *2. Be open to the Other* primarily *so WE can learn,*
> *find Truth and Goodness.*

Explanation: The primary goal of dialogue is *not* for us to teach, but for us to *learn*, to find goodness. This is the very definition of dialogue, to reach out in openness to those who think and value differently from us so *we* can learn. This is a total conversion from the hoary habit of encountering Others so as to teach them—but since in their resistence to our arrogance they hardly ever learned, we in fact never taught!

15. Exercise: (1) Describe in approximately 200 words a "typical" situation, using a concrete topic of current disagreement in society—for example, abortion—wherein both sides come to persuade the other side of their respective correctness. Share it with your instructor or e-group and participate in the ensuing dialogue.

(2) Using the same topic and points of view already expressed in (1), describe in 200 words the situation wherein both sides come primarily to learn from the other. Share it with your instructor or e-group and participate in the dialogue.

(3) Write a 200-word reflection on what difference reversing the order of coming to learn instead of to teach made. Share it with your instructor or e-group and participate in the ensuing dialogue.

Principle: Deep-Dialogue Principle 3 is:

> *3. Perceive that for us to learn, to find the good, the Others must*
> *teach and open themselves—and vice versa.*

Explanation: If we are to learn and find deeper value from this encounter with those who think and value differently from us, then the Others must open themselves and teach us their understanding of reality and grasp of goodness. We in turn open ourselves and explain how we understand and value reality, because our dialogue partner also comes to learn—from us!

16. Exercise: (1) Think up at least three slogans and three mantras (*mantra*—an Asian religious "thinking tool" [Sanskrit, *man*, "thinking," *tra*, "tool"]—related to the Latin and European languages: *mentor*; sometimes a seven-syllable phrase) to embody this principle. Example: "To teach you first have to learn!" ("Slogan"); "Learning first, I then can teach" ("Mantra").

(2) Share them with your instructor or e-group and participate in the dialogue.

(3) If on an e-group have a vote on the best in each category.

Principle: Deep-Dialogue Principle 4 is

> *4. Recognize that because Dialogue is a two-way project,*
> *we then both learn—and share the good.*

Explanation: Because we come to Dialogue to learn, then—and only then— my partners must tell us what they believe and value and why, that is, they must teach us. Conversely, since our partners come to Dialogue to learn, then—but only then!—we must explain what we understand and value and why. Thus—and only thus—do we both learn and share the good, learning and gaining what we could not by ourselves, without Dialogue.

17. Exercise: (1) Think up at least three Japanese-style haiku and three mnemonic schemes to embody this principle. Examples:

"I,
Learning in receptiveness
You,
Teaching in generosity"
(Japanese style *haiku*);
"Learning is before Teaching as *L* is before *T*." (Mnemonic scheme)

(2) Share them with your instructor or e-group and participate in the dialogue.

(3) If in an e-group, have a vote on the best in each category.

Principle: Deep-Dialogue Principle 5 is:

> *5. Learn there are Other ways of understanding,*
> *of embracing the world than our own.*

Explanation: So long as we talk only with those who think like us, we assume that our understanding and valuing of the world is not only a true picture of the world, but the *only* true picture of the world. But when we open ourselves to encounter the Other we learn time and again that there are other ways of understanding and valuing of the world than ours. Example: If we have always lived in the city, when we go to live on a farm or in the wild, we encounter other understandings and valuing of many things to do with nature. The same is true of men opening themselves up to women, Christians to Jews, rich to poor, Germans to Chinese, and so forth.

18. Exercise: (1) In 200 words write a description of how you understand and value the world. Share it with your instructor or e-group and participate in the ensuing dialogue.

(2) Write in 200 words an understanding and valuing of the world that is substantially different from yours. Share it with the instructor or the e-group and participate in the ensuing dialogue.

(3) Write a 200-word comparison of the two worldviews, and how you would go about relating them to each other. Share it with your instructor or e-group and participate in the ensuing dialogue.

Principle: Deep-Dialogue Principle 6 is:

6. Learn to recognize our commonalities and differences—and value both.

Explanation: As we come to know the Other, we find many things held in common. Psychologically it is wise to focus on these commonalities, especially in the early stages of the encounter, and during crises. We learn that there are levels of commonality that we were previously unaware of, and they now become a foundation for bonding. But we must not cover over the differences, for they too are part of reality. Very often, however, we will find that the differences are not absolutely contradictory to our values, and therefore are to be respected, and valued.[1]

19. Exercise: (1) Write a skit wherein two opponents initiate the conversation by pointing out the differences. Example: Muslims stress that God is one for them, but three for Christians.... If several persons are doing this online course together, this can then best be done in pairs.

(2) Note what the results are of such an approach. Share both the skits and the results with your instructor or e-group and participate in the ensuing dialogue.

(3) Rewrite the skit so that the two stress in the beginning what they have in common, and only then come to the differences.

(4) Note what the results are of such an approach. Share both the skits and the results with your instructor or e-group and participate in the ensuing dialogue.

Principle: Deep-Dialogue Principle 7 is:

7. Learn to move between different worlds and integrate them with care.

Explanation: We learn that each of us makes our own world, built up from our experiences, reflections, and integration thereof. In Dialogue, we increasingly become aware that each person we encounter is an entire world unto herself. Both Judaism and Islam state this dramatically in their foundational Scriptures, as we saw above: "To whomever saves a single soul [Self] it is reckoned as if s/he saved the whole world.... To whomever destroys a single soul [Self] it is reckoned as if s/he destroyed the whole world.... From this you learn that one human is worth the whole of creation" (*Mishnah*: Aboth Rabbi Nathan 31); "Whoever kills an innocent human being, it shall be as if he has killed all humankind, and whoever saves the life of one, it shall be as if he had saved the life of all humankind" (*Qur'an*: 5:32). (Note the near identity in these two different religion's "revelations"!)

20. Exercise: (1) In two paragraphs describe two differing views of the world. Example: From the point of view of a woman or a man; from the point of view of a Muslim or a Buddhist; from the point of view of a socialist or a capitalist. Share them with your instructor or e-group and participate in the ensuing dialogue.

(2) In 200 words, write a reflection on how persons from the two differing worldviews could creatively move between the two worlds and integrate them carefully. Share them with your instructor or e-group and participate in the ensuing dialogue.

Principle: Deep-Dialogue Principle 8 is

> *8. Learn that Deep-Dialogue thus gradually transforms our inner selves—and our shared lives.*

Explanation: As we proceed along the path of Deep-Dialogue, our view of reality, especially of the Other, our Self, and our relationship shifts profoundly. Gradually we realize ever more forcefully that our perception of the world is just that, our *perception* of the world. It slowly dawns on us that *we* are intimately involved in our knowledge of reality, the Other, and our Self. We really do encounter reality, but *we* encounter it, and therefore our reception of reality is partially shaped by our perceiving faculties. As noted earlier, Thomas Aquinas wrote, "Things known are in the knower according to the mode of the knower" "Cognita sunt in cognoscente secundum modum cognoscentis" (*Summa Theologiae*, II-II, Q. 1, a. 2). As our understanding of reality and ourselves deepens, our action toward ourselves and the Other is transformed accordingly.

21. Exercise: Write a 300-word essay on how Deep-Dialogue has, or has not, been transformative of your life both personally and in relationship. Share them with your instructor or e-group and participate in the ensuing dialogue.

Seven Stages of Deep-Dialogue

22. Exercise: (1) Complete subexercises 22a, 22b, and 22c (the text, the link to the photos, and exercises of the Seven Stages of Deep-Dialogue can be found both above at astro.temple.edu/~swidler/course/index.htm and on pages 57 ff.).

(2) Share them with your instructor or e-group and participate in the ensuing dialogue.

It is vital that you keep the material from each step to be able to send it in. It is important not to fudge any of the steps to "improve" them, for then you will destroy your ability to trace the progress you are making.

Subexercise 22a: (1) Read through, carefully, all seven stages, one after the other.

(2) Go back and read very carefully Stage One, making a list of the constituent salient ideas.

(3) Set aside the text and, using only your list of the constituent salient ideas, paraphrase—in your own words only!—the text.

(4) Then compare your paraphrase with the text and

(5) make any changes or additions if needed to make your paraphrase match all of the text's ideas.

(6) If you are doing this program individually, then type up in careful fashion, if you have not done so already, your list [2], paraphrase [3], and your final revised paraphrase [5] and send them to your course instructor;

(7) Do the same as above for each of the Seven Stages, sending them in one at a time to the instructor. However, if you are doing this course in a group, then send your list [2], paraphrase [3], and revised paraphrase [5] to the e-group, and participate in the online discussion. Move to each new step at the request of the instructor.

Subexercise 22b: (1) Carefully read over again the text of Stage One.

(2) Next, look very carefully at the picture of Stage One and make a list of all the points of the text that you can see in the photo.

(3) Do the same for each of the stages and photos. Try to find as many points of connection as possible between the text and the photo in each case.

(4) Type up in careful fashion your lists [2] for each of the stages and accompanying photos and send them in as above, that is, individually to the instructor, or one at a time to the e-group, while participating in the online discussion.

Subexercise 22c: (1) Write a 1,000-word personal reflection on your present understanding of the Seven Stages in relation to your own life, past, present, and future and

(2) send in to either the instructor or the e-group, and participate in the dialogue.

Exercise: Emotional-Intelligence

Explanation: As noted above, the focus of Emotional-Intelligence is learning how we humans can effectively mature "emotionally." Basically that means learning to know and understand 1) ourselves, 2) other persons, and 3) how appropriately to relate to each other. One may have learned to analyze a situation with impeccable syllogistic logic (Critical-Thinking), but be totally blind about how one's self and/or others fit(s) into the puzzle of human relations. Young children tend not to spend a great deal of time and energy reflecting on what their values are, that is, what traits/abilities they would like to have, admire in others. As we gain further experiences with age, we tend to become more conscious of these values. That is what is normally meant by becoming mature: becoming conscious of these values—or the lack thereof—in oneself and in others is a basic concern of Emotional-Intelligence. Finding, or missing, them in others is a second focus of E-I, and a third is relating ourselves, individually and in groups, to other persons and groups. These three foci will form the structure of our principles and exercises.

Principle: Emotional-Intelligence Principle 1 is

1. Know ourselves by becoming conscious of our own values.

Explanation: A fundamental way we humans come to know ourselves is by becoming conscious of our values, that is, goals, abilities that we wish to attain or acquire—in short, what we think is good and desirable. We are given innumerable values via the experiences we have from childhood through maturity from our families and surroundings. In the beginning, these values usually are simply accepted. However, with age, especially starting around puberty, we usually begin slowly to become aware of the unconscious values we have absorbed, and begin the often painful process of questioning them. This process of Emotional-Intelligence clearly is closely related to the Critical-Thinking principle of asking questions, the three *W*'s discussed above. To become a mature person, we need to become conscious of the values we hold, so that in critical fashion we can consciously affirm, modify, or reject them, and not just be controlled by them like automatons.

23. Exercise: Make a list of the most important values you hold. Think first of all of the traits you strive to attain/maintain/improve, for example, punctuality, honesty, politeness, orderliness, compassion, and so on. This should be a relatively lengthy list.

23 Subexercise a: After completing the list, put them in order of priority.

23 Subexercise b: Then, divide the priority list into five groups.

23 Subexercise c: Then, rate yourself (1 to 5, with 5 the highest) for each value.

23 Subexercise d: Fourth, multiply your rate score x 5 for each of the values in the top quintile, 4 for the second quintile, and so forth, and then come up with a total score. This could be called your values score. You could use it as a benchmark to measure growth in this area of Emotional-Intelligence. Share all this material with your instructor or e-group and participate in the dialogue.

Principle: Emotional-Intelligence Principle 2 is

2. Know other persons by learning their values.

Explanation: We usually have only superficial knowledge of persons we meet casually. To begin to know them well, we need to gradually become aware of their values. As we come to know their values, we begin to admire them if we increasingly find shared values—or the opposite.

Exercise 24: Think of three persons (not in the class) whom you admire, and another three whom you dislike, and make a list for each value you see in each of the six. Then compare the lists. What implications and conclusions do you draw from the comparisons and analyses? Share with your instructor or e-group and participate in the dialogue.

Principle: Emotional-Intelligence Principle 3 is

3. Learn that our relations with other persons and groups are directed by our and their values and their interrelationships.

Explanation: On the one hand, we are drawn to persons and groups who exemplify values we hold in high esteem, and we are repelled by the opposite. The obverse is likewise true. That is, by associating with persons and groups, we tend to be drawn to share their values, and vice versa. We need to learn to discern others' values and our own (often in light of those of others), and then make judgments concerning which values to accept and which not, and how to relate to the persons or groups involved.

Exercise 25: This exercise is really a group form of Exercise 24. Think of three groups whose values you find admirable, and three whose you do not. Reflect carefully in each case whether you are perhaps indulging in more or less stereotyping (ask youself: why are so many persons drawn to the values of the groups whose values you reject—can they all be evil or stupid?). Write down your analyses, and share with the instructor and the e-group and participate in the ensuing discussion.

Exercise: Competitive-Cooperation

Explanation: I repeat here much of what I stated above about putting into action in a consistent manner the thoughts we arrived in our thinking through Deep-Dialogue/Critical-Thinking/Emotional-Intelligence, namely, Competitive-Cooperation (see above for fuller explanation). If our actions are to be compatible with Deep-Dialogue, Critical-Thinking, and Emotional-Intelligence, they must strive toward reflecting a seemingly contradictory double term: Competitive-Cooperative. If the way we understand the world determines the way we act in the world, then action completes the circle of perception-thought-decision-action. We first perceive, then try to understand, in light of which we make a decision, and finally act, putting our perceptions, understanding, decisions into concrete behavioral form. If we have begun to engage the world in a deeply dialogical manner and have critically analyzed/synthesized our perceptions and thoughts, we will want to make decisions on their bases and carry out our actions in the world in an analogously dialogic/critical manner. I am suggesting that the most appropriate way to describe such action is "Competitive-Cooperation."

The cooperation half is relatively easy to understand. But competitive? That would seem necessarily to aim at a win-lose, a zero-sum approach. To a certain extent that is accurate. However, I am thinking first of all of this competition as being with ourself, striving to be as effective, efficient, creative as possible—to borrow from Islam the initial meaning of jihad, the Great *Jihad*: (Arabic: struggle), the competition, with ourself to live out our inner principles (placed there by God, according to Islam—and Judaism and Christianity as well). This creative competition may at times mean that one individual, one group will get the contract, will be chosen to provide the requested product or service—win-lose, zero-sum in that sense. But the "losing" creative competiion individual and group should thereby be led to create new alternatives—as, for example, renewable energy sources as alternatives to fossil fuels, or President Obama inviting Hilary Clinton into his cabinet. In the business field, an ever more human organization increasingly searches for the most creative, expansive, all-inclusive way of operating—a both-and, a win-win for both the producers and users, reflecting the creative balance of Deep-Dialogue, pro-and-con

Critical-Thinking/Emotional-Intelligence in a balance of creative competition and cooperation. (See above for further discussion.)

Principle: Competitive-Cooperation Principle 1 is

1. Do not be satisfied with the passable, but reach for the best.

Explanation: Humans by nature are open to being/doing the best. Being/doing the best does not imply being pathologically driven, a so-called Type-A person. Being the best means reaching the goal that is intrinsically set in every concrete being and circumstance. One cannot do better than reaching the goal. Someone might object, that one could perhaps reach the goal faster, more efficiently, and so on. But, what I mean here by the goal includes all of the elements, such as speed, efficiency, and a host of other factors. Reading a business manual and reading a novel on vacation will in the best way, of course, differ appropriately. Humans are open to striving to be most efficient in attaining a goal, whether it is learning a language, producing a sculpture, drafting a business plan, or resolving a health problem. We humans are open to being/doing so, but we need to cultivate the habit, the virtue of being/doing so. To do so means competing with ourselves to reach out for the best, and at the same time cooperating with our bodily and psychic strengths in overcoming our weaknesses. This is similar in relating to others. For example, a pacer can help us greatly increase our efficiency not only in racing, but in many, many endeavors. Would a pacer be designated a competitor, or a cooperator—or both?

26. Exercise: Write a 300-word reflection on the claim that habitually striving for the best will make you a better human being. Bring up, first of all, all the objections you can think of, and then, secondly, attempt to address them all as effectively as possible. Share your reflection with your instructor or e-group and participate in the ensuing dialogue.

Principle: Competitive-Cooperation Principle 2 is

2. Strive to make decisions within broader frameworks.

Explanation: Not infrequently in life we come up against what appears to be an impassable wall, a total defeat. If we stay at that level, we may well be partially or completely destroyed as a human being. However, we can turn the barrier into an opportunity if we develop the habit of stepping back and viewing the situation in a broader framework. Think of the professional athlete who will inevitably come to the end of her/his playing career. S/he can think of the sport as a whole, and perhaps go into coaching, sport broadcasting, writing, or sales.

27. Exercise: Think of and write about briefly three or more persons, prominent either in the past or the present, or whom you know or know about, who have come up against a wall in life and have turned it around and made it an opportunity to move their life forward again. A personal example: Professor

Mahmoud Ayoub from Lebanon went blind in his youth, but in response he developed a prodigious memory and learned to accept the help of others to become an excellent teacher and productive scholar—clearly an extraordinary combination of self-competitiveness and cooperation with others. Share your personal vignettes with your instructor or e-group and participate in the dialogue.

Principle: Competitive-Cooperation Principle 3 is

3. Do not be satisfied with the norm, but stress constant creativity.

Explanation: This principle is similar to Principle 1 about striving for the best, but it has its own special orientation. That special focus is on creativity, which very often springs from the cross-pollination of competition and cooperation. That is how we humans come up with something new—as in the child springing from the interaction of mother and father. Nothing is ever totally new, created *ex nihilo*, out of nothing. Christian theology claims that God accomplished that in Creation. In today's scientific worldview, God might be said to have made the Original Stuff of the universe in its initial baseball-sized condition with all the intricate laws that have been unfolding over the past 13.8 billion years built into it. But none of us mere mortals can create something from nothing. As Aristotle noted, and as his stellar student Thomas Aquinas wrote centuries later, "Nil in intellectu quod non prius in sensu" (Nothing is in the intellect which was not first in the senses). Creativity by way of setting up new linkages, new goals, new contexts is a determining characteristic of us humans. We are, consequently, a work in progress. Creativity is a major way in which we circumvent the blockages we encounter in life, but even beyond that, we strive to create the new, without needing a blockage to force us to come up with a solution. Creativity is a built-in thrust of human nature—*immer strebend* (always striving), as Johann Wolfgang von Goethe wrote. However, once again, if the creative thrust is not fostered, it will lie dormant, pushed forward only in desperate situations, if even then. Clearly, creativity transcends the blunting force of win-lose competition and the dulling force of coasting-along cooperation; it blends the best of competition and cooperation.

28. Exercise: Describe at least two persons or groups that you know of which responded in a creative manor to an blockage they encountered, and what lesson you might learn from that. Share your personal vignettes with your instructor or e-group and participate in the ensuing dialogue.

28 Subexercise a: Describe a current blockage and devise a conceivable creative solution. For example, you know of a person or entity—like Rochester, New York, which was built almost entirely on Eastman Kodak (now teetering on bankruptcy) which is attempting to resolve its problems by massive diversification. What role, if any, do you imagine for yourself in the creative solution? Share your personal reflections with your instructor or e-group and participate in the ensuing dialogue.

Principle: Competitive-Cooperation Principle 4 is

4. As much as possible, avoid zero-sum, win-lose solutions,
but seek creatively positive sum, win-win ones.

Explanation: It is normally humanly better to move in a win-win kind of solution whenever possible. Of course, as noted above, there are many situations in life that are zero sum. For example, there can be only one biological father of a child. However, even that rock-bottom physical example immediately suggests that there can be ways of being a "father" even on the physical level that can be expanded. For example, if the biological father, shortly after begetting the child, is partially or even completely incapacitated (e.g., by absence, physical or psychological defect), some other male can become the physical father in every sense other than the few seconds of conception. But that example lies at the extreme. Probably the majority of human "competitions" are better humanly resolved via a win-win route, very much including s/he who thinks s/he benefits more by a favorable zero-sum solution. (See above, where this is clearly laid out in the business field.)

29. Exercise: Describe at least one actual case in which a win-win resolution was chosen rather that a win-lose one. What lessons can be gained from this?

Share your personal vignettes with your instructor or e-group and participate in the ensuing dialogue.

29 Subexercise a: Devise one realistic case in which either a zero-sum or a positive-sum solution is thinkable, and play out the two different scenarios, and their implications and lessons. Share your personal vignettes with your instructor or e-group and participate in the ensuing dialogue.

Principle: Competitive-Cooperation Principle 5 is

5. Prefer not either-or, but both-and choices.

Explanation: As is doubtless clear by now, most of these principles are very closely related. However, is should also be obvious that there are also important differences, which makes it worthwhile to spell each one out. Far too often people think, and act, as if there were only two choices in decisions. Thinking in this black-white, either-or manner comes very naturally to many people deeply trained in the physical sciences. To be sure, I would not want to drive on a bridge built on the principle that 2+2 is sometimes 4 and sometimes 5. But most human interactions are not so black-white, either-or. Again, the positive resulting connection of competition and cooperation comes to the fore in so many cases. In fact, the vast majority of human interaction blockages are best—for both sides!—resolved in both-and choices.

30. Exercise: Describe two situations—in the public domain or based on your personal knowledge—that were resolved in either-or fashion. What were the results, and how do you evaluate them? What might an opposite, both-and solution have looked like, with what presumed results, and how would you evaluate them?

30 Subexercise a: Describe two situations—in the public domain or based on your personal knowledge—that were resolved in both-and fashion. What were the results, and how do you evaluate them? What might an opposite, either-or solution have looked like, with what presumed results, and you would you evaluate them?

Grand Summary

31. Summary Exercise: Write a 500-word essay reflecting on the links among Deep-Dialogue, Critical-Thinking, Emotional-Intelligence, Competitive-Cooperation.

31 Subexercise a: Share it with your instructor or e-group and participate in the ensuing dialogue.

Applications

This section spells out in detail some of the implications of Deep-Dialogue/ Critical-Thinking/ Emotional-Intelligence/Competitive-Cooperation, particularly in the critical areas of Education, Law, and Ethics.

Part III

Implications

17

Integrated Education through Deep-Dialogue/Critical-Thinking/Emotional-Intelligence/ Competitive-Cooperation[1]

Everything that has been discussed up this point about Deep-Dialogue/Critical-Thinking/ Emotional-Intelligence/Competitive-Cooperation is brought to bear here on putting those insights into action in a full, integrative "whole child" education program—and is spelled out in substantive detail.

Formation of the Dialogue Institute

The fundamental aim of the Dialogue Institute: Interreligious, Intercultural, International is the betterment of humanity and the world through education in the broadest sense in all the culture-shaping institutions of society, including formal education, religion, business, communications government, law, and so on. Already before I started my doctoral study of the Catholic-Protestant dialogue in Germany, the Una Sancta Movement, I was introduced to the notion and experience of education that embraces all of life in an integrating manner as a teaching assistant in the Integrated Liberal Studies (ILS) program at the University of Wisconsin, Madison, in 1956–1957—and even then the ILS program was decades old. Similarly, the Dialogue Institute is dedicated to the global pursuit of a greater religious/spiritual/ethical/dialogical awakening in all aspects of our cultural life, especially education. With more than half a century of experience and research in developing the practice and theory—the Way—of Deep-Dialogue/Critical-Thinking/Emotional-Intelligence/ Competitive-Cooperation in the broad and more formal fields of education based on a global ethic within the context of the emerging global civilization, I see the future moving ever more clearly in that direction, and as founder of the Dialogue Institute, I am working to make it into an instrument for renovating education through Deep-Dialogue/Critical-Thinking/Emotional-Intelligence/ Competitive-Cooperation—*Dia-Logos*.

To recapitulate: Deep-Dialogue is a powerful transformative process—which eventually must become a habit of mind and spirit, traditionally known as a Virtue, and eventually a whole Way of life—grounded in classical philosophical and spiritual traditions in a global context. It has been developed through a range of inter-Way encounters: interreligious, intercultural, interideological. It is a Way of entering other worlds or perspectives and returning mutually transformed, having gained a deepened sense of one's own worldview and an awakened awareness of the worldview of others. Through this awakening power of Deep-Dialogue, individuals and communities are able to experience common ground between their worlds, and thus achieve deeper personal integrity and community building.

At the same time, in order to open oneself to Deep-Dialogue, it is vital to likewise develop the skills of thinking carefully and clearly, that is, of Critical-Thinking (remember: *critical*—Greek, *krinein,* to choose, to judge). We need to learn how to understand what we—and others—really mean when we say something, why we say it, in order to choose, to judge where we believe the truth lies, and what the implications are. In brief, we must answer these three questions: What? Whence? Whither? In addition, Critical-Thinking entails at least these four elements:

a. that we work to raise our unconscious presuppositions from the *unconscious level*—where by definition they reside—to the conscious level. Only then can we deal with them fully humanly, that is, rationally reflect on and decide for, against, or partly-partly concerning them.

b. that we realize that our view of reality is a view of reality, that although it shares much with others' views of reality, it is also partially shaped by our personal lenses through which we experience and interpret reality, and hence is not absolute, but perspectival.

c. that we first learn to understand all statements in their contexts, that is, a text can be correctly understood only in its context. Only then will we be able to translate the original core meaning of the texts into our context.

d. that we learn to probe with great precision every statement, first of our own, and then also of all others, to learn precisely what they really mean. This is particularly important to do concerning simple statements, terms, and clichés because very often unconscious presuppositions lie beneath them.

This process of Critical-Thinking obviously entails a mental dialogue within our mind. Thus, at its root Critical-Thinking is dialogic—and Deep-Dialogue at its root entails clear, critical thought, which within the context of Emotional-Intelligence must issue in consequent Competitive-Cooperative action. They are four dimensions of authentic humanity: they must become Virtues, that is, habits of mind, spirit, and action.

Because Deep-Dialogue, Critical-Thinking, Emotional-Intelligence, and Competitive-Cooperation are in fact necessarily the four dimensions of one humanity, when I speak today of dialogue, I mean Deep-Dialogue, and when I speak of Deep-Dialogue, I also always mean to include Critical-Thinking, Emotional-Intelligence, and Competitive-Cooperation.

I, and the Dialogue Institute, aim at the renovation of education—from the cradle to the grave—through Deep-Dialogue/Critical-Thinking/Emotional-Intelligence/Competitive-Cooperation based on a global ethic, within an emerging global civilization (not a monolithic one, but one that is a "unity in diversity," as the previously referenced US penny has it: *E Pluribus Unum*, "Out of Many, One"). It is clear that one of the greatest challenges facing all levels of education is coping creatively with the powerful forces that arise when differing worldviews encounter each other, too often leading to a clash of civilizations. The theory and practice of Deep-Dialogue/Critical-Thinking/Emotional-Intelligence/Competitive-Cooperation will be the most effective way to meet these issues by creatively transforming education at its core.

Insights of Deep-Dialogue/Critical-Thinking/Emotional-Intelligence/ Competitive-Cooperation

I am convinced that Deep-Dialogue/Critical-Thinking/Emotional-Intelligence/Competitive-Cooperation need to be core human competencies at the center of all human life. This flows from the insight that the entire cosmos, reality itself, and therefore also our thinking about it and deciding and acting accordingly, is a dynamic, unified field of interrelations, a profound dialogic process in which all things are interconnected: a Cosmic Dance of Dialogue! Hence, there has emerged the realization that human reason, Critical-Thinking, Emotional-Intelligence, and consequent Competitive-Cooperation are dialogical at the core. Deep-Dialogue is thus the heart of our rational ability to relate to reality in action, to be in touch with the ever-changing worlds around us. Together, Deep-Dialogue, Critical-Thinking, Emotional-Intelligence, and Competitive-Cooperation are essential to becoming an authentic human; they must become a Virtue, a Way of life.

This recognition that dialogue permeates our life in every way is reflected in the awareness that we humans ourselves play a vital role in shaping our understanding of reality. The most advanced research—for example, by Bernard Lonergan, Hans-Georg Gadamer, and Paul Ricoeur—has shown that we humans inhabit worlds that we ourselves help shape (and that reciprocally shape us) through our thought processes. We humans inhabit worldviews that we make through dialogical processes of conceptualization, interpretation, imagination, construction, revision—all integral to the rational enterprise.

In this way, every aspect of our life, our experience, and the world around us takes shape in the context of a worldview that we help create—and constantly recreate!—and then inhabit. It has become clear that at the center of this human art of world making, which shapes *all* our experience, there is a fundamental dialogic dynamic between the self, or subject, and the realities that surround us. At the very foundation of our life we are situated in an interrelational structure of self and other (subject and object), which always involves modes of dialogue, interpretation, and critical thought.

Thus, it may be said that we humans are dialogical/rational beings, world-makers, interpretive beings who directly shape and reshape and participate in all phenomena that appear to us. In this deeper and expanded sense of the rational enterprise, we see that reason is essentially our ability to shape our lifeworlds, to make our experience, to analytically recognize and clarify differences, to cope with multiplicity and diversity. At the same time, it is also a capacity to syntheti-cally discern, even create, fundamental unities and common ground, harmonize differences into coherent order, and negotiate complex factors in forging our individuality, personal identity, and integrity.

Further, the dialogic structure of humanity entails not only thinking and speaking dialogically but also acting toward and with the self and others—persons and things—in ways that are also dialogic. We call the principles on which we base our actions, ethics. (In ethics, we discern a purpose, a goal for some-thing, and call any action that moves toward that goal "good" and that which moves away "bad.") Because we are living increasingly in a single world, we are correspondingly moving toward a common basis, toward—not just as Muslims or Christians or secularists, but as global citizens—a global ethic, which shapes how we treat ourselves, others, and the entire world we inhabit. (More about that below.)

The Virtue of Deep-Dialogue/Critical-Thinking/Emotional-Intelligence/ Competitive-Cooperation is at work in every aspect of our lives—in our passions, emotions, and feelings, in our understanding, judgment, and deliberations, in our relations with self, others, and our surroundings, and in our acting accord-ingly. In the art of becoming a person, an integral being (an individual, i.e., undivided), it is now more urgent than ever to cultivate core competencies, the Virtue—to follow the Way—of Deep-Dialogue/Critical-Thinking/Emotional-Intelligence/Competitive-Cooperation. These skills enable us to become whole persons who can not only harmonize a limitless diversity of worldviews, per-spectives, and identities into a coherent inner life but also negotiate our outer life, ethics, in peaceful and nonviolent ways of community with others and our surroundings.

Renewing Integral Education

Foundation

Since the capacities and skills of Deep-Dialogue/Critical-Thinking/Emotional-Intelligence/Competitive-Cooperation operate at the foundation of all our experience, they are the key ingredients in the advancement of the educational process. How we conduct our minds is all important in the quality of our life, for how we perceive the world determines how we act in the world. When we pro-ceed in the Way of Deep-Dialogue/Critical-Thinking/Emotional-Intelligence/ Competitive-Cooperation, we promote a more meaningful, coherent, and integral life. When we do not, the result is increased fragmentation, turbulence, and loss of meaning.

Since the Way of Deep-Dialogue/Critical-Thinking/Emotional-Intelligence/ Competitive-Cooperation affects every aspect of the conduct of mind—our thought process, our understanding, interpretations, judgments, deliberations, reasoning, and imagination, as well as every aspect of our use of language—and our consequent action in the world, there is no area of our experience that does not involve some mode of interpretation. To exist, to be in the world, to experience, to feel is to be in some form of reflection and interpretation. In this respect, every subject in the school curriculum, indeed, in life itself, involves the art of thought and interpretation.

Because Deep-Dialogue/Critical-Thinking/Emotional-Intelligence/ Competitive-Cooperation skills are at play in every dimension of reflection, it is not surprising that we now perceive that these core competencies are at work—or certainly should be!—in all dimensions of experience, in every subject and discipline, in every aspect of our life, and hence, in the educational curriculum as well. Therefore, Deep-Dialogue/Critical-Thinking/Emotional-Intelligence/ Competitive-Cooperation must in all education become a habit of mind, spirit, and action—a Virtue. Through the Way of Deep-Dialogue/Critical-Thinking/ Emotional-Intelligence/Competitive-Cooperation we are now able to integrate the diverse dimensions of experience—and the curriculum!—in a deep, integrated Way that was not possible before.

Here we see that globalization is directly connected with Deep-Dialogue/ Critical-Thinking/Emotional-Intelligence/Competitive-Cooperation. From the viewpoint of one schooled in the Way of Deep-Dialogue/Critical-Thinking/ Emotional-Intelligence/Competitive-Cooperation, globalization involves the growing encounter of diverse worldviews in a shared space. This is why Deep-Dialogue/Critical-Thinking/Emotional-Intelligence/Competitive-Cooperation is global dialogue—in the sense of embracing not just physical space but also all worldviews and cultures. Thus, the renewal of education in a pluralistic meeting of worlds, cultures, disciplines, and perspectives, calls for the innovations of a global classroom.

The core competencies and skills—the Virtue, the Way—of Deep-Dialogue/ Critical-Thinking/Emotional-Intelligence/Competitive-Cooperation thus enable us to reorganize and systematically integrate the diverse dimensions of the curriculum, including the following areas of life and education.

Reasoning and Critical-Thinking: The Reflective Arts

Through Deep-Dialogue/Critical-Thinking/Emotional-Intelligence/ Competitive-Cooperation, reasoning is taken to deeper levels: interpretation, making sense of things, understanding, judgment, inference are expanded in negotiating between worlds. It is one thing to process meaning and understanding within a given worldview. It is more challenging to gain access to multiple alternative worlds and hold them together in dialogical consciousness.

The capacity to negotiate multiple alternative perspectives, worldviews, ideologies, and narrative forms, to think critically between worlds is an area of education that has been underdeveloped. But in our rapidly globalizing cultures, it has become urgent to globalize our rational capacities, to inculcate the Virtue, the Way of Deep-Dialogue/Critical-Thinking/Emotional-Intelligence/Competitive-Cooperation of reflecting between worlds. It is increasingly recognized that open inquiry and truth seeking essentially involve the capacities to mediate among multiple perspectives. We need to develop discursive reflection, deliberative reflection, diversity reflection, and integral reflection.

Discursive reflection (Latin, *cursus*, run) "runs" through syllogistic steps to gain knowledge—through Deep-Dialogue/Critical-Thinking/Emotional-Intelligence/Competitive-Cooperation, it will run both within a given worldview and among worldviews.

Deliberative reflection is another name for Critical-Thinking, whereby we look at the evidence, decide, and act—through Deep-Dialogue/Critical-Thinking/Emotional-Intelligence/Competitive-Cooperation it will expand to be both within a given worldview and among worldviews.

Diversity reflection stresses the analytical skills of discerning and respecting differences within and between worlds. (Human reasoning is divided between analysis and synthesis.) Deep-Dialogue/Critical-Thinking/Emotional-Intelligence/Competitive-Cooperation recognizes differences without losing the common ground holding diversity together, thereby heightening both the analytic and synthetic abilities of discursive thought.

Integral reflection stresses the synthesizing, the unifying skills of Deep-Dialogue/Critical-Thinking/Emotional-Intelligence/Competitive-Cooperation across differences within and between worlds.

Moving between Worlds in the Language Arts

Where there is thought, there is language. Thus, all the above reflections are relevant to all aspects of the language arts. A key area often neglected in the traditional curriculum is mastering moving among worlds, religions, cultures, ideologies. All the skills of creative thinking, writing, discussing, and conversing expand to a new level through the Virtue, the Way of Deep-Dialogue/Critical-Thinking/Emotional-Intelligence/Competitive-Cooperation. For example, in literature, where widely diverse narrative forms are involved, it enables the reader to gain an ever deeper appreciation of the differences *and* commonalities within the shifting forms.

Intellectual Development and Scientific Understanding

The search for knowledge in the natural sciences was deeply impacted when humanity encountered different paradigms of interpretation and theory making (see page 146 for a fuller discussion of "paradigm shift").[2] A single way of seeking understanding was found inadequate—as today, for example, the macro world of cosmology and the micro world of quantum mechanics are incommensurable. Already during the Renaissance, the heuristic (Greek, *heuriskein*, to discover—meaning "holding a position until new evidence or line of reasoning warrants a change") experimental method was developed. Looking back, it is evident that the heuristic natural scientific experimental method is in fact on the Way of Deep-Dialogue/Critical-Thinking/Emotional-Intelligence/Competitive-Cooperation.

The spread of this heuristic natural science method of inquiry is a celebration of an aspect of the Way of Deep-Dialogue/Critical-Thinking/Emotional-Intelligence/Competitive-Cooperation. The heuristic dialogue, for example, between forming a theory and experimentally testing it leading to ongoing revisions is a central habit, Virtue of the Way of Deep-Dialogue/Critical-Thinking/ Emotional-Intelligence/Competitive-Cooperation. Further, this natural scientific heuristic method is expanding to all thought disciplines—to a broader globalized constituency: all humanity![3]

Reflective Education: Rational Awakening and Becoming Integrated

It is clear now that as the rational capacities of mind are activated through the Virtue of the Way of Deep-Dialogue/Critical-Thinking/Emotional-Intelligence/Competitive-Cooperation, the skills in becoming a whole person (which is literally what it means to be "holy") are augmented, accelerated. When persons inhabit and are inhabited by diverse worldviews, something profound happens in their inner lives. Their sense of self is challenged and can be fractured. It is clear that the Way of Deep-Dialogue/Critical-Thinking/ Emotional-Intelligence/Competitive-Cooperation will enable humans to cultivate an inner Deep-Dialogue and clarifying Critical-Thinking so as to negotiate the labyrinth of experience within and become integrated—whole/ holy persons—acting accordingly. In this, the Way of Deep-Dialogue/Critical-Thinking/Emotional-Intelligence/Competitive-Cooperation   is   essential to human flourishing in the emerging global civilization. The connection between rational awakening, personal integrity, and moral education, and ethical action now begins to become clear.

Classical education rightly understood that educating the whole person— *mens sana in corpore sano* (a healthy mind in a healthy body)—is essentially tied to moral education. Now we see that rational awakening also means becoming a more fully aware person with a deeper ability to enter with full presence into the present moment. Thus to walk the Way of Deep-Dialogue is also to develop Critical-Thinking and Emotional-Intelligence, and subsequent Competitive-Cooperation, to deepen our rational awareness, to activate our higher moral and spiritual capacities, to enter a deeper form of intellectual consciousness, to achieve greater well-being and acting in becoming a holy, integrated individual (recall: *in*-dividual = *un*-divided)—a person.

Moral and Political Education: Global Citizenship and Community

Today we see that the deepening of the inner life and personal well-being is connected with our outer life, for which, as it becomes increasingly global-ized, the Way of Deep-Dialogue/Critical-Thinking/Emotional-Intelligence/Competitive-Cooperation is more essential than ever for democratic and civil discourse and action. The key to good citizenship involves deep lis-tening, thinking clearly, speaking across diverse worldviews, and acting in Competitive-Cooperation. Moral Deep-Dialogue/Critical-Thinking/Emotional-Intelligence/Competitive-Cooperation is vital in cultivating such virtues as respect for others and for differences, indeed, for all the moral virtues. Thus, the Way of Deep-Dialogue/Critical-Thinking/Emotional-Intelligence/Competitive-Cooperation is at the heart of our inner life (intrapersonal) and outer life (interpersonal). It is thus essential that we raise our youth in the Way of Deep-Dialogue/Critical-Thinking/Emotional-Intelligence/Competitive-Cooperation.

In following the Way of Deep-Dialogue/Critical-Thinking/Emotional-Intelligence/Competitive-Cooperation, we find the foundation of a global ethic and communication across worldviews, leading to the long sought bal-ance of unity and diversity. For the Way of Deep-Dialogue/Critical-Thinking/Emotional-Intelligence/Competitive-Cooperation leads to the common ground where individuals may flourish and diversity be respected, while simultane-ously the common origin of our diverse worlds is celebrated. This is why the Way of Deep-Dialogue/Critical-Thinking/Emotional-Intelligence/Competitive-Cooperation is key to a global ethic, global citizenship, and democracy.

Peace Studies: Coexistence Education—Unity and Diversity Awakening

The many attempts recently to help youth cope creatively with issues of identity, multiplicity, diversity, difference and unity converge around being able to enter the Way of Deep-Dialogue/Critical-Thinking/Emotional-Intelligence/Competitive-Cooperation. Such attempts as diversity training, sensitivity training, toler-ance education, coexistence work, community building, peace studies, conflict resolution, and so forth are all more specialized attempts at utilizing the pow-ers of Deep-Dialogue/Critical-Thinking/Emotional-Intelligence/Competitive-Cooperation: the capacity to listen deeply to others who inhabit different worlds, to recognize and honor genuine difference, to truly enter other worlds and resist reducing the Other to one's own worldview, to develop nonviolent forms of being a Self and being in community, to create the skills of mediation and negotiation between polarized and mutually estranged views—all these grow out of the deep well of Deep-Dialogue/Critical-Thinking/Emotional-Intelligence/Competitive-Cooperation, through which we access the foundation of the many initiatives to humanize the communal space of our shared lives. Deep-Dialogue/Critical-Thinking/Emotional-Intelligence/Competitive-Cooperation is thus the source of nonviolence and a peaceful sharing of communal space.

The Aesthetic: The Creative Imagination and the Arts

Deep-Dialogue/Critical-Thinking/Emotional-Intelligence/Competitive-Cooperation lies at the heart of our aesthetic life. Our deepest esthetic creativity and capacity for beauty depends on our openness to an ever deeper encounter with beauty in diverse media. Whether through the embrace of literature, music, or the visual or the lively arts, the Way of Deep-Dialogue/Critical-Thinking/Emotional-Intelligence/Competitive-Cooperation leads to the expanding and deepening of our aesthetic capacities. This Dialogue of the Heart increasingly opens us to the Other, both person and thing.

Integral Education and the Liberal Arts

Putting the liberal arts on the Way of Deep-Dialogue/Critical-Thinking/Emotional-Intelligence/Competitive-Cooperation has deep implications for revisioning and restructuring educational priorities and practices—I am speaking not just of higher education but of all education, from the cradle to the grave. For example, it is clear that interdisciplinary, that is, intercultural, inter-Way education is not a secondary, but a primary, dimension of human understanding. The classical ideal of an integral education for the whole person becomes attainable through the Way of Deep-Dialogue/Critical-Thinking/Emotional-Intelligence/Competitive-Cooperation in educational life, through which we see deeper connections and common ground among all areas of the liberal arts—especially the natural sciences, social sciences, and humanities, as well as the professions.

Transformation of Consciousness Leads to Transformation of the World

Humanity's move in the third millennium BCE from tribes to the Age of Civilizations (Latin: civis, "city," wherein higher human capacities developed) involved a radical transformation of human consciousness. A similar radical transformation in human consciousness took place in the first millennium BCE (the Axial Period,[4] when the great primary religions and philosophies appeared from the eastern Mediterranean to the Pacific). Now, at the beginning of the third millennium CE, Humanity is entering into a third phase of radical transformation of consciousness, the Age of Global Dialogue, which is characterized by globalization and Deep-Dialogue, its obverse, Critical-Thinking/Emotional-Intelligence, and their consequent action in Competitive-Cooperation.

Just as the earlier broad development of a sense of personal responsibility with the inbreaking of the Axial Age, and the claim of the universal validity of democracy and human rights in political life now at the dawn of the Age of Global Dialogue have transformed human consciousness, and hence the world—so too will the widespread inculcation of the habit of the mind and spirit, that is, the Virtue, the Way of Deep-Dialogue/Critical-Thinking/Emotional-Intelligence/

Competitive-Cooperation, utterly and creatively transform the world—for the better!

As noted above, because the very essence of Dialogue demands community, my wife, Arlene, and I started the *Journal of Ecumenical Studies* in 1964, and then the Dialogue Institute in 1978. Here is how the latter envisions its purpose. Let it serve as a model.

Education Vision of the Dialogue institute

To research, develop, foster the habit of mind, and action, the Virtue— the Way—of Deep-Dialogue/Critical-Thinking/Emotional-Intelligence/ Competitive-Cooperation based on a global ethic in an emerging global civilization.

Education Mission of the Dialogue Institute

To introduce the Virtue, the Way of Deep-Dialogue/Critical-Thinking/ Emotional-Intelligence/Competitive-Cooperation in all aspects of education (preschool to adult); to reinvigorate integral education for whole persons and communities; to train educators in the Virtue, the Way of Deep-Dialogue/Critical-Thinking/Emotional-Intelligence/Competitive-Cooperation; to ally with organizations to research, develop, share, and encourage the habit of mind, spirit, and action, the Virtue, the Way, of Deep-Dialogue/Critical-Thinking/Emotional-Intelligence/Competitive-Cooperation; to foster a conscious development and living of a global ethic in the emerging global civilization.

18

Dialogue Institute: "Whole Child Education" Exercise in Concept Attainment

The Dialogue Institute was invited by the Ministry of Education, the Ministry of Religious Affairs, of Indonesia, and UNICEF to train in 2001 a pilot group of 75 primary school teachers and administrators in Deep-Dialogue/Critical-Thinking/Emotional-Intelligence/Competitive-Cooperation. Here is one detailed section of that highly successful training.

Rather than provide only general reflections about formal education, I would like to share a description of one concrete tool the Dialogue Institute used in training 75 primary school teachers in Indonesia in 2001 in "Whole Child Education" (we worked with the Ministry of Education, the Ministry of Religious Affairs, and UNICEF). The project was two weeks long and was very successful (the teachers were extremely enthusiastic about receiving training in Deep-Dialogue/Critical-Thinking—so much so that they quickly referred to it as DD-CT! (I had not yet developed either the concepts or terms Emotional-Intelligence or Competitive-Cooperation)—and the follow-up evaluation six months later showed that the program had "taken."

Unfortunately, in the midst of our subsequent planning to take the training to scale (I had already had discussions with the World Bank), we lost our political support when my friend President Abdurrahman Wahid was forced from office, as well as his foreign minister, Alwi Shihab (who had been a doctoral student of mine). This tool was only one of many that we used (the others can be shared simply by writing to the Dialogue Institute—dialogue@temple.edu), but it will make the previous ideas a bit more concrete.

Key Idea

Concepts are the mental tools we humans regularly use to organize the endless number of impressions that constantly pour into our minds through our senses. If we did not create concepts, every time I sent my child to the store to buy some milk, for instance, I would have to tell her to go to "that place she went to two days ago" (concept: the store) and give the "man" (concept: that tall being with two legs—I would also have to explain "legs" and "two"), take some "money" (which I could point to), that is, "buy," some of that "white" (I could point to something white) "fluid" (I could point to some fluid) called "milk." Whew! How much more efficient to simply tell her: "Eva, please go to the store and buy some milk," and trust that she understood the concepts "store," "buy," and "milk." Without concepts, we could hardly communicate with each other.

Background
The term concept comes from the Latin (con—"with" or "about"—cipere—"to grasp" or "to hold") meaning "to grasp," or "put our mind's fingers around" something. It is very much like the word "define," which also comes from the Latin (de—"around" or "about"—finere—"to end," like "finish"). So define means to "draw a line around" some idea, saying that these characteristics inside the line belong to the idea, and all those other characteristics do not. A concept is much the same: we put our mental fingers around these characteristics that belong to the concept or idea, and all those other characteristics that we do not grasp, do not belong to the concept or idea.

Goal
The goal of this exercise is *not* to give the students a definition or concept we want them to learn, but to get them to produce the concept or definition themselves. Then they themselves will "grasp" it better because they will have drawn a mental line around it, defined it. Because they worked so hard to produce it, the students also will likely remember it for the rest of their lives.

Uses
This model can be used in any subject for any age group. The concepts can be from the very simple, such as "circle" or "square," to the very complex, such as "freedom," "responsibility," "democracy." The model can also be used in every subject, such as "adjective" in language, or "exponent" in mathematics, or "chemical change" in physical science, or...

However, it is best to go through this exercise a few times first with very simple concepts—for example, "rectangle," or "domestic animal" as distinct from "wild animal"—until both teacher and students are thoroughly familiar and at ease with it. Then more complex concepts can be attacked, and the great value to both the teacher and students of this model will become increasingly apparent.

Procedure Step by Step
Following are the nine steps in this exercise. The first three are done by the teacher before the class, and the last six are done in class with the students.

Teacher Prepares Beforehand	Done in Class
1. Selects and define a concept	4. Introduce the process to class
2. Selects the attributes	5. Present samples and list attributes
3. Develops yes and no samples	6. Develop a concept definition
	7. Give additional samples
	8. Discuss the process with class
	9. Evaluate

1. *Select and define a concept:* The teacher should carefully pick a concept that is clear enough to be easily taught by the concept attainment method. The teacher should be aware of the relationships among the various related concepts. For example, when teaching the concept *apple*, the teacher should be aware of the concepts that are *coordinate* to apple: oranges, pears and apples are all *coordinate* to each other because all three belong to the *superordinate* category "fruit." However, there are many kinds of apples, as for example, McIntosh, Stayman, and Winesap, which are *subordinate* kinds of apples.

2. *Select its attributes:* As a first easy example concept to teach, let us take a "rectangle," which the teacher ahead of time will have defined for herself, perhaps as "a four-sided geometric figure containing all right angles in which the opposite sides are both equal and parallel." Then the teacher selects from that definition the essential attributes:

   Geometric figure
   Four-sided
   Containing all right angles
   Opposite sides equal
   Opposite sides parallel

3. *Develop "yes" and "no" samples:* The teacher should then create a number of different visual "yes" examples ahead of time, each of which must contain *all* the attributes. They can be blocks of wood, or paper, or drawings on the chalkboard, and so forth. The teacher should then also create a number of "no" examples, that is, different geometric shapes that are *not* rectangles (e.g., circles, triangles, parallelograms, trapezoids, etc.). Then the teacher is ready to take the exercise to class.

4. *Introduce the process to the class:* The teacher explains the exercise to the students, perhaps making it a kind of game wherein the teacher does not tell the students the name of the concept (of course, the teacher may decide it would be helpful to tell the students the name of the concept being taught). The students are told that they will be shown "yes" examples first and are to list *all* the attributes describing the examples, and then will be shown some "no" examples. Their goal is to produce a list of attributes that describes all the essential characteristics of the "yes" examples, which will lead to a clear definition of the concept.

5. *Present the examples and list the attributes:* a) Then the teacher shows a "yes" example (several "yes" examples must be used first) and has a *student* write the attributes the students call out in a list on the board (later a "no" list will be put alongside it). Remember: list *everything* the students say. This is "brainstorming," and there are no "wrong" answers in brainstorming. Let's say that the teacher showed an example of a rectangle made out of green paper. The students might volunteer the following attributes:

   Green
   Four sides
   Made of paper
   A shape
   Opposite sides are alike

b) As other "yes" examples are shown, those attributes that are *not* present are crossed out on the original list. For example, the teacher now shows a rectangular block of wood; therefore, "green" is crossed out on the original list, as is also "made of paper." Also note, although example two is made of wood, because "wood" was not present in example one, it is *not* added to the list. It is important not to erase the attributes of green and paper, but to cross them out, so in the discussion later the students can see the steps, the *process,* by which they came to define the concept.

c) Perhaps with example two, or a later "yes" example, a student will notice that *all* the "yes" examples also contain all right angles; that attribute then can be added to the list.

d) Then the teacher shows a "no" example, and a second "no" list of attributes is put on the board alongside the "yes" list of attributes. For instance, the teacher might show a trapezoid. In comparing the shape of the trapezoid with that of a rectangle, perhaps one of the students will notice that in the rectangle, opposite sides are parallel, but they are not in the trapezoid; hence, to the list of essential attributes of the original concept can be added "opposite sides are parallel."

e) The teacher should make it clear to the students that "no" examples do not eliminate attributes from the "yes" list; only "yes" examples that do not contain an attribute on the list can lead to crossing out an attribute (as the attributes "green" and "paper" were eliminated in the above example). Giving "no" examples makes the students pay attention to both similarities and differences and helps them better understand the concept's essential attributes.

Sample Lists

Yes
(Rectangle)
Green
Four sides
Made of paper
A shape
Opposite sides are alike
Contains all right angles
Opposite sides are parallel

No
(Trapezoid)
White
Four sides
Drawn on the board
A shape
Opposite sides are different
Contains several different angles
Opposite sides are not parallel

6. *Develop a concept definition*: Now that all the essential attributes of the rectangle have been determined by the students, the teacher asks them to put together a clear, precise definition of the concept (and give it a name—"rectangle" in this case—if she has not told them the name beforehand). The teacher needs to be patient and prompt the students themselves to come up with the definition. Remember, the goal is not *only* that the students themselves derive the definition, but that the students be engaged in the *process* of forming and defining concepts.

7. *Give additional examples*: Now the teacher shows the students a few more "yes" and "no" examples to test whether they can identify examples of the concept; students can also come up with examples of their own.

8. *Discuss the process with the class*: a) The teacher asks the students about *how* they arrived at the definition, making sure that they are aware of the steps they went through in order to define the concept clearly and completely—that is, listing *all* the attributes of the "yes" examples, eliminating attributes that were not present in *all* the "yes" examples, adding those attributes to the "yes" examples that they became aware of by comparison with the "no" examples.

   b) The more conscious a learner is of her or his own thinking *process*, the sharper that thinking will be. Hence, as the teacher uses this *concept attainment* model in teaching, s/he should have the students identify the point at which they understood the essential attributes of the concept and tell which examples helped the most.

9. *Evaluate:* Test periodically to see whether the students have retained the concept. Compare with teaching concepts by other methods, such as the traditional method of the teacher giving the students the definition and having them memorize it. Test to see by which method the students gain a better grasp of the concept and retain it longer.

Fosters Deep-Dialogue/Critical-Thinking/ Emotional-Intelligence/Competitive-Cooperation

a) Instead of the teacher's simply giving the students the definition of the concept to memorize, the concept attainment model fosters a dialogue both between the teacher and the students and among the students, leading them to respect the contributions both of others and themselves (Emotional-Intelligence). It also fosters a kind of dialogue between the students and the concepts and examples, as well as with their own thinking process.

b) The concept attainment model also fosters Critical-Thinking on the part of the students (and the teacher as well!) by making them *all* analyze the examples to search for the common and differentiating attributes. Their Critical-Thinking is also promoted when they have to search for the precise wording to make the definition accurate and clear. Perhaps most of all, Critical-Thinking is promoted by the students' becoming aware of their thinking process, so that they will be able deliberately and carefully to follow that process in the future when they deal with more complicated matters.

Future Implications

It does not take a great deal of fantasy to imagine how the minds of even "ordinary" children would develop if just once a week they had such a dialogic/critical-thinking/emotional-intelligence exercise. That would be 40 such experiences in first grade, another 40 in second grade, and on and on. Just by the end of eight years of primary school at age 14 they would have had 320 such Deep-Dialogue/Critical-Thinking/Emotional-Intelligence experiences, which long since would have "virtually" oriented them to Competitive-Cooperation. Imagine a work force and a citizenery so thinking and acting! A business owner would be delighted to have such creative labor! What chance would a bamboozling politician have with such a crowd of grade school graduates, let alone high school or university graduates!

Seven Stages of Deep-Dialogue/ Critical-Thinking/Emotional- Intelligence/Competitive- Cooperation—Applied to Teachers of Whole Child Education

The seven stages of Deep-Dialogue/Critical-Thinking/Emotional-Intelligence/ Competitive-Cooperation are here applied by a master teacher to a teacher of Whole Child Education.

At a training session preparing for the training of the Indonesian primary school teachers in 2001, referred to above, Launa Ellison, having been inspired by the "Seven Stages of Deep-Dialogue," developed in response these pedagogical "Seven Stages for Teachers." She taught fifth and sixth grade in the Minneapolis Public School system, and is the author of many articles and the books: *Seeing with Magic Glasses: A Teacher's View from the Front Lines* (1993); *The Personal Intelligences: Promoting Social and Emotional Learning* (2000).

Stage One: Radical Encountering of Difference

Self Faces the Other

Self faces an Other way of teaching, a different view of what is possible, a different view of teacher behavior. This Other disrupts my settled patterns of interpretation. This Other represents a different way of making sense of learning, a different way of experiencing students, a different way of experiencing important classroom processes. This new Other is disconcerting. I feel vulnerable and challenged. I must make a decision to move forward toward the change—or draw back.

Stage Two: Crossing Over—Letting Go and Entering the World of the Other

Self Transformed through Empathy

This new view of "educating the whole child processes" is very different from my own. I feel challenged to inquire, investigate, engage. I realize that I need to stand back and distance myself from my former habits, my patterns of teaching practices. I begin to realize that these new teaching practices organize and process the world very differently from my way. I realize that I must learn new habits of interpretation to make sense of "educating the whole child processes." I must translate my practices into a different form of teaching that sees education and student learning differently.

Stage Three: Inhabiting and Experiencing the World of the Other

Self Transformed into the Other

I begin to feel a new, deep connection—empathy—for these new ways. I want to let myself go, grow in this new way of "educating the whole child processes." I hold on to my prior views as much as I can, but I do advance in a conservative fashion. I experience an excitement in discovering, in inhabiting a new and different view of the teaching-learning process.

Stage Four: Crossing Back with an Expanded Vision

Self Returns Home with New Knowledge

I return to my classroom, bringing back new knowledge of how to think and act—and may even wish to adopt/adapt some of it for myself. As a result of my experience, I now realize that there are other ways of understanding the teaching-learning process. I am therefore open to rethinking how I see myself, my students, and the "educating the whole child process." My encounter with these new ways challenges my former identity, and everything begins to appear in a new light. There now begins a dramatic deepening of my sense of Self. There is no return to my former unilateral way.

Stage Five: The Dialogical Awakening

A Radical Paradigm Shift—Inwardly Transformed

As a result of the "educating the whole child process," I can no longer return to my former ways with the students. I begin to realize that the "educating the whole child process" has shaken the foundation of my former view of learning and classroom management, my former identity as teacher. Now that I am aware of the living reality of other ways of teaching/learning, other perspectives, I can no longer return to my former identity and forget these ways. I begin to realize there are other ways of teaching, other perspectives that surround me. I now open to a plurality of other views and perspectives on teacher-student relationships, and feel this irrevocably changes my sense of self.

Stage Six: The Global Awakening

The Paradigm Shift Matures

Self Related to Self, Others, the World

I have a new sense of Self and of "educating the whole child processes" that are inseparably bound together in a boundless interrelational web. This diversity enriches my Self and my teaching. I now see that all worlds are situated in a common ground of reality and that radical differences are nevertheless situated in a field of unity. I experience three related dimensions of global dialogical awakening:

a) I become aware of a deep inner dialogue within my Self. In this inner dialogue I feel increasingly more deeply rooted and grounded while I teach. My identity is enriched as I experience a more potent sense of my uniqueness and celebrate the uniqueness of each of my students.

b) As my new inner dialogue and reflective thinking evolve, I find myself in new and transformed relations with my students, parents, and school culture. This new phase of relations with my peers can be disorienting and disconcerting, for as I now dramatically grow in my new role, I find myself at an estranged distance from many of my peers. I face a new turbulence— miscommunication and misunderstanding with my colleagues—and a challenging, dramatic dialogue unfolds.

c) As this inner/outer dialogue matures, my understanding of "educating the whole child processes" enters a new phase. Dialogues arise everywhere. I have a new sense of reality, of dynamic ever-deepening relations, a new attitude toward life, of teaching.

Stage Seven: Personal and Global Transforming of Life and Behavior

Self Lives and Acts in a New Global Dialogical Consciousness

As my new understanding of "educating the whole child processes" becomes a habit of life, I find that my behavior and disposition toward myself, my students, and the school community have changed. I realize that the deepest care for my self essentially involves my care for others and my school environment. I have a deeper sense of belonging to my world, to my community, and with this a boundless sense of responsibility in all of my conduct. I now realize that I have been transformed in the deepest habits of mind and behavior. I find a deeper sense of self-realization and fulfillment and meaning in my life and my relations with others and the world around me.

20

Toward a Universal Declaration of a Global Ethic

At the global level, the implications of Deep-Dialogue/Critical-Thinking/ Emotional-Intelligence/Competitive-Cooperation lead to the need for a global ethic, that is, fundamental ethical principles shared de facto by persons of all religions and ethical systems.

Humans tend to group themselves in communities with similar understandings of the meaning of life and how to act accordingly. For the most part, in past history such large communities, called cultures or civilizations, have tended on the one hand to live unto themselves, and on the other to dominate and, if possible, absorb the other cultures they encountered. For example, Christendom, Islam, China.

The Meaning of Religion (Ideology)

At the heart of each culture is what is traditionally called a religion, that is, as seen above, "An explanation of the ultimate meaning of life, and how to live accordingly, based on some notion and experience of the Transcendent." Normally all religions contain the four "C's": creed, code, cult, community structure, and are based on the notion and experience of the transcendent.

> *Creed* refers to the cognitive aspect of a religion; it is every-thing that goes into the explanation of the ultimate meaning of life.
>
> *Code* of behavior or ethics includes all the rules and customs of action that somehow follow from one aspect or another of the *Creed*.
>
> *Cult* means all the ritual activities that relate the follower to one aspect or other of the Transcendent, either directly or in-directly, prayer being an example of the former and certain formal behavior toward representatives of the Transcendent, like priests, of the latter.
>
> *Community-structure* refers to the relationships among the followers; this can vary widely, from a very egalitarian relationship, as among Quakers, through a "republican" structure like Presbyterians have, to a monarchical one, as with some Hasidic Jews vis-à-vis their Rebbe.

The **Transcendent**, as the roots of the word indicate, means "that which goes beyond" the everyday, the ordinary, the surface experience of reality. It can refer to spirits, gods, a personal God, an impersonal God, emptiness, and so forth.

Especially in modern times there have developed "explanations of the ultimate meaning of life, and how to live accordingly" which are not based on a notion of the Transcendent, for example, secular humanism, Marxism. Although in every respect these "explanations" function as religions traditionally have in human life, because the idea of the Transcendent, however it is understood, plays such a central role in religion, but not in these "explanations," for the sake of accuracy it is best to give these "explanations" not based on notion of the Transcendent a separate name; the name often used is: *Ideology*. Much, though not all, of the following will, *mutatis mutandis*, also apply to Ideology even when the term is not used.

From the Age of Monologue to the Age of Dialogue

A Radically New Age

Those scholars who earlier in the twentieth century with a great show of scholarship and historical/sociological analysis predicted the impending demise of Western civilization were dead wrong. After World War I, in 1922, Oswald Spengler wrote his widely acclaimed book, *The Decline of the West*.[1] After the beginning of World War II, Pitirim A. Sorokin published in 1941 his likewise popular book, *The Crisis of Our Age*.[2] Given the massive, worldwide scale of the unprecedented destruction and horror of the world's first global war, 1914–1918, and the even vastly greater of the second global conflict, 1939–1945, the pessimistic predictions of these scholars and the great following they found are not ununderstandable.

In fact, however, those vast world conflagrations were manifestations of the dark side of the unique breakthrough in the history of humankind in the modern development of Christendom-become-Western-Civilization, now becoming Global-Civilization. Never before had there been world wars; likewise, never before had there been world political organizations (League of Nations, United Nations). Never before did humanity possess the real possibility of destroying all human life—whether through nuclear or ecological catastrophe. These unique negative realities/potentialities were possible, however, only because of the correspondingly unique accomplishments of Christendom-Western-Global-Civilization—the likes of which the world has never before seen. On the negative side, from now on it will always be true that humankind could self-destruct. Still, there are solid empirical grounds for reasonable hope that the inherent, infinity-directed life force of humankind will nevertheless prevail over the parallel death force.

The prophets of doom were correct, however, in their understanding that humanity is entering into a radically new age. Earlier in the twentieth century the naysayers usually spoke of the doom of only Western Civilization (e.g., Spengler,

Sorokin), but after the advent of nuclear power and the Cold War, the new generation of pessimists—as said, not without warrant: *corruptio optimae pessima* ("destruction of the best become the worst")—warned of *global* disaster. This emerging awareness of global disaster is a clear, albeit negative, sign that something profoundly, radically new is entering onto the stage of human history.

There have, of course, also recently been a number of more positive signs that we humans are entering a radically new age. In the 1960s, there was much talk of the Age of Aquarius, and there still is today the continuing fad of New Age consciousness (there is, of course, also a serious dimension to it). Some may be put off by the idea of an emerging radically new age because they perceive such talk to be simply that of fringe groups. I would argue, however, that the presence of "the crazies" around the edge of any idea or movement, far from being a sign of the invalidity of that idea or movement, is, on the contrary, a confirmation precisely of its validity, at least in its core concern. I would further argue that if people are involved with a movement that does not eventually develop its crazies, its extremists, the movement is not touching the core of humankind's concerns—they should get out of the movement; they are wasting their time!

Moreover, there have likewise recently been a number of very serious scholarly analyses pointing to the emergence of a radically new age in human history. Two of them will be dealt with in some detail. The first is the concept of the paradigm shift, particularly as expounded by Hans Küng.[3] The second is the notion of the "Second Axial Period," as articulated by Ewert Cousins.[4] Then, including these two, but setting them in a still larger context, I shall lay out my own analysis, which I see as the movement of humankind out of a millennia-long "Age of Monologue" into the newly inbreaking "Age of Dialogue," indeed, an inbreaking "Age of Global Dialogue."

Of course there is a great deal of continuity in human life throughout the shift from one major paradigm to another, from one period to another, from one age to another. Nevertheless, even more striking than this continuity is the ensuing break, albeit largely on a different level than the continuity. This relationship of continuity and break in human history is analogous to the transition of water from solid to fluid to gas with an increase in temperature. With water there is throughout on the chemical level the continuity of H^2O. However, for those who have to deal with the water, it makes a fantastic difference whether the H^2O is ice, water, or steam! In the case of the major changes in humankind, the physical base remains the same, but on the level of consciousness the change is massive. And here too it makes a fantastic difference whether we are dealing with humans whose consciousness is formed within one paradigm or within another, whose consciousness is Pre-Axial, Axial-I or Axial-II, whose consciousness is monologic or dialogic.

A Major Paradigm Shift

Thomas Kuhn revolutionized our understanding of the development of scientific thinking with his notion of paradigm shifts. He painstakingly showed that fundamental paradigms or "exemplary models" are the large thought frames within which we place and interpret all observed data, and that scientific advancement inevitably brings about eventual paradigm shifts—from geocentrism to heliocentrism, for example, or from Newtonian to Einsteinian physics—which are always vigorously resisted at first, as was the thought of Galileo, but finally prevail.[5] This insight, however, is not only valid for the development of thought in the natural sciences but also applicable to all major disciplines of human thought, including religious thought. For example, the move from the Semitic thought world of Jesus and his followers into the Hellenistic world of early Christianity and then into the Byzantine and medieval Western Christian worlds, and further, generated a number of greater and lesser paradigm shifts in European religion and culture over the centuries.

The Modern Major Paradigm Shift

Since the eighteenth-century European Enlightenment, Christendom-now-become-Western-Civilization has been undergoing a major paradigm shift, especially in how we humans understand our process of understanding and what meaning and status we attribute to truth, that is, to our statements about reality—in other words, to our epistemology. This new epistemological paradigm is increasingly determining how we perceive, conceive, think about, and subsequently decide and act on things.

It is difficult to overestimate the importance of the role in religion, in the "ultimate understanding of reality and how to live accordingly," played by the conceptual paradigm or model one has of reality. The paradigm within which we perceive reality not only profoundly affects our theoretical understanding of reality but also has immense practical consequences. For example, in Western medicine the body is usually conceived of as a highly nuanced, living machine, and therefore if one part wears out, the obvious thing to do is to replace the worn part—hence, organ transplants originated in Western, but not in Oriental, medicine.

However, in Oriental, Chinese, medicine, the body is conceived of as a finely balanced harmony: pressure exerted on one part of the body is assumed to have an opposite effect in some other part of the body—hence, acupuncture originated in Oriental, but not in Western, medicine.[6] Our conceptual paradigms have concrete consequences.

Furthermore, obviously some particular paradigms or models for perceiving reality will fit the data better than others, and they will then be preferred—for example, the shift from the geocentric to the heliocentric model in astronomy. But sometimes differing models will *each* in its own way "fit" the data more or less adequately, as in the example of Western and Oriental medicine. The differing models are then viewed as complementary. Clearly it would be foolish to limit one's perception of reality to only one of the complementary paradigms.

Let me turn now, once again, to the post-Enlightenment epistemological paradigm shift. Whereas the Western notion of truth was largely absolute, static, and monologic or exclusive up to the past century, it has since become deabsolutized, dynamic, and dialogic—in a word, it has become "relational."[7] This new view of truth came about in at least six different, but closely related, ways. In brief they are

1. **Historicism:** Truth is deabsolutized by the perception that reality is always described in terms of the circumstances of the time in which it is expressed.
2. **Intentionality:** Seeking the truth with the intention of acting accordingly deabsolutizes the statement.
3. **Sociology of knowledge:** Truth is deabsolutized in terms of geography, culture, and social standing.
4. **Limits of language:** Truth as the meaning of something and especially as talk about the transcendent is deabsolutized by the nature of human language.
5. **Hermeneutics:** All truth, knowledge is seen as interpreted truth, knowledge, and hence is deabsolutized by the observer, who is always also interpreter.
6. **Dialogue:** The knower engages reality in a dialogue in a language the knower provides, thereby deabsolutizing all statements about reality.[8]

In sum, our understanding of truth and reality has been undergoing a radical shift. This new paradigm that is being born understands all statements about reality, especially about the meaning of things, to be historical, intentional, perspectival, partial, interpretive, and dialogic. What is common to all these qualities is the notion of *relationality*, that is, that all expressions or understandings of reality are in some fundamental way related to the speaker or knower. It is while bearing this paradigm shift in mind that we proceed with our analysis.

0. Before the nineteenth century in Europe, truth, that is, a statement about reality, was conceived in quite an absolute, static, exclusivistic either-or manner. If something was true at one time, it was always true. Not only empirical facts but also the meaning of things or the oughtness that was said to flow from them were thought of in this way. At bottom, the notion of truth was based exclusively on the Aristotelian principle of contradiction: a thing could not be true and not true in the same way at the same time. Truth was defined by way of exclusion: A was A because it could be shown not to be not-A. Truth was thus understood to be absolute, static, exclusivistically either-or. This is a classicist or absolutist view of truth.

1. Historicism: In the nineteenth century, many scholars came to perceive all statements about the truth of the meaning of something as partially the products of their historical circumstances. Those concrete circumstances helped determine the fact that the statement under study was even called forth, that it was couched in particular intellectual categories (for example, abstract Platonic, or concrete legal, language), particular literary forms (for example, mythic or metaphysical language), and particular psychological settings (such as a polemical response to a specific attack). These scholars argued that only if the truth statements were placed in their historical situation, their historical *Sitz im Leben*, could they be properly understood. The understanding of the text could be found only in context. To express that same original meaning in a later *Sitz im Leben*, one would require a proportionately different statement. Thus, all statements about the meaning of things were now seen to be deabsolutized in terms of time.

This is a historical view of truth. Clearly at its heart is a notion of relationality: any statement about the truth of the meaning of something has to be understood in relationship to its historical context.

2. Intentionality: Later thinkers like Max Scheler added a corollary to this historicizing of knowledge; it concerned not the past but the future. Such scholars also saw truth as having an element of intentionality at its base, as being oriented ultimately toward action, praxis. They argued that we perceive certain things as questions to be answered and set goals to pursue specific knowledge because we wish to do something about those matters; we intend to live according to the truth and meaning that we hope to discern in the answers to the questions we pose, in the knowledge we decide to seek. The truth of the meaning of things was thus seen as deabsolutized by the action-oriented intentionality of the thinker-speaker.

This is an intentional or praxis view of truth, and it too is basically relational: a statement has to be understood in relationship to the action-oriented intention of the speaker.

3. The sociology of knowledge: As statements of truth of the meaning of things were seen by some thinkers to be historically deabsolutized in time, so too, starting in this century with scholars like Karl Mannheim, such statements began to be seen as deabsolutized by such things as the culture, class, and gender of the thinker-speaker, regardless of time. All reality was said to be perceived from the perspective of the perceiver's own worldview. Any statement of the truth of the meaning of something was seen to be perspectival, "standpoint-bound," as Mannheim put it, and thus deabsolutized.

This is a perspectival view of truth and is likewise relational: all statements are fundamentally related to the standpoint of the speaker.

4. The limitations of language: Following Ludwig Wittgenstein and others, many thinkers have come to see that any statement about the truth of things can be at most only a partial description of the reality it is trying to describe. Although reality can be seen from an almost limitless number of perspectives, human language can express things from only one perspective. If this is now seen to be true of what we call "scientific truths," it is so much the more true of statements about the truth of the meaning of things. The very fact of dealing with the truth of the meaning of something indicates that the knower is essentially involved and hence reflects the perspectival character of all such statements.

A statement may be true, of course—it may accurately describe the extra-mental reality it refers to—but it will always be cast in particular categories, language, concerns, and so forth, of a particular standpoint, and in that sense will be limited, deabsolutized.

This also is a perspectival view of truth, and therefore also relational.

This limited and limiting, as well as liberating, quality of language is especially clear in talk of the transcendent. The transcendent is by definition that which goes beyond our experience. Any statements about the transcendent must thus be deabsolutized and limited far beyond the perspectival character seen in ordinary statements.

5. Hermeneutics: Bernard Lonergan, Hans-Georg Gadamer, and Paul Riceour recently led the way in developing the science of hermeneutics, which, by arguing that all knowledge of a text is at the same time an *interpretation* of the text, further deabsolutizes claims about the "true" meaning of the text. But this basic insight goes beyond knowledge of texts and applies to all knowledge. In all knowledge, I come to know something; the object comes into me in a certain way, namely, through the lens that I use to perceive it. As St. Thomas Aquinas stated, "Things known are in the knower according to the mode of the knower—*cognita sunt in cognoscente secundum modum cognoscentis.*"[9]

This is an interpretive view of truth. It is clear that relationality pervades this hermeneutical, interpretative, view of truth.

6. Dialogue: A further development of this basic insight is that I learn not by being merely passively open or receptive to, but by being in dialogue with, extramental reality. I not only "hear" or receive reality, but I also—and, I think, first of all—"speak" to reality. I ask it questions, I stimulate it to speak back to me, to answer my questions. In the process I give reality the specific categories and language in which to respond to me. The "answers" that I receive back from reality will always be in the language, the thought categories, of the questions I put to it. It can speak to me, can really communicate with my mind, only in a language and categories that I understand.

When the speaking, the responding, grows less and less understandable, if the answers are sometimes confused and unsatisfying, then I probably need to learn to speak a more appropriate language when I put questions to reality. If, for example, I ask the question, "How far is yellow?" of course, I will receive a nonsense answer. Or if I ask questions about living things in mechanical categories, I will receive confusing and unsatisfying answers.

This is a dialogic view of truth, whose very name reflects its relationality.

With this new, irreversible understanding of the meaning of truth, the critical thinker has undergone a radical Copernican turn. Just as the vigorously resisted shift in astronomy from geocentrism to heliocentrism revolutionized that science, the paradigm shift in the understanding of truth statements has revolutionized all the humanities, including theology-ideology. The macroparadigm with which critical thinkers operate today is characterized by historical, social, linguistic, hermeneutical, praxis and dialogic—relational—consciousness. This paradigm shift is far advanced among thinkers and doers, but as in the case of Copernicus, and even more dramatically of Galileo, there are still many resisters in positions of great institutional power.

With the deabsolutized view of the truth of the meaning of things, we come face to face with the specter of relativism, the opposite pole of absolutism. Unlike relationality, a neutral term that merely denotes the quality of being in relationship, relativism, like so many "isms," is a basically negative term. If it can no longer be claimed that any statement of the truth of the meaning of things is absolute, totally objective, because the claim does not square with our experience of reality, it is equally impossible to claim that every statement of the truth of the meaning of things is completely relative, totally subjective, for that also does not square with our experience of reality, and of course would logically lead to an atomizing isolation that would stop all discourse, all statements to others.

Our perception, and hence description, of reality is like our view of an object in the center of a circle of viewers. My view and description of the object, or reality, will be true, but it will not include what someone on the other side of the circle perceives and describes, which will also be true. So, neither of our perceptions and descriptions of reality is total, complete—absolute in that sense—or objective in the sense of not in any way being dependent on a "subject" or viewer. At the same time, however, it is also obvious that there is an objective, doubtless "true" aspect to each perception and description, even though each is relational to the perceiver-subject.

But if we can no longer hold to an absolutist view of the truth of the meaning of things, we must take certain steps so as not to be logically forced into the silence of total relativism. First, besides striving to be as accurate and fair as possible in gathering and assessing information and submitting it to the critiques of our peers and other thinkers and scholars, we need also to dredge out, state clearly, and analyze our own presuppositions—a constant, ongoing task. Even in this of course we will be operating from a particular "standpoint."

Therefore, we need, secondly, to complement our constantly critiqued statements with statements from different "standpoints." That is, we need to engage in dialogue with those who have differing cultural, philosophical, social, religious viewpoints so as to strive toward an ever fuller perception of the truth of the meaning of things. If we do not engage in such dialogue, we will not only be trapped within the perspective of our own standpoint but will now also be aware of our lack. We will no longer with integrity be able to remain deliberately turned in on ourselves. Our search for the truth of the meaning of things makes it a necessity for us as human beings to engage in dialogue. Knowingly to refuse dialogue today could be an act of fundamental human irresponsibility—in Judeo-Christian terms, a sin.

The Second Axial Period[10]

It was the German philosopher Karl Jaspers who over a half-century ago in his book *The Origin and Goal of History*[11] pointed to the "axial" quality of the transformation of consciousness that occurred in the ancient world. He called the period from 800–200 BCE the "Axial Period" because "it gave birth to everything which, since then, man has been able to be." It is here in this period "that we meet with the most deepcut dividing line in history. Man, as we know him today, came into being. For short, we may style this the 'Axial Period.'"[12]

Although the leaders who effected this change were philosophers and religious teachers, the change was so radical that it affected all aspects of culture, for it transformed consciousness itself. It was within the horizons of this form of consciousness that the great civilizations of Asia, the Middle East, and Europe developed. Although within these horizons many developments occurred through the subsequent centuries, the horizons themselves did not change. It was this form of consciousness that spread to other regions through migration and exploration, thus becoming the dominant, although not exclusive, form of consciousness in the world. To this day, whether we were born and raised in the culture of China, India, Europe, or the Americas, we bear the structure of consciousness that was shaped in this Axial Period.

What is this structure of consciousness and how does it differ from pre-Axial consciousness? Prior to the Axial Period, the dominant form of consciousness was cosmic, collective, tribal, mythic, and ritualistic. This is the characteristic form of consciousness of primal peoples. It is true that between these traditional cultures and the Axial Period there emerged great empires in Egypt, China, and Mesopotamia, but they did not yet produce the full consciousness of the Axial Period.

The consciousness of the tribal cultures was intimately related to the cosmos and to the fertility cycles of nature. Thus there was established a rich and creative harmony between primal peoples and the world of nature, a harmony that was explored, expressed, and celebrated in myth and ritual. Just as they felt themselves part of nature, so they experienced themselves as part of the tribe. It was precisely the web of interrelationships within the tribe that sustained them psychologically, energizing all aspects of their lives. To be separated from the tribe threatened them with death, not only physical but psychological as well. However, their relation to the collectivity often did not extend beyond their own tribe, for they often looked upon other tribes as hostile. Yet within their tribe they felt organically related to their group as a whole, to the life cycles of birth and death and to nature and the cosmos.

The Axial Period ushered in a radically new form of consciousness. Whereas primal consciousness was tribal, Axial consciousness was individual. "Know thyself" became the watchword of Greece; the Upanishads identified the *atman*, the transcendent center of the self; Gautama charted the way of individual enlightenment; Confucius laid out the individual's ethical path; the Jewish prophets awakened individual moral responsibility for powerless persons. This sense of individual identity, as distinct from the tribe and from nature, is the most characteristic mark of Axial consciousness.

From this flow other characteristics: consciousness that is self-reflective, analytic, and that can be applied to nature in the form of scientific theories, to society in the form of social critique, to knowledge in the form of philosophy, to religion in the form of mapping an individual spiritual journey. This self-reflective, analytic, critical consciousness stood in sharp contrast to primal mythic and ritualistic consciousness. When self-reflective *logos* emerged in the Axial Period, it tended to oppose the traditional *mythos*. Of course, mythic and ritualistic forms of consciousness survive in the post-Axial Period even to this day, but they are often submerged, surfacing chiefly in dreams, literature, and art.

Following the lead of Ewert Cousins, if we shift our gaze from the first millennium BCE to the beginning of the twenty-first century, we can discern another transformation of consciousness, which is so profound and far reaching that he calls it the "Second Axial Period."[13] Like the first, it is happening simultaneously around the earth, and like the first it will shape the horizon of consciousness for future centuries. Not surprisingly, too, it will have great significance for world religions, which were formed in the First Axial Period. However, the new form of consciousness is different from that of the First Axial Period. Then it was individual consciousness; now it is global consciousness.

This global consciousness that is generated on a "horizontal" level through the worldwide meeting of cultures and religions, is only one of the global characteristics of the Second Axial Period. The consciousness of this period is global in another sense, namely, in rediscovering its roots in the earth. At the moment at which various cultures and religions are meeting each other and creating a new global community, our life on the planet is being threatened. The very tools that we have used to bring about this convergence—industrialization and technology—are undercutting the biological support system that sustains life on our planet. The future of consciousness, even life on the earth, is shrouded in a cloud of uncertainty.

Cousins is not suggesting a romantic attempt to live in the past, but rather that the evolution of consciousness proceeds by way of recapitulation. Having developed self-reflective, analytic, critical consciousness in the First Axial Period, we must now, while retaining these values, reappropriate and integrate into that consciousness the collective and cosmic dimensions of the pre-Axial consciousness. We must recapture the unity of tribal consciousness by seeing humanity as a single tribe.

Further, we must see this single tribe related organically to the total cosmos. This means that the consciousness of the twenty-first century will be global from two perspectives: (1) from a horizontal perspective, cultures and religions must meet each other on the surface of the globe, entering into creative encounters that will produce a complexified collective consciousness; (2) from a vertical perspective, they must plunge their roots deep into the earth in order to provide a stable and secure base for future development. This new global consciousness must be organically ecological, supported by structures that will insure justice and peace. The voices of the oppressed must be heard and heeded: the poor, women, racial and ethnic minorities. These groups, along with the earth itself, can be looked upon as the prophets and teachers of the Second Axial Period. This emerging twofold global consciousness is not only a creative possibility to enhance the twenty-first century but is an absolute necessity if we are to survive.

Globalization

Since the sixteenth-century European "Age of Discovery," the earth has tended more and more to become, as Wendell Wilkie put it in 1940, "One World." This increasingly happened in the form of Christendom dominating and colonizing the rest of the world. In the nineteenth century, however, Christendom became less and less Christian and more and more the secular West, shaped by a secular ideology, or ideologies, alternative to Christianity. Still, the religious and ideological cultures of the West, even as they struggled with each other, dealt with other cultures and their religions in the customary manner of ignoring them or attempting to dominate, and even absorb, them—although it became increasingly obvious that the latter was not likely to happen.

As the twentieth century drew to a close, however, all of those ways of relating became increasingly impossible to sustain. For example: what happened in other cultures quickly led young men and women of the West to die on the volcanic ash of Iwo Jima or the desert sands of Kuwait. But more than that, the West could no longer escape what was done in the First World, such as the production of acid rain, in the Second World, such as the Chernobyl nuclear accident, or in the Third World, such as the mass destruction of the Amazon rain forest, "the world's lungs."

At the same time, the world has been slowly, painfully emerging from the millennia-long Age of Monologue into the Age of Dialogue. As noted above, until a century or so ago, each religion, and then ideology—each culture—tended to be very certain that it alone had the complete "explanation of the ultimate meaning of life, and how to live accordingly." Then through a series of revolutions in understanding, which began in the West but ultimately spread more and more throughout the whole world, the limitedness of all statements about the meaning of things began to dawn on isolated thinkers, and then increasingly on the middle and even grass-roots levels of humankind: the epistemological revolutions of historicism, pragmatism, sociology of knowledge, language analysis, hermeneutics, and finally dialogue.

Now that it is increasingly understood that the Muslim, Christian, secularist, Buddhist, and so on perception of the meaning of things is necessarily limited, the Muslim, Christian, secularist, Buddhist increasingly feels not only no longer driven to replace, or at least dominate, all other religions, ideologies, cultures, but even drawn to enter into dialogue with them, so as to expand, deepen, enrich each of their necessarily limited perceptions of the meaning of things. Thus, often with squinting, blurry eyes, humankind is emerging from the relative darkness of the Age of Monologue into the dawning Age of Dialogue—dialogue understood as a conversation with someone who differs from us so *we* can learn, because of course since we now growingly realize that our understanding of the meaning of reality is necessarily limited, we might learn more about reality's meaning through someone else's perception of it.

The Age of Global Dialogue

Cousins has basically affirmed everything Hans Küng has described as the newly emerging contemporary paradigm shift, but Cousins sees the present shift as much more profound than simply another in a series of major paradigm shifts of human history. He sees the current transformation as a shift of the magnitude of the First Axial Period, which will similarly reshape human consciousness. I too want to basically affirm what Küng sees as the emerging contemporary major paradigm shift, as well as with Cousins that this shift is so profound as to match in magnitude the transformation of human consciousness of the Axial Period, so that it should be referred to as a Second Axial Period.

More than that, however, I am persuaded that what humankind is entering into now is not just the latest in a long series of major paradigm shifts, as Küng has so carefully and clearly analyzed. I am also persuaded that it is even more than the massive move into the consciousness-transforming Second Axial Period, as Cousins has so thoroughly demonstrated. Beyond these two radical shifts, although of course including both of them, humankind is emerging out of the from-the beginning-until-now millennia-long Age of Monologue into the newly dawning Age of Dialogue.

The turn toward dialogue is, in my judgment, the most fundamental, the most radical and utterly transformative of the key elements of the newly emerging paradigm, which Küng has so penetratingly outlined, and which Cousins also perceptively discerns as one of the central constituents of the Second Axial Age. However, that shift from monologue to dialogue constitutes such a radical reversal in human consciousness, is so utterly new in the history of humankind from the beginning, that it must be designated as literally "revolutionary," that is, it turns everything absolutely around. In brief, as noted above: dialogue is a whole new way of thinking in human history.

To sum up and reiterate, in the latter part of the twentieth century humankind underwent a macro paradigm shift (Küng). More than that, humankind moved into a transformative shift in consciousness of the magnitude of the Axial Period (800–200 BCE) so that we had to speak of an emerging Second Axial Period (Cousins). Even more profound, however, now early in the Third Millennium, humankind is slipping out of the shadowy Age of Monologue, where it has been since its beginning, into the dawn of the Age of Global Dialogue (Leonard Swidler). Into this new Age of Global Dialogue Küng's macro paradigm shift and Cousins's Second Axial Period are sublated, that is, taken up and transformed. Moreover, as Cousins has already detailed, humankind's consciousness is becoming increasingly global. Hence, our dialogue partners necessarily must also be increasingly global. In this new Age of Global Dialogue, dialogue on a global basis is now not only a possibility but also a necessity. As I noted in the title of a recent book—humankind is faced with ultimately with two choices: Dialogue or Death![14]

Need for a Global Ethic

When the fact of the epistemological revolutions that are leading to the growing necessity of interreligious, interideological, intercultural dialogue is coupled with the fact of all humankind's interdependency—such that any significant part of humanity could precipitate the whole of the globe into a social, economic, nuclear, environmental or other catastrophe—there arises the pressing need to focus the energy of these dialogues on not only how humans perceive and understand the world and its meaning but also on how they should act in relationship to themselves, to other persons, and to nature, within the context of reality's undergirding, pervasive, overarching source, energy, and goal, however understood. In brief, humankind increasingly desperately needs to engage in a dialogue on the development of, not a Buddhist ethic, a Christian ethic, a Marxist ethic, and so on, but a global ethic—and I believe a key instrument in that direction will be the shaping of a Universal Declaration of a Global Ethic.

I say ethic in the singular rather than ethics in the plural, because what is needed is not a full-blown global ethics that is spelled out in great detail—indeed, such would not even be possible—but a global consensus on the fundamental attitude toward good and evil and the basic and middle principles to put it into action. Clearly also, this ethic must be global. It will not be sufficient to have a common ethic for Westerners or Africans or Asians, and so on. The destruction, for example, of the ozone layer or the loosing of a destructive gene mutation by any one group will be disastrous for all.

I say also that this Universal Declaration of a Global Ethic must be arrived at by consensus through dialogue. Attempts at the imposition of a unitary ethics by various kinds of force have been had aplenty, and they have inevitably fallen miserably short of globality. The most recent failures can be seen in the widespread collapse of communism, and in an inverse way in the resounding rejection of secularism by resurgent Islamism.

That the need for a global ethic is most urgent is becoming increasingly apparent to all. Humankind no longer has the luxury of letting such an ethic slowly and haphazardly grow by itself, as will willy nilly gradually happen. It is vital that there be a conscious focusing of energy on such a development. Immediate action is necessary.

1) Every scholarly institution, whether related to a religion or ideology or not, needs to press its experts of the widest variety of disciplines to use their creativity among themselves and in conjunction with scholars from other institutions, both religiously related and not, in formulating a global ethic.

2) Every major religion and ethics group needs to commission its expert scholars to focus their research and reflection on articulating a global ethic from the perspective of their religion or ethics group—in dialogue with all other religions and ethics groups.

3) Collaborative working groups of scholars in the field of ethics, which are very deliberately interreligious and interideological, need to be formed specifically to tackle this momentous task, and those that already exist need to focus their energies on it.

4) Beyond that there needs to be a major permanent global ethics research center, which will have some of the best experts from the world's major religions and ethics groups in residence, perhaps for years at a stretch, pursuing precisely this topic in its multiple ramifications.

When the Universal Declaration of a Global Ethic is finally drafted—after multiple consultations, revisions, and eventual acceptance by the full range of religious and ethics institutions—it will then serve as a minimal ethical standard for humankind to live up to, much as the United Nation's 1948 *Universal Declaration of Human Rights*. Through the former, the moral force of the world's religious/ethics institutions can be brought to bear especially on issues that are not susceptible to the legal and political force of the latter. Such an undertaking by the religions and ideologies of the world would be different from, but complementary to, the work of the United Nations.

After the initial period, which doubtless would last several years, the global ethic research center could serve as an authoritative religious and ideological scholarly locus to which always-new specific problems of a global ethic could be submitted for evaluation, analysis, and response. The weightiness of the responses would be substantive, not formal. That is, its solutions would carry weight because of their inherent persuasiveness coming from their intellectual and spiritual insight and wisdom.

Principles of a Universal Declaration of a Global Ethic

Let me first offer some suggestions of the general notions that I believe ought to shape a Universal Declaration of Global Ethic, and then offer a tentative draft constructed in their light:

1. The Declaration should use language and images that are acceptable to all major religions and ethics groups; hence, its language ought to be humanity based, rather than from authoritative religious books. It should be from "below," not from "above."
2. Therefore, it should be anthropocentric, indeed more, it must be anthropocosmocentric, for we cannot be fully human except within the context of the whole of reality.
3. The affirmations should be dynamic in form, in the sense that they will be susceptible to being sublated. That is, they might properly be reinterpreted by being taken up into a larger framework.
4. The Declaration needs to set inviolable minimums, but also open-ended maximums to be striven for. However, maximums may not be required, for they might violate the freedom-minimums of some persons.
5. It could well start with—although not limit itself to—elements of the so-called Golden Rule: treat others as we would be treated.

Excursus: the "Golden Rule"

A glimpse of just how pervasive the Golden Rule is, albeit in various forms and expressions, in the world's religions and ideologies, great and small, can be garnered from this partial listing:

1) Perhaps the oldest recorded version—which is cast in a positive form—stems from Zoroaster (628–551 BCE): "That which is good for all and any

one, for whomsoever—that is good for me...what I hold good for self, I should for all. Only Law Universal is true Law" (*Gathas*, 43.1).

2) The Greek Thales of Milet, around 600 BCE, asked: "How can we conduct the best and most righteous life? By refraining from doing what we blame in others."[15]

3) Pittakos, a contemporary of Thales, advised: "Don't do yourself that others make you angry at!"[16]

4) Confucius (551–479 BCE), when asked, "Is there one word which may serve as a rule of practice for all one's life?" said, "Do not to others what you do not want done to yourself" (*Analects*, 12.2 & 15.23). Confucius also stated in a variant version, "What I do not wish others to do to me, that also I wish not to do to them" (*Analects*, 5.11).

5) A contemporary of Confucius was Laozi, the founder of Taoism, which taught: "Consider your neighbor's happiness and suffering as your own happiness and suffering and strive to increase his wellbeing as your own."[17]

6) The founder of Jainism was Vardhamana, known as Maha-vira ("Great Hero—540–468 BCE). The various scriptures of Jainism, however, derived from a later period: "A man should wander about treating all creatures as he himself would be treated" (*Sutrakritanga* 1.11.33). "One who you think should be hit is none else but you.... Therefore, neither does he cause violence to others nor does he make others do so" (*Acaranga-sutra* 5.101–2).

7) Buddhism's founder was Siddhartha Gautama, known as Buddha ("Enlightened One"—563–483 BCE). The various scriptures of Buddhism derived from a later period: "Comparing oneself to others in such terms as 'Just as I am so are they, just as they are so am I,' he should neither kill nor cause others to kill" *Sutta Nipata* 705). "Here am I fond of my life, not wanting to die, fond of pleasure and averse from pain. Suppose someone should rob me of my life.... If I in turn should rob of his life one fond of his life.... How could I inflict that upon another?" (*Samyutta Nikaya* v.353).

8) Herodotus (484—425 BCE), the Father of History in Greece, wrote: "For what I reproach the neighbor, I won't do to the best of my ability."[18]

9) The Hindu epic poem, the third century BCE *Mahabharata*, states that its Golden Rule, which is expressed in both positive and negative form, is the summary of all Hindu teaching, "the whole Dharma": "Vyasa says: Do not to others what you do not wish done to yourself; and wish for others too what you desire and long for for yourself—this is the whole of Dharma; heed it well" (*Mahabharata*, Anusasana Parva 113.8).

10) In the biblical book of Leviticus (composed in the fifth century BCE, although some of its material may be more ancient), the Hebrew version of the Golden Rule is stated positively: "You shall love your neighbor as yourself" (Lev. 19: 18).

11) The deuterocanonical biblical Tobit was written around the year 200 BCE and contains a negative version—as most are—of the Golden Rule: "Never do to anyone else anything that you would not want someone to do to you" (Tobit 4:15).

12) The major founder of Rabbinic Judaism, Hillel, who lived about a generation before Jesus, although he may also have been his teacher, taught that the Golden Rule—his version being both positive and negative—was the heart of the Torah; "all the rest was commentary": "Do not do to others what you would not have done to yourself" (*Btalmud*, Shabbath 31a).

13) Following in this Jewish tradition, Jesus stated the Golden Rule in a positive form, saying that it summed up the whole Torah and prophets: "Do for others just what you want them to do for you" (Luke 6:31); "Do for others what you want them to do for you: this is the meaning of the Law of Moses [*Torah*] and of the teachings of the prophets" (Matthew 7:12).

14) In the seventh century CE, Mohammed is said to have claimed that the Golden Rule is the "noblest Religion": "Noblest Religion is this—that you should like for others what you like for yourself; and what you feel painful for yourself, hold that as painful for all others too." Again: "No man is a true believer unless he desires for his brother that which he desires for himself."[19]

15) Guru Angad (1504–1552 CE) recommends to the Sikhs: "Treat others as you would like to be treated yourself."[20]

16) The Golden Rule is likewise found in some nonliterate religions: "One going to take a pointed stick to pinch a baby bird should first try it on himself to feel how it hurts"[21]

17) The eighteenth-century Western philosopher Immanuel Kant provided a "rational" version of the Golden Rule in his famous Categorical Imperative, or Law of Universal Fairness: "Act on maxims which can at the same time have for their object themselves as universal laws of nature.... Treat humanity in every case as an end, never as a means only."[22]

18) The late-nineteenth-century founder of Baha'ism, Baha'ullah, wrote: "He should not wish for others that which he doth not wish for himself, nor promise that which he doth not fulfill."[23]

19) In 1915, a new version of Buddhism, Won Buddhism, was founded in Korea by the Great Master Sotaesan. In the teachings he left behind are found variants of the Golden Rule: "Be right yourself before you correct others. Instruct yourself first before you teach others. Do favors for others before you seek favors from them." "Ordinary people may appear smart in doing things only for themselves, but they are really suffering a loss. Buddhas and *Bodhisattvas* may appear to be stupid in doing things only for others, but eventually they benefit themselves."[24]

It is clear that the core of the world's major religions, the Golden Rule, "does not attempt the futile and impossible task of abolishing and annihilating the authentic ego. On the contrary, it tends to make concern for the authentic ego the *measure* of altruism. 'Do not foster the *ego* more than the *alter*; care for the *alter* as much as for the *ego*.' To abolish egoism is to abolish altruism also; and *vice versa*."[25] Authentic egoism and authentic altruism then are not in conflict with each other; the former necessarily moves to the latter, even possibly "giving one's life for one's friend." This, however, is the last and highest stage of human development. It is the stage of the (w)holy person, the saint, the arahat, the bodhisattva, the sage. Such a stage cannot be the foundation of human society; rather, it must be the goal of it. The foundation of human society must be first authentic self-love, which not only includes moving outward to loving others, but of its very nature is endlessly self-expansive so that the *primus ego* always reaches toward an ever farther *alter ego*!

Not recognizing this foundation of authentic self-love is the fundamental flaw of those idealistic systems, such as communism, that try to build a society on the foundation of altruism. A human and humanizing society should lead toward (w)holiness, toward altruism, but it cannot be built on the assumption that its citizens are (w)holy and altruistic to start with. Such an altruism must grow out of an ever developing authentic self-love; it cannot be assumed, and surely it cannot be forced (as was tried for decades—with disastrous dehumanizing results).

6. As humans ineluctably seek ever more knowledge, truth, so too they seek to draw what they perceive as the good to themselves (that is, they love). Usually this self is expanded to include the family, and then friends. It needs to continue its natural expansion to the community, nation, world and cosmos, and the source and goal of all reality.

7. But this human love necessarily must start with self-love, for one can love one's "neighbor" only as one loves oneself. But since one becomes human only by interhuman mutuality, loving others fulfills one's own humanity, and hence is also the greatest act of authentic self-love.

8. Another aspect of the Golden Rule is that humans are always to be treated as ends, never as mere means, that is, as subjects, never as mere objects.

9. Yet another implication of the Golden Rule is that those who cannot protect themselves ought to be protected by those who can.

10. A further ring of the expanding circles of the Golden Rule is that nonhuman beings are also to be reverenced and treated with respect because of their being.

11. It is important that not only basic but also middle ethical principles be spelled out in this Declaration. Although most of the middle ethical principles that need to be articulated here are already embedded in juridical form in the United Nations' 1948 Universal Declaration of Human Rights, it is vital that the religions and ethical traditions expressly state and approve them. Then the world, including both adherents and outsiders to the various religions and ethical traditions, will know to what ethical standards all are committing themselves.

12. If a Universal Declaration of a Global Ethic is to be meaningful and effective, however, its framers must resist the temptation to pack too many details and special interests into it. It can function best as a kind of constitutional set of basic and middle ethical principles from which more detailed applications can be constantly be drawn.

A Plan of Action

Such general suggestions need to be discussed, confirmed, rejected, modified, supplemented. Beyond that, it is vital that all the disciplines contribute what from their perspectives ought to be included in the Declaration, how that should be formulated, what is to be avoided—and this is beginning to happen. The year 1993 was the hundredth anniversary of the 1893 World Parliament of Religions, which took place in Chicago and marked the beginning of what became a world-wide interreligious dialogue. As a consequence, a number of international conferences took place, and in the center of them was the launching and developing of a Universal Declaration of a Global Ethic.

The first was held in New Delhi, India, in February 1993; the second in August of the same year in Bangalore, India; and the third that same year in September in Chicago. For that huge (over 6,000 participants) September 1993 Chicago "Parliament of the World's Religions" Professor Hans Küng drafted a Declaration Toward a Global Ethic (www.weltethos.org/index-en.php), which the Parliament adopted.[26]

Beyond that, the text below, having been commissioned by the January 1992 meeting in Atlanta, Georgia, of the International Scholars' Annual Trialogue—ISAT (Jewish-Christian-Muslim), was drafted by Professor Leonard Swidler and analyzed and approved at the January 1993 meeting of ISAT in Graz, Austria. It was focused on during the spring 1993 semester graduate seminar that the author held at Temple University, entitled "Global Ethics-Human Rights-World Religions." It was also a major focus of the First International Conference on Universalism in August 1993, in Warsaw; a consultation of the American Academy of Religion in November 1993, in Washington D.C. was devoted to the topic; the sixth International Scholars' Annual Trialogue in January 1994 concentrated for a second year on the Universal Declaration; in May 1994, it was the subject of a conference sponsored by the International Association of Asian Philosophy and Religion—IAAPR in Seoul, Korea; the World Conference on Religion and Peace—WCRP in part focused on it in its fall 1994 World Assembly in Rome/Riva del Garda, Italy; and on June 20–21, 1995, it was the subject of a conference in San Francisco in honor of the fiftieth anniversary of the founding of the United Nations, entitled "Celebrating the Spirit: Towards a Global Ethic."

In March 1997, the Philosophy and Ethics Division of UNESCO held in Paris the first meeting of its newly established committee to work toward a universal ethic. Its second meeting was held in December 1997 in Naples, in conjunction with the Instituto Italiano degli Studii Filosofici. Both the above two drafts (as well as the one described next) were submitted to this UNESCO committee.

Later, Küng drafted a third text (see: www.weltethos.org/index-en.php), this time within the context of the InterAction Council, entitled "A Universal Declaration of Human Responsibilities." The InterAction Council is a committee made up of former heads of states, chaired by retired Chancellor Helmut Schmidt of Germany. All three of these texts have been subjected to numerous consultations and comments by scholars and thinkers from multiple philosophical, religious, and other backgrounds.

To summarize: it is imperative that various religious and ethical communities, ethnic groups, geographical regions—in fact, every kind of group, small and large, including all who are reading these words!—discuss and write out your own version of a Universal Declaration of a Global Ethic. That is, what you (!)—not somebody else—consider your own basic ethical principles, which at the same time you believe people of all other religious and ethical traditions could also affirm. The three already existing drafts should certainly be made use of in this process. But all communities and regions need to make their own contributions to the final Declaration, and in the process of wrestling with the issues and forging the wording, you will make the concern for a global ethic your own, and will thus better be able to mediate it to your constituents and enhance the likelihood of the Declaration's in fact being adhered to in practice.

What must be stressed is that this project cannot be done only by the scholars and leaders of the world's religious and ethical communities, although obviously the vigorous participation of these elements is vital. The ideas and sensitivities must also come from the grassroots.

Moreover, it is also at the grassroots, as well at the levels of scholars and leaders, that, first, consciousnesses must be raised on the desperate need for the deliberate development of a global ethic, and then once drafted and accepted, the conviction of its validity must be gained. The most carefully thought out and sensitively crafted Declaration will be of no use if those who are to adhere to it do not believe in it. A global ethic must work on all three levels: scholars, leaders, grassroots. Otherwise, it will not work at all. Hence, I urge

- first, all religious, ethical, ethnic, and geographical communities and organizations, including classes, clubs… (either alone or in concert with others, but always in a dialogic spirit)—and most especially the myriad NGOs of the world—need to move seriously but quickly to the drawing up of their own draft of a Universal Declaration of a Global Ethic;
- second, these groups need to strategize on how to maneuver their drafts to gain the greatest influence in all the theaters in which they each work: the UN, other NGOs, scholarly groups, religious groups, the vast world of the Internet, myriads of grass-roots organizations—in short, wherever aroused imaginations will lead;
- third, each group should send their draft of a Universal Declaration of a Global Ethic to the Center for Global Ethics (Professor Leonard Swidler, *Journal of Ecumenical Studies*, Temple University, Philadelphia, PA 19122; globalethic.org; email dialogue@temple.edu), and the Weltethos Stiftung; www.weltethos.org will serve first as a collection and distribution centers and, when the time is appropriate, facilitators in the process of synthesizing a final draft and devising in as democratic manner as possible a process of worldwide adoption.

In sum, having studied, listened, and thought, I challenge us all to take up this vital task and act!

21

A Universal Declaration of a Global Ethic

Here is laid out one possible draft of a global ethic. It needs to be carefully studied, rearticulated multiple times, and shared across the globe, until eventually a consensus text can be universally affirmed—analogous to the United Nations 1948 Declaration of Human Rights.

Rationale

We women and men from various ethical and religious traditions commit ourselves to the following Universal Declaration of a Global Ethic. We speak here not of ethics in the plural, which implies rather great detail, but of ethic in the singular, that is, the fundamental attitude toward good and evil, and the basic and middle principles needed to put it into action.

We make this commitment not despite our differences but arising out of our distinct perspectives, recognizing nevertheless in our diverse ethical and religious traditions common convictions that lead us to speak out against all forms of inhumanity and for humaneness in our treatment of ourselves, one another, and the world around us. We find in each of our traditions

a) grounds in support of universal human rights,
b) a call to work for justice and peace, and
c) concern for conservation of the earth.

We confirm and applaud the positive human values that are, at times painfully slowly, but nevertheless increasingly, being accepted and advocated in our world: freedom, equality, democracy, recognition of interdependence, commitment to justice and human rights. We also believe that conditions in our world encourage, indeed require, us to look beyond what divides us and to speak as one on matters that are crucial for the survival of and respect for the earth. Therefore we advocate movement toward a global order that reflects the best values found in our myriad traditions.

We are convinced that a just global order can be built only upon a global ethic that clearly states universally recognized norms and principles, and that such an ethic presumes a readiness and intention on the part of people to act justly—that is, a movement of the heart. Secondly, a global ethic requires a thoughtful presentation of principles that are held up to open investigation and critique—a movement of the head.

Each of our traditions holds commitments beyond what is expressed here, but we find that within our ethical and religious traditions, the world community is in the process of discovering elements of a fundamental minimal consensus on ethics that is convincing to all women and men of goodwill, religious and non-religious alike, and that will provide us with a moral framework within which we can relate to ourselves, each other, and the world in a just and respectful manner.

In order to build a humanity-wide consensus, we find it is essential to develop and use a language that is humanity based, although each religious and ethical tradition also has its own language for what is expressed in this Declaration.

Furthermore, none of our traditions, ethical or religious, is satisfied with minimums, vital as they are; rather, because humans are endlessly self-transcending, our traditions also provide maximums to be striven for. Consequently, this Declaration does the same. The maximums, however, clearly are ideals to be striven for, and therefore cannot be required, lest the essential freedoms and rights of some thereby be violated.

Presuppositions

As a Universal Declaration of a Global Ethic, which we believe must undergird any affirmation of human rights and respect for the earth, this document affirms and supports the rights and corresponding responsibilities enumerated in the 1948 *Universal Declaration of Human Rights* of the United Nations. In conjunction with that first United Nations Declaration, we believe there are five general presuppositions that are indispensable for a global ethic:

a) Every human possesses inalienable and inviolable dignity; individuals, states, and other social entities are obliged to respect and protect the dignity of each person.

b) No person or social entity exists beyond the scope of morality; everyone—individuals and social organizations—is obliged to do good and avoid evil.

c) Humans are endowed with reason and conscience—the great challenge of being human is to act conscientiously; communities, states and other social organizations are obliged to protect and foster these capabilities.

d) Communities, states, and other social organizations that contribute to the good of humans and of the world have a right to exist and flourish; this right should be respected by all.

e) Humans are a part of nature, not apart from nature; ethical concerns extend beyond humanity to the rest of the earth, and indeed the cosmos. In brief: this Declaration, in reflection of reality, is not just anthropocentric, but anthropocosmocentric.

A Fundamental Rule

We propose the Golden Rule, which for thousands of years has been affirmed in many religious and ethical traditions, as a fundamental principle upon which to base a global ethic: "What you do not wish done to yourself, do not do to others," or in positive terms, "What you wish done to yourself, do to others." This rule should be valid not only for one's own family, friends, community, and nation but also for all other individuals, families, communities, nations, the entire world, the cosmos.

Basic Principles

1. Because freedom is of the essence of being human, every person is free to exercise and develop every capacity, so long as it does not infringe on the rights of other persons or express a lack of due respect for things living or nonliving. In addition, human freedom should be exercised in such a way as to enhance both the freedom of all humans and due respect for all things, living and nonliving.

2. Because of their inherent equal dignity, all humans should always be treated as ends, never as mere means. In addition, all humans in every encounter with others should strive to enhance to the fullest the intrinsic dignity of all involved.

3. Although humans have greater intrinsic value than nonhumans, all such things, living and nonliving, do possess intrinsic value simply because of their existence and, as such, are to be treated with due respect. In addition, all humans in every encounter with nonhumans, living and nonliving, should strive to respect them to the fullest of their intrinsic value.

4. As humans necessarily seek ever more truth, so too do they seek to unite themselves, that is, their "selves," with what they perceive as the good: in brief, they love. Usually this self is expanded/transcended to include their own family and friends, seeking the good for them. In addition, as with the Golden Rule, this loving/loved self needs to continue its natural expansion/ transcendence to embrace the community, nation, world, and cosmos.

5. Thus true human love is authentic self-love and other-love corelatively linked in such a way that ultimately it is drawn to become all inclusive. This expansive and inclusive nature of love should be recognized as an active principle in personal and global interaction.

6. Those who hold responsibility for others are obliged to help those for whom they hold responsibility. In addition, the Golden Rule implies, if we were

in serious difficulty wherein we could not help ourselves, we would want those who could help us to do so, even if they held no responsibility for us; therefore, we should help others in serious difficulty who cannot help themselves, even though we hold no responsibility for them.

7. Because all humans are equally entitled to hold their religion or belief—that is, their explanation of the ultimate meaning of life and how to live accordingly—as true, every human's religion or belief should be granted its due freedom and respect.

8. In addition, dialogue—that is, conversation whose *primary* aim is to learn from the other—is a necessary means whereby women and men learn to respect the other, ceaselessly to expand and deepen their own explanation of the meaning of life, and to develop an ever broadening consensus whereby men and women can live together on this globe in an authentically human manner.

Middle Principles

The following Middle Ethical Principles are in fact those that underlie the 1948 United Nations *Universal Declaration of Human* Rights, formally approved by almost every nation in the world.

Legal Rights/Responsibilities

Because all humans have an inherent equal dignity, all should be treated equally before the law and provided with its equal protection.

At the same time, all individuals and communities should follow all just laws, obeying not only the letter but most especially the spirit of the law.

Rights/Responsibilities Concerning Conscience and Religion or Belief

Because humans are thinking, and therefore essentially free-deciding beings, all have the right to freedom of thought, speech, conscience, and religion or belief.

At the same time, all humans should exercise their rights of freedom of thought, speech, conscience, and religion or belief in ways that will respect themselves and all others and strive to produce maximum benefit, broadly understood, for both themselves and their fellow humans.

Rights/Responsibilities Concerning Speech and Information

Because humans are thinking beings with the ability to perceive reality and express it, all individuals and communities have both the right and the responsibility, as far as possible, to learn the truth and express it honestly.

At the same time everyone should avoid cover-ups, distortions, manipulations of others, and inappropriate intrusions into personal privacy; this freedom and responsibility is especially true of the mass media, artists, scientists, politicians, and religious leaders.

Rights/Responsibilities Concerning Participation in All Decision-making Affecting Oneself or Those for Whom One is Responsible

Because humans are free-deciding beings, all adults have the right to a voice, direct or indirect, in all decisions that affect them, including a meaningful participation in choosing their leaders and holding them accountable, as well as the right of equal access to all leadership positions for which their talents qualify them.

At the same time, all humans should strive to exercise their right, and obligation, to participate in self-governance so as to produce maximum benefit, widely understood, for both themselves and their fellow humans.

Rights/Responsibilities Concerning the Relationship between Women and Men

Because women and men are inherently equal, all men and women have an equal right to the full development of all their talents as well as the freedom to marry, with equal rights for all women and men in living out or dissolving marriage.

At the same time, all men and women should act toward each other outside of and within marriage in ways that will respect the intrinsic dignity, equality, freedom, and responsibilities of themselves and others.

Rights/Responsibilities Concerning Property

Because humans are free, and bodily and social in nature, all individual humans and communities have the right to own property of various sorts.

At the same time, society should be so organized that property will be dealt with respectfully, striving to produce maximum benefit not only for the owners but also for their fellow humans, as well as for the world at large.

Rights/Responsibilities Concerning Work and Leisure

Because to lead an authentic human life all humans should normally have both meaningful work and recreative leisure, individuals and communities should strive to organize society so as to provide these two dimensions of an authentic human life both for themselves and all the members of their communities.

At the same time, all individuals have an obligation to work appropriately for their recompense, and, with all communities, to strive for ever more creative work and recreative leisure for themselves, their communities, and other individuals and communities.

Rights/Responsibilities Concerning Children and Education

Children are first of all not responsible for their coming into existence or for their socialization and education; their parents are. Where for whatever reason they fail, the wider community, relatives, and civil community have an obligation to provide the most humane care possible, physical, mental, moral/spiritual, and social for children.

Because humans can become authentically human only through education in the broad sense, and today increasingly can flourish only with extensive education in the formal sense, all individuals and communities should strive to provide an education for all children and adult women and men which is directed to the full development of the human person, respect for human rights and fundamental freedoms, the promotion of understanding, dialogue, and friendship among all humans—regardless of racial, ethnic, religious, belief, sexual or other differences—and respect for the earth.

At the same time, all individuals and communities have the obligation to contribute appropriately to providing the means necessary for this education for themselves and their communities, and beyond that to strive to provide the same for all humans.

Rights/Responsibilities Concerning Peace

Because peace as both the absence of violence and the presence of justice for all humans is the necessary condition for the complete development of the full humanity of all humans, individually and communally, all individuals and communities should strive constantly to further the growth of peace on all levels, personal, interpersonal, local, regional, national, and international, granting that

1) the necessary basis of peace is justice for all concerned;
2) violence is to be vigorously avoided, being resorted to only when its absence would cause a greater evil;
3) when peace is ruptured, all efforts should be bent to its rapid restoration—on the necessary basis of justice for all.

At the same time, it should be recognized that peace, like liberty, is a positive value which should be constantly cultivated, and therefore all individuals and communities should make the necessary prior efforts not only to avoid its breakdown but also to strengthen its steady development and growth.

Rights/Responsibilities Concerning the Preservation of the Environment

Because things, living and nonliving, have an intrinsic value simply because of their existence, and also because humans cannot develop fully as humans, or even survive, if the environment is severely damaged, all individuals and communities should respect the ecosphere within which "we all live, move and have our being," and act so that

1) nothing, living or nonliving, will be destroyed in its natural form except when used for some greater good, as, for example, the use of plants/animals for food;
2) if at all possible, only replaceable material will be destroyed in its natural form.

At the same time, all individuals and communities should constantly be vigilant to protect our fragile universe, particularly from the exploding human population and increasing technological possibilities which threaten it in an ever expanding fashion.

June 14, 1995 Revision

Send revisions to: Prof. Leonard Swidler, Religion Department, Temple University, Philadelphia, PA 19122, USA; E-mail: dialogue@temple.edu

22

The Law and Global Ethics[1]

The relationship between ethics—the internal ought—and the law—the external ought—is carefully laid out, leading to the need for articulating not just international, global law but also a global ethic.

The Meaning of Ethics and Law

Human beings are persons, that is, beings who can know endlessly, choose freely, and love. Hence, when we speak of ethics we are talking about the principles of behavior of free beings, of humans. We do not speak of our pets having ethics, or complain that trees do not follow their ethics. Because only humans have freedom, only humans can choose whether or not to act in a certain way. This is what we mean when we talk of ethics: the principles by which free beings, humans, choose to act one way or another.

When we speak of law in the most general sense, we are talking about the operation of the principle of cause and effect. Thus, we speak of the laws of nature, the law of gravity, and the like. Step out a tenth-story window, and the law of gravity operates to dash us to the ground at a certain rate of acceleration and a certain force—with the consequences being quite predictably smashing. Cause: stepping out the tenth-story window; effect: being dashed to earth—unless, of course, something intervenes, such as a strong awning appropriately placed on the ninth floor.

When the term law is used in a societal context, the same fundamental notion applies. Commit murder (cause), and we are punished by execution or incarceration (effect)—again, unless something intervenes, such as, our not being found out. In a way, the same basic principle of cause and effect operates in the field of ethics as well. We say in English that we "ought" to choose good and avoid evil; we speak of being "obliged" to choose the good. Our English word obliged comes from a Latin root, *obligare*, "to be bound to." Hence, we are bound to, obliged to, do the good, which will bring about a good result. If, however, we as free beings choose instead to do evil, we are likewise bound to suffer the evil consequences—again, unless something intervenes, such as being forgiven by the person offended. (Parenthetically, it is worth noting that the Latin root of the term religion is fundamentally the same as that of oblige, i.e., *religare*, "to be bound back.")

The Relationship between Ethics and Law

Basically the relationship between law and ethics in human society is that the law is a public expression of an ethical requirement (law operates in the external forum, while ethics operates in the internal forum). Thus, all law is a particular, overt specification of some aspect of ethics. Ethics is the broader category. Normally, everything required by law is required by ethics, but not everything required by ethics is required by law.[2]

Often in human history the law of a society has largely reflected the ethics of a particular portion of the society, which frequently in a variety of ways dominated the rest of the society, with whose ethics theirs was at variance. In that case, "might made right." A prevailing societal ethics, of course, is ultimately determined by the fact that all government exists at the sufferance of the governed. Even in those extremely savage dictatorships in which the elite, operating according to their ethics, killed right and left, the abused population for the time accepted the ethics of the elite as the lesser of evils—but it nevertheless accepted it rather than rebel to the point of their utter self-destruction.

In such situations there obviously exists a kind of schizophrenia, a splintered society wherein the freedom, and hence creativity, of the majority of the population is greatly restricted rather than given rein and fostered. Obviously such a "split-personality" condition is at least as destructive for a society as it is for an individual. Just as for the good of the individual person, so also for the good of the whole society, such a split needs to be overcome. The freedom and creativity of both the individual and society need to be released and encouraged.

Clearly those persons concerned about the welfare of not only individual persons but also of human society in general must commit themselves to overcoming that societal split and promoting the freedom and creativity of all. In fact, the long stretch of human history shows clearly that this process is well underway. The move of humankind from a primitive tribal state to the gradual founding of civilizations, to the fantastic, relatively simultaneous great leap forward of the Axial Period (800–200 BCE) in China, India, the Near East, and Europe,[3] to the breakthrough of modernity in the eighteenth-century Enlightenment, and now to the dawning of the Age of Global Dialogue,[4] creating a new global civilization. Freedom and responsible self-governance, that is, democracy, for all was not even a dream or *desideratum* until the Enlightenment. Now it is becoming a global reality for rapidly increasing numbers. People can be suppressed, but they cannot be satisfied. Humankind is coming of age, beoming an adult—with all the agonies and ecstasies of that process of maturation.

In this new age, the continued imposition by law of the ethics of a privileged elite is no longer acceptable. The age-old way of dominance by the few is waning. The age-old striving for freedom and responsibility for the many is waxing. Law now is increasingly expected to reflect the ethics of freedom and responsibility of all.

Nature of Religion and Validation of Societal Ethics

In those situations where a law is contrary to the ethical principles of the many, the claim is made that law does not oblige ethically, as was noted already by Thomas Aquinas in his treatise *"De lege,"* and even far earlier by Cicero.[5] However, the sanction, the effect, of the cause of an ethically invalid law may still be carried out if the law is violated—as in the case of Martin Luther King's being jailed when nonviolently disobeying US racial segregation laws—or not carried out if successfully avoided by flight, force, and the like.

The question then arises, where does the effect, the sanction, resulting from violating an ethical principle come from? It arises from what we in the West have called religion, or its functional equivalent, an ideology, for example, atheistic Marxism. For example, in the Abrahamic religions, Judaism, Christianity, and Islam, traditionally understood, good behavior merits continued existence after death in the Kingdom of Heaven. In Indian religions, Hinduism, Buddhism, and so on, traditionally understood, the law of karma operates: every human action has its consequences in a future existence. Some similar cause and effect procedure exists in every religion and ideology, including very critical-thinking modern versions of each older religion.

Whence, then, comes the validation of a religion? The answer lies in the nature of religion. As noted above, religion is an "explanation of the ultimate meaning of life, and how to live accordingly, based on some notion and experience of the Transcendent."[6] Normally all religions contain the four "C's": Creed, Code, Cult, Community-structure:

> **Creed** refers to the cognitive aspect of a religion; it is everything that goes into the explanation of the ultimate meaning of life.
>
> **Code** of behavior or ethics includes all the rules and customs of action that somehow follow from one aspect or another of the Creed.
>
> **Cult** means all the ritual activities that relate the follower to one aspect or the other of the Transcendent, either directly or indirectly, prayer being an example of the former and certain formal behavior toward representatives of the Transcendent, such as priests, of the latter.
>
> **Community-structure** refers to the relationships among the followers; this can vary widely, from a very egalitarian relationship, as among Quakers, through a republican structure like Presbyterians have, to a monarchical one, as with some Hasidic Jews vis-à-vis their Rebbe.
>
> The **Transcendent**, as the roots of the word indicate, means "that which goes beyond" the everyday, ordinary, surface experience of reality. It can refer to spirits, gods, a personal God, an impersonal God, Emptiness, and so forth.

Especially in modern times there have arisen "explanations of the ultimate meaning of life, and how to live accordingly" that are *not* based on a notion of the Transcendent, for example, secular humanism, Marxism. Although in every respect these explanations function as religions traditionally have in human life, because the idea of the Transcendent, however it is understood, plays such a central role in religion, but not in these explanations, for the sake of accuracy it is best to give these explanations not based on a notion of the Transcendent a separate name. The name often used is ideology.

From the very constitutive structure of religion/ideology the validation of its ethics flows: a religion's ethics are the necessary behavioral principles resulting from the religion's explanation of the ultimate meaning of life.

There will, then, be a basically one-to-one relationship between the law and the ethics of the society—in the sense that all laws will/should be ethically acceptable, that is, if there is but one religion or ideology pervading that society. But what of a society in which there are several influential religions and/or ideologies: what will the relationship be between the law and the ethics flowing from the disparate religions and/or ideologies?

Global Civilization and Religions/Ideologies-in-Dialogue"

In past history the answer to that question was basically that one religion/ideology and its ethics prevailed, with minor concessions reluctantly granted to the other religions/ideologies. This condition began to change radically with the Enlightenment, as reflected first in the American and then the French Revolution. On July 4, 1776, the 13 English American colonies issued their Declaration of Independence (drafted by Thomas Jefferson, from Virginia), which declared that "All men are created equal, that they are endowed by their Creator with certain unalienable Rights, that among these are Life, Liberty and the pursuit of happiness." Even before that, the Bill of Rights of the Constitution of Virginia adopted on June 12, 1776, drafted largely by George Mason, rang out: "All men are by nature equally free and independent, and have certain inherent rights...namely, the enjoyment of life and liberty, with the means of acquiring and possessing property, and pursuing and obtaining happiness and safety....All power is vested in, and consequently derived from, the people."[7]

Among the many human rights listed were complete religious liberty for all, choice of leaders, due process of law, and, for the first time in any document of constitutional import, freedom of the press. After winning the War of Independence in 1781, the United States of America was governed by the Articles of Confederation, which proved inadequate, and so in 1787 a new Constitution was drafted, including a Bill of Rights, drafted by James Madison (also from Virginia) and submitted to Congress on July 28, 1789. Slightly later, another landmark document in the history of human rights was forged at the beginning of the French Revolution—the Declaration des Droits des Hommes et Citoyens (Declaration of the Rights of Humans and Citizens), passed on August 27, 1789.

The French Declaration largely repeated the preceding American and English precedents, as is clear even from the language used:

> [It] proclaims, in the presence and under the auspices of the Supreme Being, the following rights of man and the citizen. 1. Men are born and remain free and equal in rights...preservation of the natural and inalienable rights of man; these rights are liberty, property, security, and resistance to oppression. 3. The source of all sovereignty resides essentially in the nation...Law is the expression of the general will....No man may be accused, arrested, or detained except in the cases determined by law, and according to the forms prescribed thereby.

As the German historian Martin Göhring noted, "It was not wholly without significance that the soldier of freedom, La Fayette, who had fought for the independence of America and had been present when the American declaration was proclaimed, was the first to propose a declaration of rights to the National Assembly."[8]

Still, at the start of this period of religious liberty, the ethics shaping American and French law were predominantly Christian—Protestant and Catholic, respectively. Only gradually have the ethics, and resultant laws, opened themselves to the influence of other religions and ideologies. That process is one that proceeds by way of dialogue, and is unending.

As the third millennium moves forward, it is evident to all that humankind as a whole is rapidly moving into a global civilization made up of many cultures. In 1993, Harvard University Professor Samuel Huntington wrote of the coming clash of civilizations, cultures.[9] He was partially accurate. We have seen the violent clash of cultures: Catholicism-Protestantism in Northern Ireland, Islam-Catholicism-Orthodox Christianity in Bosnia, Islam-Orthodox Christianity in Azerbaijan-Armenia, Buddhism-Hinduism in Sri Lanka, Judaism-Islam in the Near East.

All previous civilizations have had a religion (or in recent modern times occasionally its functional equivalent, an ideology) at its heart, shaping and reflecting its understanding of the ultimate meaning of life and the outflowing values. But what now of the burgeoning global civilization? What religion or ideology will be at its heart? For it too will need a spiritual life-giving vision and consequent values—otherwise it will die aborning.

The heart of the emerging global civilization will be no specific religion or ideology, but it will be religions/ideologies-in-dialogue. This heart began to take shape at the beginning of the twentieth century with the launching of the Christian ecumenical movement in 1910, gradually drawing the Christian churches into intense dialogue. It was further developed in the 1960s by the initiation of widespread interreligious/interideological dialogue, led especially by the Catholic Church in its watershed event of the Second Vatican Council (1962–1965).

Global Law and Global Ethic

Both those sets of dialogues, intra-Christian and interreligious/ideological, have increased at a geometric rate, shifting to another level once more in 1991 when Professor Hans Küng and I issued the call for the drafting and eventual adoption of a Universal Declaration of a Global Ethic, as discussed above.[10] What then ought the relationship to be between the developing global ethic and the law on the global level? Global law needs to faithfully reflect global ethic; global law should also contribute to the shaping of global ethic. To fulfill both parts of its responsibility, the global law profession needs to have its experts in global law be in close and constant dialogue with the other major shapers of global ethic. This will include all disciplines, professions, and walks of life, but in a special way it will concentrate on the dialogue with thinkers and scholars of religious and philosophical ethics.

As part of that vital enterprise, I proposed that the Union Internationale des Avocats take a leadership role and join together with the Dialogue Institute in forming an ongoing committee of legal experts and experts in ethics, religion, and philosophy.

Potential Applications

All of the principles and practices of *Deep-Dialogue/Critical-Thinking/ Emotional-Intelligence/Competitive-Cooperation* can and should be applied to myriad human situations and structures. This section lays out three concrete possible programs as stimulating examples. Each reader and group needs to employ her/his/its own creativity to produce—and share—their own practical applications.

Part IV

Potential Applications

Eleven-Step Program to Deep-Dialogue/Critical-Thinking/ Emotional-Intelligence/ Competitive-Cooperation

Here is an eleven-step program for any group of any sort to follow, leading not just to a successful dialogical encounter, but one with a beginning full embrace of Deep-Dialogue/Critical-Thinking/ Emotional-Intelligence/Competitive-Cooperation.

Introduction to Deep-Dialogue/Critical-Thinking

It has been said, "We have met the enemy—and he is us!" We are just beginning to emerge from the millennia-long Age of Monologue, when we talked only with those who think as we think—or should! We are now standing at the dawn of the Age of Global Dialogue, wherein we must listen to and talk with those who think differently from us, those who are truly Other—or we will perish! For example, in the business world we individually *and* corporately are beginning to realize that we need to radically change the way we think and encounter both ourselves and others, as well as the world in which we all live—or we, and those who depend on us, will surely fail rather than flourish.

Following are the fundamental steps we *all* must take on this journey out of self-centered monologue into an openness to our deeper Self, to Others, and to the world around us, that is, to Deep-Dialogue/Critical-Thinking/Emotional-Intelligence/Competitive-Cooperation.

a. Deep-Dialogue is a way of encountering and understanding—Ourselves, Others, and the world at the deepest levels.
b. Deep-Dialogue opens up possibilities of grasping the fundamental meanings of life, individually and corporately, and its various dimensions.
c. Deep-Dialogue will transform the way we deal with Ourselves, Others, and the World.

d. Deep-Dialogue thus is a whole new Way of thinking and acting, of understanding and behaving in the world.

The counterpart to Deep-Dialogue is Critical-Thinking/Emotional-Intelligence, which is then implemented by Competitive-Cooperation. Together they comprise a whole new Way of thinking, and consequently acting. To open oneself to Deep-Dialogue, one must also develop the skills of thinking carefully and clearly, of Critical-Thinking (critical, from the Greek, *krinein*, to choose, judge), and then Emotional-Intelligence. However, because Deep-Dialogue, Critical-Thinking, Emotional-Intelligence, Competitive-Cooperation are in fact necessarily four dimensions of one reality, when I speak of Deep-Dialogue, I automatically mean to include Critical-Thinking, Emotional-Intelligence, and Competitive-Cooperation. This should be borne in mind when reading all the Dialogue Institute materials in this book, or elsewhere. In brief, for the sake of simplicity, I will often use the term Deep-Dialogue alone, and include within it Critical-Thinking Emotional-Intelligence, and Competitive-Cooperation as well.

Preparation for Dialogue

First Step: Opening to the Other
Participants see that it's worthwhile to meet with the Other, even perceived opponents.

This is the indispensable first, and most difficult, step—which, only if taken, makes the next ten possible. It launches us into self-critical-thinking
Second Step: *Mutual Learning*
Participants perceive that they might at least learn something from this sympathetic opening up, even from opponents—self-critical-thinking has begun.

Since dialogue, which is different from debate, is an encounter primarily so that each person can learn from the other, this second step is likewise essential, for without it there will be no dialogue, only fruitless argument. But once taken, all the rest of the steps will sooner or later follow—if the participants persistently follow the groundrules of the Dialogue Decalogue. With this orientation, the participants are now prepared to enter into Stage One of Deep-Dialogue outlined above.

Encounter—Entry into Deep-Dialogue

Third Step: Personal Trust
Begin to build personal trust by discussing, first, issues likely to reveal things held in common—acknowledging at the same time that there are differences.

The opening stress on likely commonalities will begin to break down stereotypes and build personal trust, which is critical, for only through personal trust can one approach Deep-Dialogue. Openly acknowledging differences will quiet the fear that the swallowing of separate identities is a covert aim of Deep-Dialogue. It is important to build and maintain the momentum of finding commonalities, for this strengthens the personal bonding on the human level that will be necessary to weather the turbulence of entering another worldview. Participants will typically find themselves in Stage One and the beginning of Stage Two of Deep-Dialogue.

Fourth Step: Shared Living

Participants develop even deeper bonds beyond words through shared living.

There is something almost magical about how material things can draw even hostile parties together. Simply sitting around a table tends to bring us together, sharing food even more so, and sleeping overnight in the same place still more. Sharing of work, play, and ritual has a bonding effect that can be transformative individually and corporately. It carries on a kind of subliminal dialogue. Participants will typically find themselves in Stage Two and at the beginning of Stage Three of Deep-Dialogue.

Fifth Step: Common Project

Undertake together a project of common concern that all agree needs doing.

Doing things together reaches another level of our humanity and hence deepens the dialogue, cements the bonding between the partners ever more firmly. Participants will typically find themselves in Stage Two/Three of Deep-Dialogue.

Sixth Step: The Other Home

Visit together one another's emotional/spiritual home.

There are several ways to visit an emotional/spiritual home: on-site (e.g., shareholder and union meetings), immersion in sacred texts (e.g., the Gita or Qur'an), aesthetic experiences, and so forth. Particular positions do not arise in isolation, nor are they often held solely because of abstract principles. Rather, they are set in a context of a whole human life flourishing in a community with emotional and meaning-of-life/spiritual supports. These visits let us walk with our Deep-Dialogue partners into these deep resources. Participants will typically find themselves in Stage Two or Three of Deep-Dialogue.

Seventh Step: Role Playing

Organize role-playing skits related to controversial issues, with partners taking roles opposite to their own inclination.

This procedure will help the dialogue partners get a better "feel" for the other's stance. Even though one may not be intellectually persuaded, each will always gain a greater sympathy, a "feeling-with," the partner's position. Participants will typically find themselves in Stages Three through Five of Deep-Dialogue.

Eighth Step: Dialogue at Work

Prepare for the next dialogue sessions jointly in pairs or groups.

This procedure teaches the dialogue partners how to actually prepare dialogues rather than debates—which usually are the result of preparations done in isolation. Preparing dialogues in cooperation models the principle of dialogue and joint critical-thinking, and already begins the dialogue at the root.

Participants will typically find themselves in Stages Three through Five of Deep-Dialogue.

Ninth Step: Revision

As partners advance in Deep-Dialogue, they revisit difficult issues, seeing them now with transformed vision as a result of their mutual critical-thinking; this opens up new creative possibilities for decision and action.

Groundrule six of the Dialogue Decalogue provides a helpful way to approach issues wherein common positions are *not* clear prospects: "Agree with your partner as far as possible with integrity; where you can agree no farther, *there* is the point of real difference." This common-sense rule trains the dialogue partners further in listening sympathetically to the Other. This is a vital skill to have if the rough rapids of reaching out to the Other—even of controversy—and the returning home enriched are to be safely navigated. Participants will typically find themselves in Stages Three through Five of Deep-Dialogue.

Tenth Step: Truer Results

Begin to take up the thorniest issues for dialogue.

Approached now from new perspectives forged in Deep-Dialogue, unsuspected agreement will be uncovered even on the thorniest issues. Now both the commonalities and the real differences will come to the surface; often those differences will be seen to be complementary, although occasionally some may be found to be mutually exclusive. But always clarity of positions will emerge from this joint critical-thinking, which will provide a truer basis for action. Participants will typically find themselves in Stage Six of Deep-Dialogue.

Summarizing and Looking Ahead

Eleventh Step: Reassessment

Both separately and jointly draw up a new assessment of the issues.

a. Note common ground, and articulate it to mutual satisfaction.
b. Note where clear disagreements have been discerned, and articulate them to mutual satisfaction, indicating their complementary or mutually exclusive character.
c. Note where further clarifying dialogue is needed, and articulate those issues to mutual satisfaction.

The Deep-Dialogue experience is thereby brought to a holistic synthesis, summarizing the entire evolutionary process and drawing conclusions. This fixes the insights gained, with the result that they will never be forgotten—nor will the deep friendships that will have been forged. Participants will typically be in Stage Six of Deep-Dialogue.

24

An Executives' Encounter through Deep-Dialogue/Critical-Thinking/Emotional-Intelligence/Competitive-Cooperation

This is a 32-hour step-by-step program designed for business leaders, leading them through Deep-Dialogue/Critical-Thinking/Emotional-Intelligence/Competitive-Cooperation, which will focus on the concrete issues the individual participants are dealing with, including in-depth follow-up.

While it is vital that all persons learn and practice Deep-Dialogue/Critical-Thinking/Emotional-Intelligence/Competitive-Cooperation, it is especially important that those in key leadership positions do so because they can promote, or preclude, it and its benefits for hundreds, thousands, millions, perhaps even hundreds of millions of other people. What is presented here is one model—definitely not *the* model—of how a number of such executives could be brought together for brief, intensive training in Deep-Dialogue/Critical-Thinking/Emotional-Intelligence/Competitive-Cooperation. The executives could be from for-profit or nonprofit business, government, religion, education. They could all be from one organization, or any creative combination. A copy of this book, or at least select portions, should be made available to and read by the executives before they come to the encounter.

*   *   *

A 32-hour Seminar for Twelve Senior Executives
Conducted by the Dialogue Institute

10 AM Monday—4 PM Tuesday

Prologue

1. Receive the names and addresses of 12 senior executives.
2. Send them a brief questionnaire with four to five questions, including
   a) tell us your title and three key responsibilities;
   b) tell us your previous title and responsibilities;
   c) tell us the "human" problems that most weigh on you in your job responsibilities, for example, improving pro-/declivity, securing and encouraging the right people, dealing with prejudice among workers;
   d) tell us the title of the story of one of your most difficult job-related human issues—we will ask for details in the follow-up phone call;
   e) suggest possible 30-minute time slots for the follow-up phone call.
3. Follow up with a scheduled telephone conversation with each executive—schedule 30 minutes, and request permission to tape for private use only, then to be destroyed—asking the same questions, drawing out more of the details so as to get a better feel for where the executive's passion and concerns lie.

Event

4. At the beginning of the day, spend 30 minutes having the executives introduce themselves overtly to us, and covertly to each other. From phone conversations, pick the first one to model and set the tone—speak to her/him ahead of time.
5. Spend a half hour giving an overview of Deep-Dialogue/Critical-Thinking/Emotional-Intelligence/Competitive-Cooperation and how it will bear on this organization.
6. Silence—and place everyone in the Deep-Listening Mode.
   Read aloud the Seven Stages of Deep-Dialogue/Critical-Thinking/Emotional-Intelligence/Competitive-Cooperation and the Dialogue Decalogue.
7. Spend the next hour telling a paradigmatic story (perhaps straight or masked, or even an amalgamation—whose specific circumstances might be changed during the session) of difficult human problems the executives have encountered; all of them enter into dialogue about the issues, how they are, or are not, similar to what others' experience, possible resolutions.
8. Break for lunch.
9. After lunch, the executives are paired and asked to walk and chat for a half hour about the morning's story and try to arrive at a *joint* resolution.
10. Report back in plenary session the six resolutions, and discuss their similarities or dissimilarities.
11. A key issue that surfaced in the preevent questionnaires and phone conversations will be chosen for role-playing encounter scenarios. For

example, an encounter between a North American Caucasian and an African Black concerning whether to offer bribery to get a contract when it is illegal for the American and the African is basically honest but cannot exist on the wages s/he receives.

12. The twelve executives are divided into two groups, and they each pick one of their number to play the protagonist's role (as much as possible taking the position they are *not* inclined toward). Each team will be instructed by the Dialogue Institute leader as to what the "facts" are and told to completely suspend their own sentiments and immerse themselves in the mental and emotional world of their protagonist. Each team jointly devises the strategy for their lead role player.

13. The first encounter will be in the form of an adversarial debate, with each side trying to put forth her/his side's position as authentically persuasively—*not* bombastically—as possible.

14. Then the teams will change sides and again prepare their strategy—choosing a different player—and once again engage in an adversarial debate.

15. Coffee Break

16. The executives are instructed more thoroughly on Deep-Dialogue. The executives are then broken up into different teams of six, and this time are given the task of retaining the same set of facts and strategizing for the third encounter. However, now the teams are instructed to maintain the authenticity of their roles, but to strive with integrity to enter into a Deep-Dialogue with the other side—a real challenge.

17. Again the teams are instructed to reverse roles, choose different role players, and strategize on how to enter into an authentic Deep-Dialogue—and do so. Make certain each executive plays at least one protagonist role.

18. A half hour before dinner break, each executive pairs off—but with a different partner from the one after lunch—to walk and chat about the role-playing experiences. No solutions sought, just reflections and digesting. Preliminary diagnosis.

19. Dinner

20. For the first 45 minutes after dinner, begin the diagnosis comparing the adversarial and Deep-Dialogue encounters.

21. For the next 45 minutes, brainstorm on a project for the common good that the executives can jointly carry out in the ensuing three months.

22. Social time for the rest of the evening.

23. Second morning, continue the diagnosis, asking whether the Deep-Dialogue approach succeeded where the adversarial did not. If so, why, how, where the dialogue failed, where opportunities were seized or missed, how it could have been improved, and the like.

24. Next, focus on how the Deep-Dialogue/Critical-Thinking/Emotional-Intelligence/Competitive-Cooperation approach might be helpfully utilized in the story related and discussed the first morning.

25. Then look for the general principles of dialogue, critical thought, and competitive cooperation that can be distilled from the stories and role-playing experienced, getting the executives to come up with their own articulated list of principles, which may or may not match exactly the Deep-Dialogue/Critical-Thinking/Emotional-Intelligence/Competitive-Cooperation principles of the Dialogue Institute.

26. During the last half hour before lunch, firm up plans for a joint project for the general common good.

27. Lunch

28. First hour after lunch: Ask each executive how s/he might use the Deep-Dialogue/Critical-Thinking/Emotional-Intelligence/Competitive-Cooperation approach to address issues s/he is facing that were not part of the above-related and discussed story.

29. Second hour: Plans for future contact and follow-up (email, newsletter, and telephone), and

30. Final hour: Suggestions for the future, and evaluation. Close with a bonding liturgy.

32*. Three months later (date set now), reassemble the executives and the Dialogue Institute team to reanalyze results and plan for long-term future.

25

Business in Dialogue: Network for Business Ethical/Spiritual Values

Here is laid out the mission, vision, structure, and action of "Business in Dialogue: Network for Business Ethical/Spiritual Values."

Prologue

The evolution of human history is largely directed by its foundational institutions, such as religion, politics, law, science, the arts, and business. The change from localized agrarian societies to those based on industry, and now increasingly to a global one founded on the boundaryless spread of knowledge, has thrust business into the center of shaping the future of humankind and the earth. The revivification of late nineteenth-century globalization—after the horrible period of two World Wars and a Cold War—creates both tremendous opportunities and huge problems, epitomized in massive poverty alongside overwhelming wealth and the devastating violence fueled by religion, which ought to be a harmonizing force: the Middle East, Sri Lanka, Kashmir, and so on.

The purpose of humanity is to live well, however defined by the billions of individuals and the thousands of groupings, religious and other. The purpose of business is to create wealth. As long as the understanding of living well was commonly shared, then business could get on with creating wealth. But in our suddenly global world wherein such a fundamental shared understanding is missing, both business and humankind in general are severely crippled. A shared understanding of what it means to live well, which both affirms what we hold in common and respects our rich humanizing differences, is badly needed by business, humankind, and the earth. This shared understanding on how to live well—another name for a global ethic—can come only through dialogue, Deep-Dialogue/Critical-Thinking/Emotional-Intelligence/Competitive-Cooperation and Networking.

The Dialogue Institute: Interreligious, Intercultural, International was founded to develop and apply the principles of Deep-Dialogue/Critical-Thinking/Emotional-Intelligence/Competitive-Cooperation. At the heart of its work is the Global Ethic Project, and from that flows the Global Business Ethic Project. The Dialogue Institute outreach instrument for that project is Business in Dialogue: The Global Dialogue Network for Ethical and Spiritual Values in Business.

Vision

Business in Dialogue: The Global Dialogue Network for Ethical and Spiritual Values in Business assists business leaders in developing, implementing, and monitoring their own business ethic programs; it also operates as a global facilitating and coordinating agency, with the aid of spiritual and civic leaders and scholars, to articulate, implement, and monitor a global business ethic, enhancing thereby the creation of wealth and the living well of all humankind and the earth.

Mission

The mission of Business in Dialogue is to facilitate Deep-Dialogue/Critical-Thinking/Emotional-Intelligence/Competitive-Cooperation among the world's business leaders and with spiritual and civic leaders and scholars in order to enhance the creation of wealth and the living well of all humankind and the Earth.

Action

Business in Dialogue avoids repeating the work of the many corporations and organizations already active in this area. Rather, it networks with them to further develop a worldview that speeds up the movement toward a global business ethic. Specific efforts include

a. fostering Deep-Dialogue/Critical-Thinking/Emotional-Intelligence/ Competitive-Cooperation and Networking among business leaders as well as spiritual and civic leaders and scholars locally, regionally, nationally, and globally; and
b. working with business, spiritual, and civic leaders, scholars, and organizations to further the integration of worldwide ethical standards, leading to the articulation, implementation, and monitoring of a global business ethic.

Structure

Business in Dialogue: The Global Dialogue Network for Ethical and Spiritual Values in Business is the outreach arm of the Dialogue Institute: Interreligious, Intercultural, International. Business in Dialogue's structure consists of business leaders, along with leaders and scholars of civic and spiritual institutions, and it maintains alliances with appropriate organizations worldwide. Business in Dialogue invites the endorsement and involvement of all.

"Business in Dialogue within a Global Business Ethic"

26

Conclusion

The conclusion places the next move in the heads, hands, and hearts of the readers and invites them to share their thoughts and actions with each other through the author—in Dialogue.

I have written here all I have to say about Dialogue, about Deep-Dialogue/Critical-Thinking/Emotional-Intelligence/Competitive-Cooperation, at the present time, although I am sure from my past half-century and counting of concentration on Dialogue that—should I be even more fortunate than up to now and live some more healthy years beyond my present 85—I will have even more yet to say about Dialogue—if anyone wants to listen and engage me in Dialogue.

Let me close for now and urge you readers to pursue diligently Deep-Dialogue/Critical-Thinking/Emotional-Intelligence/Competitive-Cooperation, by thinking dialogically and critically, relating intelligently, and acting accordingly—competitively-cooperatively. Work at doing so every day, all the time, so that it becomes a Virtue, a Way of Life, and let your watchword be *Dia-Logos*.

My email address is dialogue@temple.edu. I invite you to come dialogue with me.

Notes

1 Dialogue on Dialogue: Introduction to the *Virtue* and *Way* of Deep-Dialogue/Critical-Thinking/Emotional-Intelligence/ Competitive-Cooperation—*Dia-Logos*

1. See Leonard Swidler, "Christian-Marxist Dialogue: A Historical Overview and Analysis," Leonard Swidler and Edward James Grace, eds., *Catholic-Communist Collaboration in Italy* (Lanham, MD: University Press of America, 1988), pp. 7–26.
2. See Leonard Swidler, *The Ecumenical Vanguard* (Pittsburgh: Duquesne University Press, 1965), in which I detailed the history of the Una Sancta Movement.
3. Samuel Huntington, "The Clash of Civilizations?" *Foreign Affairs* (Summer, 1993); see also his later book: *The Clash of Civilizations and the Remaking of World Order* (New York: Simon and Schuster, 1993).
4. See Leonard Swidler and Paul Mojzes, *The Study of Religion in an Age of Global Dialogue* (Philadelphia: Temple University Press, 2000), and Leonard Swidler, *Quanqiu Duihua de Shidai: The Age of Global Dialogue*. Lihua Liu, trans. (Beijing: China Social Science Press, 2006).
5. Leonard Swidler, (1) *After the Absolute: The Dialogical Future of Religious Reflection* (Minneapolis: Fortress Press, 1990); (2) *Death or Dialogue: From the Age of Monologue to the Age of Dialogue* (editor and author, with John Cobb, Monika Hellwig, and Paul Knitter (Philadelphia: Trinity Press International, 1990); (3) *Bursting the Bonds: A Jewish-Christian Dialogue on Jesus and Paul*, editor, and author, with Gerard Sloyan, Lewis Eron, and Lester Dean (Maryknoll, NY: Orbis Books, 1990); (4) *Attitudes of Religions and Ideologies towards the Outsider: The Other*, coeditor and author, with Paul Mojzes (New York: Edwin Mellen Press, 1990); (5) *A Bridge to Buddhist-Christian Dialogue*, coauthor with and translator of Seiichi Yagi (Mahwah NJ: Paulist Press, 1990); (6) *Christian Mission and Interreligious Dialogue*, coeditor and author with Paul Mojzes (New York: Edwin Mellen Press, 1990); (7) *Human Rights: Christians Marxists and Others in Dialogue*, editor and author (New York: Paragon House, 1991); (8) *Der umstrittene Jesus* (Stuttgart: Quell Verlag, 1991; Kaiser Taschenbuch, Gütersloh: Chr. Kaiser/Gütersloher Verlagshaus, 1993); (9) *Muslims in Dialogue: The Evolution of a Dialogue over a Generation*, editor and author (New York: Mellen Press 1992); (10) *The Meaning of Life at the Edge of the Third Millennium* (Mahwah, NJ: Paulist Press, 1992); (11) *Die Zukunft der Theologie im Dialog der Religionen und Weltanschauungen* (Regensburg/Munich: Pustet/Kaiser Verlag, 1992); (12) *Introduzione al buddismo: Paralleli con l'etica ebraico-cristiana*, coauthor, with Antony Fernando (Bologna: Edizioni Dehoniane,1992).
6. One more reminder: As mentioned above, since much of the material in this book was developed as stand-alone items, there will be a certain amount of repetition of

explanation of basic terms. I decided not to always eliminate them so that if a reader wished to copy one or another section for personal use, it would still "stand alone." In addition, as reminded above: *Repetitio est mater studiorum!*

2   What Is Religion?

1. See Swidler and Mojzes, *The Study of Religion*, for a thorough study of the meaning and study of religion.
2. Acts 9:2; 19:9, 23; 22:4; 24:14, 22.
3. See, e.g., Swidler, *After the Absolute*; and Swidler, *Quanqiu Duihua de Shidai.*
4. Swidler and Mojzes, *Study of Religion*, p. 135.

3   The Cosmic Dance of Dialogue:
Dialogue of the Head, Hands, Heart, the Holy

1. See Leonard Swidler, http://www.youtube.com/watch?v=Nu4ssQHRLP0, reflections at the Scottish Parliament, March 19, 2009. It should also be noted that these general reflections at the beginning of this volume still tend to use the term dialogue rather than Deep-Dialogue, let alone Critical-Thinking, Competitive-Cooperation, and *Dia-Logos*. Those expansions will be more fully introduced in the pages below, and from then on regularly used.
2. See Swidler and Mojzes, *The Study of Religion*, for greater detail. When defining "religion," I also wrote of those "explanations of the ultimate meaning of life, and how to live accordingly," which are not based on a notion of the Transcendent, and suggested that they be referred to as "ideologies."
3. For general information, see http://en.wikipedia.org/wiki/Bernard_Lonergan. His major works were *Insight: A Study of Human Understanding* (1957); and *Theological Method* (1972).
4. For general information see http://en.wikipedia.org/wiki/Gadamer. Hans-Georg Gadamer's magnum opus was, *Truth and Method.* 2nd rev. ed., trans. J. Weinsheimer and D.G. Marshall (New York: Crossroad, 1989).
5. For general information, see http://en.wikipedia.org/wiki/Paul_Ric%C5%93ur. Paul Ricoeur's more influential work was *Time and Narrative* (*Temps et Récit*), 3 vols. trans. Kathleen McLaughlin and David Pellaue. (Chicago: University of Chicago Press, 1984, 1985, 1988 [1983, 1984, 1985]).
6. The term "Holy" is related to "salvation," and in its Latin form, *salvatio*, it comes from the root "*salus*" (the Greek form is *soterion/soteria* from *saos*), meaning wholeness, health or well-being—hence, such English terms as "salutary," "salubrious," "salute." The same is true of the Germanic root of the word, *Heil*, "salvation," which as an adjective is *heilig*, "holy"—whence the English cognates: health, hale, heal, whole, holy. To be "holy" means to be "whole," to lead a whole, a full life. When we lead a whole, full life, we are holy; we attain salvation, wholeness, (w)holiness. Indeed, for German-speaking Christians Jesus (Yeshua in Hebrew), is called our *Heiland*, Savior.

   The very name of Yeshua has very interesting significance in this regard. The name of *Yeshua* is made up of two parts. The first part, "Ye," is an abbreviated form of the Hebrew proper name for God, *Yahweh*. The second part, *shua*, is the Hebrew word for salvation. Where the root meaning of the Indo-European words for salvation is fullness, wholeness, the root meaning of the Semitic word used here, *"shua,"* is that of capaciousness, openness. Salvation then means the opposite of being in straits; it means being free in wide open space. This makes it close to, although not precisely the same as, the Indo-European root meaning.

7. Those who know Western medieval philosophy will recognize that these are the "metaphysicals," the four aspects of Being Itself perceived from different perspectives: The One, the True, the Good, the Beautiful.

4   What Is Dialogue?

1. See above, notes 8, 9, and 10.

2. Thomas Aquinas, *Summa Theologiae*, II-II, Q. 1, a. 2.

3. "Decree on Ecumenism" (*Unitatis Reintegratio*), 4,5, Vatican II.

4. Klaus Klostermeier, "Interreligious Dialogue as a Method for the Study of Religion" *Journal of Ecumenical Studies*, 21,4 (Fall, 1984), pp. 755–759.

5. Secretariatus pro Non-credenti, *Humanae personae dignitatem*, August 28, 1968; quoted in full in Austin Flannery, ed., *Vatican Council II* (Collegeville, MN: The Liturgical Press, 1975), pp. 1007, 1010. (Emphasis added.)

6. See, e.g, www.arcc-catholic-rights.net for the Association for the Rights of Catholics in the Church (ARCC), which I cofounded in 1980.

7. Thomas Aquinas, *Summa Theologiae*, I-II, Q. 91, a. 2: "Among other things, however, the rational creature submits to divine providence in a more excellent manner in so far as it participates itself in providence by acting as providence both for itself and for others." "Inter cetera autem rationalis creature excellentiori quondam modo divinae providentiae subiacet, inquantum et ipsa fit providentiae particeps, sibi ipsi et aliis providens."

8. See Hans Küng and Karl-Josef Kuschel, eds., *A Global Ethic* (New York: Continuum, 1993); Leonard Swidler, ed., *For All Life: Toward Universal Declaration of a Global Ethic. An Inter-religious Dialogue* (Ashland, OR: White Cloud Press, 1998); and Leonard Swidler, ed., *A Global Ethic*. Special Issue of *Journal of Ecumenical Studies*, 42,3 (Summer, 2007).

9. Flannery, *Humanae personae*, p. 1003. (Emphasis added.)

5   Deep-Dialogue/Critical-Thinking/Emotional-Intelligence/Competitive-Cooperation: The Most Authentic Way to Be Human

1. See Leonard Swidler, with John Cobb, Monika Hellwig, and Paul Knitter, *Death or Dialogue: From the Age of Monologue to the Age of Dialogue* (Philadelphia: Trinity Press International, 1990).

2. Those who know Western medieval philosophy will recognize that these are the "Metaphysicals," the four aspects of Being Itself, perceived from different perspectives: the one, the true, the good, the beautiful.

3. *Think* comes from the Germanic side of the English (Anglo-Saxon) language: *denken* is "to think," "to cogitate" (Latin: *cogitare* = to think).

4. See, e.g., Leonard Swidler, "Nobody Knows Everything about Anything! The Cosmic Dance of Dialogue," *Journal of Ecumenical Studies*, 45, 2 (Spring, 2010), 175–177, and Reflections at the Scottish Parliament at www.youtube.com/watch?v=Nu4ssQHRLP0.

5. Steven Pinker, *The Better Angels of Our Nature. Why Violence Has Declined* (New York: Viking Books, 2011), Chapter 9. Amazingly, it is a massively proven fact that the US popular IQ level has steadily gone up over the past century in the area of abstract thinking.
6. See Bernard Lonergan, *Method in Theology* (New York: Herder and Herder, 1972), p. 253. More details in Swidler, *After the Absolute.*

6   The Dialogue Decalogue: Ground Rules for Interreligious, Interideological Dialogue

1. The first version of just four ground rules was published as "Ground Rules for Interreligious Dialogue," in the *Journal of Ecumenical Studies*15, 3 (Summer, 1978), pp. 413f., and expanded to the "The Dialogue Decalogue: Groundrules for Interreligious Dialogue," *Journal of Ecumenical Studies* 20,1 (Winter, 1983): 1–4; from 1984 onward the title was "Dialogue Decalogue: Ground Rules for Interreligious, Interideological Dialogue." It has been reproduced in at least 39 different publications in at least 9 different languages. An expanded version, titled "Deep-Dialogue Decalogue" is found later in this volume. These commonsense guidelines were named "Dialogue Decalogue" for mnemonic pedagogical reasons: members of the Abrahamic religions—Judaism, Christianity, Islam—will all recognize and easily remember the term the Decalogue, the Ten Commandments. In addition, the alliteration of D...D also aids recall.
2. Cf. John S. Dunne, *The Way of All the Earth* (New York: Macmillan, 1972).

7   Dialogue Decalogue: Pastoral Applications

* Robert L. Kinast, Professor of Pastoral Theology, Catholic University of America, in *Journal of Ecumenical Studies* 21:2 (Spring, 1984), pp. 311–318. After Robert Kinast read the Dialogue Decalogue in *JES*, he telephoned me and said that there were many extraordinary overlaps between my principles of interreligious dialogue as articulated in the Dialogue Decalogue and the principles that he and his colleagues used in the teaching of pastoral theology—and would I be interested in seeing the latter written up. I said yes, and they were thus subsequently published in *JES*, and are reproduced here.

Rabbi Richard A. Freund, after reading the Dialogue Decalogue and Robert Kinast's application of it to the teaching of pastoral theology in JES 21:2, reproduced here, likewise sent in his application of the Dialogue Decalogue to the then current interreligious dialogue situation in Latin America. Obviously the situation has changed there in the past more than quarter of a century, but nevertheless, much of his reflection (which sees conditions for interreligious dialogue largely negative) is still informative for today. It can be found at: "Applications of the 'Dialogue Decalogue' for Latin American Interreligious Dialogue," *Journal of Ecumenical Studies* 23:4 (Fall, 1986), pp. 671–675.

1. See Regis A. Duffy, *A Roman Catholic Theology of Pastoral Care* (Philadelphia: Fortress Press, 1983), pp. 12–25.
2. See, e.g., Gerard Egan, *The Skilled Helper* (Monterey, CA: Brooks/Cole, 1975); and Howard Clinebell, *Basic Types of Pastoral Counseling* (Nashville: Abingdon Press, 1966).

3. See Gerald R. Niklas, *The Making of a Pastoral Person* (Staten Island, NY: Alba House, 1981). For a comparison with standard forms of theological education, see Robert L. Kinast, "Theological Reflection in Ministry Preparation," in James E. Hug, ed., *Tracing the Spirit* (New York and Ramsey, NJ: Paulist Press, 1983), pp. 83–99.

4. One of the most challenging exposés of pastoral control is Juan Luis Segundo's *The Hidden Motives of Pastoral Action*, tr. John Drury (Maryknoll, NY: Orbis Books, 1978). On the meaning of pastoral care, see William V. Arnold, *Introduction to Pastoral Care* (Philadelphia: Westminister Press, 1982); Alastair V. Campbell, *Rediscovering Pastoral Care* (Philadelphia: Westminster Press, 1981).

5. See C. W. Brister, *The Promise of Pastoral Counseling* (New York: Harper and Row, 1978), pp. 51–66; Melvin C. Blanchette, "Theological Foundations of Pastoral Counseling," in *Pastoral Counseling* (Englewood Cliffs, NJ: Prentice-Hall, 1983), pp. 19–37.

6. The writings of Erik Erikson, Carl Jung, and Abraham Maslow are especially favored. See, e.g, James and Evelyn Eaton Whitehead, *Christian Life Patterns* (Garden City, NY: Doubleday, 1979); Donald Capps, *Pastoral Care* (Philadelphia: Westminster Press, 1979); and the numerous works of John Sanford and Morton Kelsey.

7. See Gordon E. Jackson, *Pastoral Care and Process Theology* (Washington, DC: University Press of America, 1981).

8. The action outcome is an essential feature of current models of theological reflection on pastoral experience. See, e.g., James and Evelyn Whitehead, *Method in Ministry* (New York: Seabury Press, 1980), pp. 99–113; Robert L. Kinast, "A Process Model of Theological Reflection," *The Journal of Pastoral Care* 37 (June, 1983): 144–156.

9. See Don S. Browning, ed., *Practical Theology* (New York: Harper and Row, 1983). For another suggestion on how pastoral theology can mediate between experience and theology, see Robert L. Kinast, "Orthopraxis: Starting Point for Theology," Catholic Theological Society of America *Proceedings* (1983).

10. Recognition of this tendency prompted Paul Pruyser to write his influential *The Minister as Diagnostician* (Philadelphia: Westminster Press, 1976).

11. See Michael Emmons and David Richardson, *The Assertive Christian* (Minneapolis: Winston Press, 1980); and David Augsberger, *Caring Enough to Confront* (Stottsdale, PA: Herald Press, 1980).

12. See James and Evelyn Eaton Whitehead, *Community of Faith* (New York: Seabury Press, 1982), pp. 49–63.

13. See Sean Sammon, *Growing Pains in Ministry* (Whitinsville, MA: Affirmation Books, 1983).

14. See Capps, *Pastoral Care*, pp. 79–107.

15. See James and Evelyn Whitehead, *Method in Ministry*, chap. 5, especially the "additional resources" section.

16. Applicants also generally provide a self-assessment or personal history, prior to any one else's observations and perceptions, which remains a basis for the ongoing experience of dialogue and interaction.

17. For a suggestion for how this might work, se Robert L. Kinast, "How Pastoral Theology Functions," *Theology Today* 37 (January, 1981): 425–439.

10   The Background of the "Way" of Deep-Dialogue/ Critical-Thinking/Emotional-Intelligence/Competitive-Cooperation

1. Acts 9:2; 19:9, 23; 22:4; 24:14, 22.

2. Note, there is no substantive difference in meaning between "ethics" and "morals," and their derivatives. "Ethics" comes from the Greek (*ethike*), and "morals" from the Latin (*mos, moris*), and both mean "custom." Often in English usage one speaks of business ethics, but of sexual morality; however, this frequent, but not consistent, distinction is—to engage in a bit of wordplay—merely customary. Both terms are used to designate the interior rules a person or group of persons affirms that determine whether certain actions are judged good or bad. More about that below.

3. See, e.g., Leonard Swidler, "Nobody Knows Everything about Anything! The Cosmic Dance of Dialogue," *Journal of Ecumenical Studies*, 45,2 (Spring, 2010), 175–177, and Reflections at the Scottish Parliament at www.youtube.com/watch?v=Nu4ssQHRLP0.

4. Steven Pinker, *The Better Angels of Our Nature. Why Violence Has Declined* (New York: Viking Books, 2011), Chapter 9. Amazingly, it is a massively proven fact that the US popular IQ level has steadily gone up over the past century in the area of abstract reasoning.

5. See Bernard Lonergan, *Method in Theology* (New York: Herder and Herder, 1972), p. 253. More details in Leonard Swidler, *After the Absolute* (Minneapolis, MN: Fortress Press, 1990).

11   Theory Underlying Deep-Dialogue/ Critical-Thinking/Emotional-Intelligence/ Competitive-Cooperation

1. The term was coined by Elizabeth Anscombe (a convert to Catholicism), "Modern Moral Philosophy," *Philosophy*, 33, 124 (January, 1958), although she herself disagreed with it.

2. The term "deontology" (Greek: *deon*, obligation, *logos*, study of) was invented in 1930 by C.D. Broad, *Five Types of Ethical Theory* (New York: Harcourt Brace, 1930).

3. The International Theological Commission of the Vatican issued a new study on the Natural Law in 2009. See *À la recherche d'une éthique universelle. Nouveau regard sur la loi naturelle* (Paris: Le édition du Cerf), 2009; the original French and an Italian translation of the text alone are found at: http://www.vatican.va/roman_curia/congregations/cfaith/cti_index.htm (without any supplementary material found in the book).

4. Elizabeth Anscombe in the article listed in note 58 above is usually credited with launching the modern reemphasis on the developing of *virtus*, that is, on "virtue ethics."

5. Karen Armstrong, *A History of God: The 4000-Year Quest of Judaism, Christianity, and Islam* (New York: Alfred A. Knopf, 1993), p. 140.

16   Online Course in Deep-Dialogue/ Critical-Thinking/Emotional-Intelligence/ Competitive-Cooperation

1. See above for a brief discussion of differences. For a detailed discussion, see Swidler, *After the Absolute*.

17   Integrated Education through Deep-Dialogue/Critical-Thinking/ Emotional-Intelligence/Competitive-Cooperation

1. I am particularly grateful to Ashok Gangedean for drawing up an initial draft of this document, which we then edited and modified together, and I again have considerably further developed it here.
2. See Thomas Kuhn, *The Structure of Scientific Revolutions* (Chicago: University of Chicago Press, 1962). For general information on Kuhn and his explanation of "paradigm shifts" in the natural sciences, which notion has subsequently be applied to all fields of knowledge, see http://en.wikipedia.org/wiki/Thomas_Kuhn.
3. See, e.g., Hans Küng, *Theologie im Aufbruch* (Munich: Piper Verlag, 1999); Leonard Swidler, *Club Modernity. For Reluctant Christians* (Philadelphia: Ecumenical Press, 2011).
4. See Karl Jaspers, *Vom Ursprung und Ziel der Geschichte* (Zurich: Artemis, 1949), pp. 1943; trans. Michael Bullock, *The Origin and Goal of History* (New Haven: Yale University Press, 1953).

20   Toward a Universal Declaration of a Global Ethic

1. Oswald Spengler, *Der Untergang des Abendlandes* (Munich: Beck, 1922–23), 2 vols.
2. Pitirim A. Sorokin, *The Crisis of Our Age* (New York: Dutton, 1941).
3. See, among others, Hans Küng, *Theologie im Aufbruch* (Munich: Piper Verlag, 1987), esp. pp. 153 ff.
4. See especially Ewert Cousins, "Judaism-Christianity-Islam: Facing Modernity Together, *Journal of Ecumenical Studies*, 30:3–4 (Summer-Fall, 1993), pp. 417–425.
5. Thomas Kuhn, *The Structure of Scientific Revolutions* (Chicago: University of Chicago Press, 2nd ed., 1970).
6. I am grateful for this exemplary comparison to Henry Rosemont, whom I met when he was the Fulbright Professor of Philosophy at Fudan University, Shanghai, 1982–1984.
7. Already more than two millennia ago, some Hindu and Buddhist thinkers held a nonabsolutistic epistemology, but that fact had no significant impact on the West. Because of the relative cultural eclipse of those civilizations in the modern period and the dominance of the Western scientific worldview, these ancient nonabsolutistic epistemologies have until now played no significant role in the emerging global society—although in the context of dialogue, they should in the future. Since the middle of the nineteenth century, Eastern thought has become increasingly better known in the West, and proportionately influential. This knowledge and influence appear to be increasing geometrically in recent decades. It is even beginning to move into the hardest of our so-called hard sciences, nuclear physics, as evidenced by the popular book of the theoretical physicist Fritjof Capra, *The Tao of Physics* (Boulder, CO: Shambhala, 2nd ed., 1983).
8. For a full discussion of these epistemological issues and related matters, see my *After the Absolute: The Dialogical Future of Religious Reflection.* (Minneapolis: Fortress Press, 1990).
9. Thomas Aquinas, *Summa Theologiae*, II-II, Q. 1, a. 2.

10. I am in this section especially indebted to Ewert Cousins's essay "Judaism-Christianity-Islam: Facing Modernity Together, *Journal of Ecumenical Studies*, 30:3–4 (Summer-Fall, 1993), pp. 417–425.

11. Karl Jaspers, *Vom Ursprung und Ziel der Geschichte* (Zurich: Artemis, 1949), pp. 19–43.

12. Ibid., p. 19; trans. Michael Bullock, *The Origin and Goal of History* (New Haven: Yale University Press, 1953), p. 1. For the ongoing academic discussion of Jaspers' position on the Axial Period, see *Wisdom, Revelation, and Doubt: Perspectives on the First Millennium B.C., Daedalus* (Spring, 1975); and *The Origins and Diversity of Axial Age Civilizations*, ed. S.N. Eisenstadt (New York: SUNY Press, 1989).

13. For a more comprehensive treatment of Cousins's concept of the Second Axial Period, see his book *Christ of the 21st Century* (Rockport, MA: Element, 1992).

14. Leonard Swidler et al., *Death or Dialogue* (Philadelphia: Trinity Press International, 1990).

15. H.-U. Hoche, "Die Goldene Regel. Neue Aspekte eines alten Moralprinzips." *Zeitschrift für philosophische Forschung* 32(1978), pp. 355–375, p. 371.

16. Ibid., p. 372.

17. Ibid.

18. Ibid.

19. Hadith: Muslim, chapter on *iman*, 71–72; Ibn Madja, Introduction, 9; Al-Darimi, chapter on *riqaq*; Hambal 3, 1976. The first quotation is cited in Bhagavan Das, *The Essential Unity of All Religions* (1934), p. 298.

20. N. J. Hein, "Goldene Regel. 1. Religionsgeschichtlich," in: *Religion in Geschichte und Gegenwart*, 1958, col. 1688.

21. A Yoruba Proverb (Nigeria), cited in Andrew Wilson, ed., *World Scripture* (New York: Paragon House, 1991), p. 114.

22. Immanuel Kant, *Critique of Practical Reason*, A 54; and *Groundwork of the Metaphysics of Ethics*, BA 66f.

23. Baha'hula, *Gleanings from the Writings of Baha'u'llah*, trans. by Shoghi Effendi (Wilmette, IL: Baha'i Publishing Trust, 2nd ed., 1976).

24. *The Scripture of Won Buddhism* (Iri, Korea: Won Kwang Publishing Co., rev. ed. 1988), pp. 309f.

25. Bhagavan Das, *The Essential Unity of All Religions* (1934), p. 303.

26. Hans Küng and Karl-Josef Kuschel, eds., *A Global Ethic* (New York: Continuum, 1993).

22   The Law and Global Ethics

1. Leonard Swidler, Lecture delivered before the International Senate of the *Union Internationale des Avocats*, in the Eschenbach Palace, Vienna, on "The Relationship Between the Law and a Global Ethic," February 21, 1998.

2. Many cultures have spoken of all human law as (or should be) a reflection the Divine Law. For example, such a notion is at the foundation of Confucianism, as in the tenet of *T'ien-ming*, the "Mandate of Heaven." It is found as well in Roman thinkers, such as first-century BCE Cicero: "Law is the highest reason, implanted by Nature which commands what ought to be done and forbids the opposite. . . . Law is not a product of human thought, nor is it any enactment of peoples, but something eternal which rules the whole universe by its wisdom in command and prohibition. Thus they have been accustomed to say that Law is the primal and ultimate

mind of Jupiter." *De legibus*, in Donald S. Greenberg, *Classics of Western Thought*, vol. I *The Ancient World*, (New York: Harcourt, Brace Jovanovich, 4th ed., 1988), pp. 434f.

3. See Karl Jaspers, *Vom Ursprung und Ziel der Geschichte* (Zurich: Artemis, 1949), pp. 19–43; trans. Michael Bullock, *The Origin and Goal of History* (New Haven: Yale University Press, 1953).

4. "The Age of Global Dialogue," *Marburg Zeitschrift für Religionswissenschaft*, vol. 1, no. 2 (July 1996): http://www.unimarburg.de/fb11/religionswissenschaft/journal/swidler.html.

5. Thomas Aquinas, *Summa Theologiae*, I,II, q.90,a.3. See also Cicero, *De legibus*, where he says, "Laws were invented for the safety of citizens, the preservation of States, and the tranquillity and happiness of human life…and when such rules were drawn up and put into force, it is clear that men called them 'laws.' From this point of view it can be understood that those who formulated wicked and unjust statutes for nations, thereby breaking their promises and agreements, put into effect anything but 'laws.'" In Greenberg, *Classics of Western Thought*, vol. I, pp. 437f.

6. See Leonard Swidler and Paul Mojzes, *The Study of Religion in the Age of Global Dialogue* (Philadelphia: Temple University Press, 2000) for greater detail.

7. Richard L. Perry, ed., *Sources of Our Liberties* (Chicago: American Bar Foundation, rev. ed., 1978), p. 311.

8. Martin Göhring, *Weg und Sieg der modernen Staatsidee in Frankreich* (Tübingen: Mohr-Siebeck, 1946), p. 280.

9. See Samuel P. Huntington, "Clash of Civilizations?" *Foreign Affairs*, Summer, 1993, pp. 22–49.

10. See Leonard Swidler, ed., *For All Life. Toward Universal Declaration of a Global Ethic. An Interreligious Dialogue* (Ashland, OR: White Cloud Press, 1998).

Index

Abrahamic, 9, 68, 73, 179, 200
abstract, 33, 35, 42, 43, 78, 83, 108, 114,
    153, 187, 200, 202
adamah, 75
aesthetic, 17, 25, 29, 38, 50, 68, 106,
    137, 187
Africa, 16, 17, 42, 78, 161, 191
Age of Aquarius, 151
    of discovery, 158
    of Global Dialogue, 4, 15, 16, 137, 151,
        159, 160, 178, 185, 197
    of Monologue, 16, 150, 151, 159, 160,
        185, 197, 199
alter ego, 103, 164, 165
altruism, 164, 165
Amazon, 159
analysis, 20, 39, 44, 79, 108, 112, 134, 150,
    151, 153, 159, 162, 197
Anderson, Arlene Swidler, 3
Anscombe, Elizabeth, 202
Anthropology/Anthropos/
    anthropocentric, 12, 15, 39,
    162, 171
Aquinas, Thomas, 22, 33, 84, 85, 108, 118,
    123, 155, 179, 199, 203, 205
Aristotle, 83–5, 108, 123
Armenia, 181
Armstrong, Karen, 86, 202
Arnold, William V., 200
Atlanta, 166
atman, 157
Augsberger, David, 201
Augustine of Hippo, 40, 42, 77, 84, 113
Axial Period, 83, 137, 151, 159, 160, 178,
    203, 204
    Second Axial Period, 151,
        156–60, 204
Ayoub, Mahmoud, 123
Azerbaijan, 181

Baha'ism, 164, 204
Baha'hula, 164, 204
Barth, Karl, 8
beauty, 17, 19, 38, 50, 67, 68, 106, 137, 199
Bhakti, 10, 29, 74
Bible, 11, 16, 36, 75, 110, 163
Blanchette, Melvin C., 201
bodhisattva, 29, 164, 165
Bosnia, 181
Brister, C. W., 201
Browning, Don S., 201
Bullock, Michael, 203, 204
Buddhism, 3, 10, 26, 27, 31, 74, 86, 117, 159,
    161, 163, 164, 179, 181, 197, 203, 204
business, 2–4, 43, 44, 79, 103, 108,
    121, 122, 124, 129, 144, 185, 189,
    193–4, 201
Byzantine, 152

Calvin, John, 40, 113
Campbell, Alastair V., 200
Canon, 44, 79, 84
Capps, Donald, 201
Capra, Fritjof, 203
Catholic, 3, 11, 23–5, 30, 32, 34–7, 47, 62,
    84, 96, 129, 181, 197, 199–202
Central Intelligence Agency, 4
Centro Pro Unione, 3
Chernobyl, 159
Chicago, 166, 198, 203, 205
children, 31, 119, 144, 174
Chinese, 10, 29, 31, 37, 43, 62, 74, 86, 116,
    149, 152, 157, 178, 197
Christian, 1, 3, 8, 9, 11, 12, 24, 26–9, 31–4,
    40, 43, 48–51, 66, 73, 79, 84, 85, 87,
    96, 113, 116, 117, 121, 123, 132, 152,
    156, 158, 159, 161, 166, 179, 181, 182,
    197, 198, 200–3
    Christian-Marxist dialogue, 1, 48, 197

Cicero, 84, 179, 204, 205
Clinebell, Howard, 200
civilization, 4, 73, 85, 88, 129, 131, 135,
    137, 138, 149, 150, 152, 156, 178, 180,
    181, 197, 203–5
Clash of Civilizations, 4, 131, 181, 197, 205
Clinton, Hilary, 43, 79, 121
Cobb, John, 26, 197, 199
Code, 7, 8, 149, 179
cognitive, 7, 9, 17, 25, 29, 30, 38, 41, 50, 92,
    149, 179
comparative religion, 11, 13
competitive-cooperation, 1–5, 35, 42–4,
    45, 61–8, 71, 72–5, 77–81, 83–5,
    89–97, 99–106, 121–3, 125, 129–39,
    143–5, 182, 185, 186, 189–95, 197–9,
    201, 202
commandment, 47, 48, 49, 50, 53, 54, 55,
    56, 57, 58, 200
conflict, 32, 56, 57, 71, 136, 150, 164
confucius, 10, 65, 66, 74, 83, 86, 157, 163,
    204, 206
consciousness, 9, 25, 26, 33, 39, 41,
    62–5, 76, 86, 88, 90–2, 94, 96,
    102, 104, 106, 107, 110, 119, 120,
    130, 133, 135, 137, 138, 143, 147, 151,
    155–61, 167
concept, 13, 17, 38, 42, 44, 78, 79, 87, 108,
    131, 139–43, 151, 152, 204
    concept attainment, 139–43
Constitution, 180
convergence, 16, 37, 158
Cosmos, 3, 37, 39, 43, 61, 75, 78, 84, 85, 87,
    90, 92, 93, 95, 111, 131, 135, 157, 158,
    165, 171
    Cosmic dance, 3, 15–18, 37–9, 75, 86,
    92, 93, 95, 131, 198, 199, 201
Cousins, Ewert, 151, 157–60, 203, 204
Creed, 7, 8, 44, 79, 149, 179
critical-thinking, 1–4, 35, 39, 41–5, 61–8,
    71–81, 83–91, 93–7, 99–114, 119–22,
    125, 129–39, 143–5, 179, 182, 185–95,
    197–9, 201, 202
Cult, 7, 8, 149, 179

Das, Bhagavan, 204
deabsolutized, 21, 22, 24, 152–5
Dean, Lester, 197
debate, 1, 24, 47, 48, 54, 55, 62–4, 186,
    187, 191

Deep-Dialogue, 1–4, 19, 35, 37, 39,
    42–45, 47, 61–8, 71–8, 80, 81, 83–97,
    99–107, 109, 111, 113–19, 121, 123,
    125, 129–39, 143–5, 182, 185–95,
    197–202
Declaration of Independence, 110, 180
    of human rights, 33, 34, 162, 165, 169,
    170, 172
democracy, 44, 80, 108, 109, 113, 136, 137,
    140, 169, 178
denken, 39
deontology, 84, 202
Dharma, 163
Dia-Logos, 1–4, 83, 87–90, 92–4, 102, 129,
    195, 197, 198
Dialogue Decalogue, 29, 47, 53, 55, 59, 61,
    63, 97, 186, 188, 190, 200
Dialogue Institute, 2, 3, 97, 102, 129, 131,
    138, 139, 141, 182, 189, 191–4
difference, 12, 13, 26–32, 54, 56, 85, 87, 96,
    97, 99–101, 104, 107, 109–11, 115, 117,
    124, 132, 134, 136, 142, 145, 147, 151,
    169, 174, 186, 188, 193, 201, 202
divergence, 16, 37
Drury, John, 200
Duffy, Regis A., 200
Dunne, John, 25, 50, 200
dynamic, 16, 21, 34, 37, 49, 54, 66, 84, 87,
    88, 90, 93, 94, 102, 131, 147, 153, 162

Eastman Kodak, 123
ecology, 71, 87, 101, 102, 200
education, 2, 12, 21, 23, 34, 53, 54, 55,
    56, 57, 58, 59, 71, 84, 106, 125, 129,
    131–48, 174, 189, 200, 202
Effendi, Shoghi, 204
Egan, Gerard, 200
Egypt, 157
Einstein, Albert, 16, 37, 85, 152
eisegesis, 109, 110
    See also exegesis
Emmons, Michael, 101
Emotional-Intelligence, 1–4, 35, 41–5,
    61–8, 71–5, 77–81, 83–5, 88–91, 93–7,
    99–104, 106, 119–22, 125, 129–39,
    143–5, 182, 185–6, 189–95, 197, 199,
    201, 202
empathy, 57, 59, 100, 146
enlightenment, 12, 42, 78, 152, 157,
    178, 180

environment, 102, 147, 160, 174
ethics, 2, 7, 8, 30, 84, 96, 97, 102, 103, 114,
    125, 132, 149, 161, 162, 166, 167, 169,
    170, 177–82, 201, 202, 204
  global ethics, 2, 30, 161, 166, 167,
    177, 204
  virtue ethics, 84, 202
equal, 16, 24, 29, 33, 37, 38, 49, 58,
    59, 66, 83, 84, 141, 156, 169, 171–3,
    180, 181
Erikson, Erik, 201
Eron, Lewis, 197
Europe, 21, 26, 86, 87, 115, 152, 153, 156–8,
    178, 198, 199
executive, 189, 190, 191, 192
exegesis, 109, 110

faith, 23, 24, 39, 40, 48, 59, 112, 182,
    201, 202
Fernando, Antony, 197
fides, 40, 112
framework, 45, 64, 71, 80, 105, 122,
    162, 170
Fudan University, 203
Fulbright, 203

Gadamer, Hans-Georg, 15, 22, 131,
    155, 198
Galileo, Galilei, 152, 155
Gandhi, Mohandas, 63
Gautama, Siddhartha, 10, 63, 74,
    157, 163
geocentrism, 152, 155
Goethe, Johann Wolfgang, 123
Germany, 3, 25, 109, 129, 166
Gilbert, Rabbi Arthur, 3
Gita, 16, 187
globality, 96, 161
global dialogue, 3, 4, 15, 16, 81, 133,
    137, 151, 159, 160, 178, 185, 194, 197,
    204, 205
global ethic, 2, 30, 34, 96, 129, 131, 132,
    136, 138, 149, 160–2, 165–75, 177, 182,
    193, 199, 203–5
God, 8–11, 16, 27, 29, 30, 31, 40, 42, 43,
    73–5, 77, 79, 85, 86, 87, 113, 117, 121,
    123, 150, 179, 198, 202
Göhring, Martin, 181, 205
Golden Rule, 40, 49, 66, 113, 162–4,
    165, 171

good, 7, 11, 15, 17, 38, 42–4, 67, 77–9,
    84, 89, 92, 104, 108, 111, 112, 114–16,
    120, 132, 136, 161–3, 165, 169–71, 175,
    177–9, 191, 192, 199, 201
Gratian, 84
Graz, 166
Greece, 157, 163
Greenberg, Donald S., 204
Guru Angad, 164

Hadith, 204
Haight, Roger, 23
haiku, 116
Halacha, 9, 29, 73, 74
Halloran, Harry, 3
hands, 3, 16–19, 25, 29, 30, 37, 38, 50, 58,
    67, 95, 96, 195, 198
Harvard University, 181
Haverford College, 3
head, 11, 15–19, 25, 26, 29, 30, 37, 38, 47,
    50, 61, 95, 170, 195, 198
heart, 9–11, 15–17, 19, 25, 29, 37–9, 50, 67,
    83, 95, 96, 131, 136, 137, 149, 154, 164,
    170, 181, 193, 195, 198
Hein, N. J., 204
heliocentrism, 152, 155
Hellwig, Monika, 197, 199
hermeneutics, 22, 49, 155, 159
Herodotus, 163
Hillel, 164
Hindu, 3, 10, 27–9, 31, 32, 49, 62, 64, 66,
    74, 86, 163, 179, 181, 203
historicism, 153, 159
Hoche, H.-U., 204
hodos, 9, 29, 73
Hohmah, 86–88
holy, 15, 18, 19, 25, 29, 30, 37, 50, 84, 92,
    95, 135, 165, 198
Homo sapiens, 42, 78
human, 4, 8–11, 13, 15–17, 20, 22, 25,
    29–40, 42–5, 49, 50, 55, 61–3, 65, 68,
    71, 73–80, 83, 84, 86–8, 90–4, 96, 97,
    99, 105, 106, 111, 113, 114, 117, 119,
    121–4, 129–32, 134–7, 139, 149–56,
    158–62, 164–6, 169–75, 177–82, 187,
    190, 193, 194, 197–9, 204, 205
human rights, 33, 34, 44, 80, 84, 137, 162,
    165, 166, 169, 170, 172, 174, 180, 197
Huntington, Samuel, 197, 205
Hug, James E., 200

Ibn Madja, 204
ideology, 4, 8, 25, 29, 32, 34, 36, 50, 80, 97, 149, 150, 155, 159, 161, 179–81
idiot savant, 42, 77
idolatry, 9, 11
Imago Dei, 75
individual, 1, 4, 7, 15, 16, 27–9, 32, 37, 43, 49, 50, 55, 57, 63, 67, 68, 74, 79, 80, 81, 85, 87, 88, 95–7, 103, 111, 119, 121, 130, 132, 135, 136, 157, 158, 170–5, 178, 185, 187, 189, 193
integral education, 132, 137, 138
Integrated Liberal Studies, 129
integrative, 25, 27, 50, 89–91, 129
intentionality, 22, 154
interreligious, 3, 11–13, 16, 20, 23–6, 27, 30, 34, 47–50, 54–9, 68, 95, 102, 103, 129, 130, 160, 161, 166, 181, 182, 193, 194, 197, 199, 200, 202, 205
interior, 10, 11, 29, 67, 97, 201
Iowa, University, 12
Iwo Jima, 159

Jackson, Gordon E., 201
Jaspers, Karl, 156, 203, 204
Jesus, 9, 11, 40, 63, 73, 113, 152, 164, 197, 198
Jews, 8, 11, 32, 49, 65, 66, 116, 149, 179
Jewish-Christian dialogue, 3, 49, 197
Jewish-Christian-Muslim dialogue, 3, 166
Jihad, 43, 79, 121
Jnana, 10, 74
Journal of Ecumenical Studies, 3, 35, 138, 167, 199, 200, 201, 203
Judaism, 9–11, 32, 43, 51, 73, 74, 79, 111, 117, 121, 164, 179, 181, 200, 202, 203
Jung, Carl, 201
justice, 50, 158, 169, 174

Kabbalah, 29
Kaku, Ryuzabura, 44, 79, 80
kalam, 11
Kant, Immanuel, 85, 164, 204
kavanah, 10, 11
Karma, 10, 74, 179
Kashmir, 193
Kelsey, Morton, 201
Klostermeier, Klaus, 26, 199
Knitter, Paul, 197, 199
Kortsch, Uli, 3

krinein, 39, 41, 62, 76, 96, 104, 107, 130, 186
Küng, Hans, 23, 34, 151, 182, 199, 203, 204
Kuhn, Thomas, 151, 203
Kuschel, Karl-Josef, 199, 204
Kuwait, 159
Kyosei, 44, 45, 79, 80

language, 8, 22, 33, 39, 61, 83, 85, 86, 87, 100, 106, 109, 115, 122, 133, 134, 140, 153–5, 159, 162, 170, 181, 199, 200
Latin, 3, 7, 8, 27, 28, 30, 36, 40, 41, 42, 75, 78, 83, 84, 97, 106, 108, 112, 114, 115, 134, 137, 140, 177–9, 182, 195, 198, 199, 201
law, 2, 22, 30, 33, 40, 84, 112, 113, 123, 125, 129, 163, 164, 165, 172, 177–82, 193, 202, 204, 205
leisure, 111, 173
Leviticus, 163
liberal arts, 163
Lonergan, Bernard, 15, 22, 43, 78, 131, 155, 198, 200, 202
logos, 2, 39, 80, 86–8, 202
-logy, 4, 8, 12, 15, 21, 39, 87, 152, 153
Luther, Martin, 16, 40, 113

Magga, 10, 74
Mahabharata, 163
Maha-vira, 163
Majjhima Patipada, 10, 74
Mannheim, Karl, 21, 154
mantra, 15, 115
Marga, 10, 29, 74
marriage, 173
Marshall, D. G., 198
Marxism, 3, 8, 20, 150, 179, 180
Maslow, Abraham, 201
Mason, George, 180
Matthew, 164
McLaughlin, Kathleen, 198
Mencius, 83
Mesopotamia, 157
Messiah, 11
Mishnah, 111, 117
mnemonic, 116, 200
Mohammed, 164
Mojzes, Paul, 197, 198, 205
Moksha, 10, 31, 74

moral, 75, 102, 106, 135, 136, 157, 162, 170, 174, 201, 202, 204
Muller, Max, 12
Muslim, 3, 9, 11, 28, 29, 32, 33, 36, 49, 62, 64, 66, 74, 117, 132, 159, 166, 197, 204
Mutombo, 36
mutuality, 93, 94, 165
mythos, 157

Nazi, 25, 32
network, 90, 92, 101, 105, 111, 193, 194
New Delhi, 166
Newton, Isaac, 152
Niklas, Gerald R., 200

Obama, Barack, 43, 79, 121
Oklahoma, 3

Pali, 10, 74
paradigm shift, 21, 101, 102, 134, 146, 147, 151–3, 155, 159, 160, 203
Pascal, Blaise, 17, 38
pass over, 67
pastoral, 53–9, 200, 201
peace, 43, 44, 72, 78, 80, 132, 136, 158, 166, 169, 174
Pellaue, David, 198
Perlmutter, Howard, 4
person, 2–4, 8–10, 11, 13, 16, 19, 20, 23, 24, 26–8, 30–3, 36, 42, 47, 48, 50, 54–9, 61, 63, 65, 71, 74–7, 80, 81, 83, 84, 90–2, 95–7, 99, 102, 103, 105–7, 109, 111, 113, 114, 117–25, 130, 132, 135–8, 145, 147, 149, 150, 157, 161, 162, 165, 170–2, 174, 177–9, 186, 187, 189, 198, 199–201
Phan, Peter, 23
phenomena, 13, 21, 85, 132
Philadelphia, 3, 167, 175, 197, 199, 200, 201, 203–5
Pinker, Steven, 43, 78, 200, 202
Pittakos, 163
Plato, 29, 83, 153
political, 33, 36, 71, 75, 136, 137, 139, 150, 162
pope, 16, 34, 36
pragmatism, 12, 159
presupposition, 40, 41, 56, 62, 64, 65, 91, 96, 104, 106, 107, 110, 113, 114, 130, 156, 170

prima facie, 114
primal principle, 83, 85, 86
primus ego, 103, 165
property, 173, 180, 181
Pruyser, Paul, 201
psychology, 12, 39, 53, 55, 87

Quaker, 3, 8, 149, 179
Qur'an, 16, 36, 110, 111, 117, 187

Rabbi, 3, 9, 10, 11, 73, 111, 117, 164
Ricoeur, Paul, 15, 131, 198
reductio ad absurdum, 40, 112–14
reformation, 3
relationality, 87, 101, 102, 153–5
relativism, 155, 156
Religionswissenschaft, 12, 13, 204
religion, 2, 3, 4, 7–13, 15, 16, 18–20, 23–7, 29, 31–4, 36, 38, 47, 48, 50, 51, 54, 55, 68, 73, 74, 96, 97, 101, 102, 111, 117, 129, 134, 137, 149, 150, 152, 157–9, 161, 162–5, 166, 172, 175, 178–82, 189, 193, 197–200, 204, 205
Ren, 10
Richardson, David, 201
Rosemont, Henry, 203
ruach, 75

salus, 30, 198
Sammon, Sean, 201
Sanford, John, 201
San Francisco, 166
satori, 31
Scheler, Max, 154
Second World, 159
secular, 10, 34, 55, 66, 80, 96, 132, 150, 158, 159, 161, 180
Segundo, Juan, 23, 200
self, 1, 3, 9, 13, 16, 19, 23, 26, 28, 29, 31, 35–7, 40–4, 48–51, 54–6, 58, 62–4, 66, 67, 74, 75, 77, 79, 81, 83, 85, 90, 94, 95, 96, 99, 100–3, 105, 106, 111, 113, 117–21, 123, 130–2, 135, 141, 145–8, 150, 156–8, 163–5, 170, 171, 173, 178, 185, 186, 199, 201, 202
self-critical, 29, 50, 56, 63, 66, 67, 99, 186
semitic, 9, 11, 27, 31, 73, 152, 199
Seoul, 166
seven stages, 50, 68, 72, 97, 99–102, 118, 119, 145, 190

Shafer, Ingrid, 3, 99
Shang-Ti, 29
Shar'ia, 9, 29
Shihab, Alwi, 139
Shin-to, 10, 74
silver screen, 110
Sloyan, Gerard, 197
sociology of knowledge, 21, 154, 159
Socrates, 63
solipsism, 36
Sorokin, Pitirim A., 150, 151, 203
Sotaesan, 164
Soviet Union, 1, 4
Spengler, Oswald, 150, 203
spiritual, 17, 25, 29, 30, 38, 50, 59, 63, 67, 68, 71, 75, 80, 90, 96, 97, 129, 130, 135, 157, 162, 174, 181, 187, 193, 194
Sri Lanka, 181, 193
stoics, 84
Sunyata, 27, 31, 86, 87
Sufis, 29, 63
suttee, 27, 28, 31, 32, 49
syllogism, 40, 76, 112
syncretism, 51
synthesis, 39, 134, 188

Tao, 10, 29, 31, 50, 74, 86–8, 163, 203
Temple University, 12, 166, 167, 175, 197, 205
Thales of Milet, 163
Theos, 8, 10, 29, 30, 74
Third World, 159
T'ien, 10, 74, 204
Tikun olam, 38
Tobit, 163
Torah, 9, 73, 164
transcendent, 7–9, 15, 20, 22, 36, 149, 150, 153–155, 157, 179, 180, 198
trust, 28, 29, 40, 41, 48–50, 56, 57, 64, 65, 112, 113, 140, 186, 204
trialogue, 166
truth, 10, 11, 16, 17, 19–22, 24, 30, 32, 36, 40, 41, 47, 50, 51, 62, 63, 74, 76, 90, 96, 104, 107, 113–15, 130, 134, 152, 153, 154, 155, 156, 165, 171, 172, 198

ultimate, 2, 7–9, 12, 15, 20, 29, 30–3, 36, 47, 48, 54, 55, 61, 85, 86, 87, 88, 90, 91, 92, 103, 114, 149, 150, 152, 154, 159, 160, 171, 172, 178–81, 198, 204

Una Sancta, 3, 25, 197
University of Pennsylvania, 4
University of Science and Arts, 3
Unbelievers, 30
UNESCO, 166
UNICEF, 139
United Nations, 33, 34, 150, 162, 165, 166, 169, 170, 172
universe, 10, 16, 37, 74, 86, 175, 202, 204
Union Internationale des Avocats, 182, 204
Upanishads, 157
Ur-Prinzip, 83, 85–8, 93

Vatican, 3, 23–5, 30, 34, 35, 49, 181, 199, 202
Vedas, 36
virtue, 1–4, 63, 68, 73–6, 80, 83, 84, 86, 89, 91, 97, 102, 103, 105, 122, 130–8, 195, 197, 202

Warsaw, 166
Wahid, Abdurrahman, 139
western, 7, 8, 21, 39, 73, 83, 84, 150, 152, 161, 164, 199, 203–5
Whitehead, James and Evelyn, 201
Weinsheimer, J., 198
Wilson, Andrew, 204
Wittgenstein, Ludwig, 22, 154
Wilkie, Wendell, 158
Wisconsin, University of, 129
women, 41, 83, 84, 96, 106, 116, 158, 159, 169, 170, 172–4
World Bank, 139
World Wars, 3, 150, 193
World Parliament of Religions, 166
work, 10, 15, 17, 24, 25, 32, 38, 44, 54, 56, 58, 64, 67, 71, 74, 75, 79, 82, 84, 87, 90, 95, 97, 111, 123, 129, 130, 132, 133, 136, 139, 140, 144, 161, 162, 166, 167, 169, 173, 187, 193, 194, 195, 198, 201

Yagi, Seiichi, 197
Yeshua, 9, 73, 198

zero-sum, 35, 43, 45, 49, 80, 105, 121, 124, 202
Zoroaster, 162

CPSIA information can be obtained
at www.ICGtesting.com
Printed in the USA
LVOW01s1957241115

464048LV00004B/91/P